I0875866

PERSONALITY PSYCHOLOGY

THE BASICS

Personality Psychology: The Basics, 2nd Edition, offers a comprehensive yet accessible exploration of the field of personality psychology. This updated edition, authored by Stanley O. Gaines, Jr., with contributions from Manuel Ramirez, III, and Norma Rodriguez, delves into the major schools of thought – psychodynamic, behaviourist, humanistic/existential, trait, and the newly combined cognitive/biological perspectives.

Building on the strengths of the first edition, this second edition retains its engaging, jargon-free style and informative breakout boxes, making complex theories easy to understand. It continues to explore why individuals think, feel, and act differently in similar situations, while incorporating fascinating case studies to illustrate key concepts. A significant enhancement in this edition is the inclusion of a groundbreaking chapter, 'Past, present, and future in personality psychology: On "Racial," Cultural, and Ethnic Diversity.' Here, Ramirez and Rodriguez bring their expertise in Latina/o psychology to propose a shift from individual-centric to community-centric perspectives, fully embracing multiculturalism.

Designed for high school students and beginning undergraduates, and suitable for use on A-level courses in the UK, this book is written in accordance with the British Psychological Society's guidelines. By rigorously examining influential theories, cutting-edge research, and future trends, *Personality Psychology: The Basics*, 2nd Edition, provides an essential introduction to the discipline, offering fresh insights into the complexities of human behaviour.

Stanley O. Gaines, Jr., PhD. is Senior Lecturer in Psychology, Centre for Culture and Evolution, Brunel University of London (UK).

with

Manuel Ramirez, III, PhD. is Professor Emeritus of Psychology, Psychology Department, University of Texas at Austin, USA.

Norma Rodriguez, PhD. is Flora Sanborn Pitzer Professor of Psychology, Psychology Field Group, Pitzer College in Claremont, CA, USA.

The Basics Series

The Basics is a highly successful series of accessible guidebooks which provide an overview of the fundamental principles of a subject area in a jargon-free and undaunting format.

Intended for students approaching a subject for the first time, the books both introduce the essentials of a subject and provide an ideal springboard for further study. With over 50 titles spanning subjects from artificial intelligence (AI) to women's studies, The Basics are an ideal starting point for students seeking to understand a subject area.

Each text comes with recommendations for further study and gradually introduces the complexities and nuances within a subject.

APHASIA
JANE MARSHALL

POSITIVE HEALTH: THE BASICS
JOLANTA BURKE, PADRAIC J. DUNNE, ELAINE BYRNE, & CIARAN A. O'BOYLE

PSYCHOLOGY: THE BASICS (2ND EDITION)
ROLF REBER

PERSONALITY PSYCHOLOGY: THE BASICS (2ND EDITION)
STANLEY O. GAINES, JR.

For more information about this series, please visit: www.routledge.com/Routledge-The-Basics-Series/book-series/B

PSYCHOLOGY: THE BASICS (3RD EDITION)

PERSONALITY PSYCHOLOGY: THE BASICS (2ND EDITION)

For more information about this series, please visit: www.routledge.com/Routledge-The-Basics/book-series/B

PERSONALITY PSYCHOLOGY

THE BASICS

SECOND EDITION

Stanley O. Gaines, Jr. with
Manuel Ramirez, III and Norma Rodriguez

Routledge
Taylor & Francis Group
LONDON AND NEW YORK

Designed cover image: Getty Images / Yifei Fang

Second edition published 2027
by Routledge
4 Park Square, Milton Park, Abingdon, Oxon, OX14 4RN

and by Routledge
605 Third Avenue, New York, NY 10158

Routledge is an imprint of the Taylor & Francis Group, an informa business

© 2027 Stanley O. Gaines, Jr., Manuel Ramirez III and Norma Rodriguez

The right of Stanley O. Gaines, Jr., Manuel Ramirez III and Norma Rodriguez to be identified as authors of this work has been asserted in accordance with sections 77 and 78 of the Copyright, Designs and Patents Act 1988.

All rights reserved. No part of this book may be reprinted or reproduced or utilised in any form or by any electronic, mechanical, or other means, now known or hereafter invented, including photocopying and recording, or in any information storage or retrieval system, without permission in writing from the publishers.

For Product Safety Concerns and Information please contact our EU representative GPSR@taylorandfrancis.com. Taylor & Francis Verlag GmbH, Kaufingerstraße 24, 80331 München, Germany.

Trademark notice: Product or corporate names may be trademarks or registered trademarks, and are used only for identification and explanation without intent to infringe.

First edition published by Routledge 2019

British Library Cataloguing-in-Publication Data
A catalogue record for this book is available from the British Library

ISBN: 9781032989907 (hbk)
ISBN: 9781032989808 (pbk)
ISBN: 9781003601777 (ebk)

DOI: 10.4324/9781003601777

Typeset in Bembo
by Newgen Publishing UK

CONTENTS

ACKNOWLEDGEMENTS

To past and present members of the Routledge editorial team (e.g., Ruth Bourne, Emilie Coin, Paul Dukes, Emma Harder-Collins, Helena Parkinson, Jade Ridgill, and Yashika Tanwar) who shepherded the development of this book from inception to completion, our sincerest thanks.

FOREWORD

The challenges faced by textbook authors would be familiar to art museum curators. In both professions, one must display classics that are well known, must represent diverse bodies of work that are less well-known (perhaps only because their creators reside in parts of the globe with lesser economic power and prominence), and must develop a narrative, that is, a coherent storyline that enables audiences to understand how the different contributions, from different times and places, thematically interconnect. Achieving all three goals is difficult, particularly if there are space constraints: a compact art gallery or, as in the present work, a relatively brief book of "basics."

Dr. Stan Gaines proves to be a master curator. He wisely begins by grounding personality psychology's current concerns in the long history of the field and also related fields of scholarship; card-carrying personality psychologists are not the only scholars who have informed our understanding of persons and the differences among them. His Chapters 2–5 then present, concisely yet comprehensively, twentieth-century classics: contributions to the psychodynamic, behaviouristic, humanistic and existential, and trait perspectives that dominated the previous century's discourse and remain valuable today.

Chapter 6 does something distinctive. Dr. Gaines abandons the outdated distinction between "cognitive perspectives" and "biological perspectives" because, he recognizes, the viewpoints have "begun to coalesce within modern-day personality psychology." One modern viewpoint that is integrative, he explains, is the study of *personality architecture*, the design and operating characteristics of those systems of mind that contribute to people's distinctive, coherent personal tendencies. For some elements of personality architecture, individual differences are primarily grounded in biologically based temperament. For others, they arise from socioculturally acquired cognitive structures (beliefs, goals, self-evaluative standards). These different elements of personality architecture functionally interact. Models of personality architecture thus yield holistic portraits of thinking-and-feeling persons – portraits that do not fit the old "cognitive versus biological perspectives" dichotomy.

Chapter 7 represents diversity. In collaboration with Ramirez and Rodriguez, Gaines reviews scholarly efforts in personality science that respect "differentness." The diverse peoples of the world, situated as they are in cultures with distinctive meaning systems and communities with unique histories, cannot be understood merely by administering scales measuring purportedly universal constructs and comparing mean-level scores across cultures. People must be understood on their own terms. Their experiences and behaviours do not spring forth from universal personality constructs. They are guided, instead, by an aspect of cognition: world views that are shaped by the practices and values of a culture. In complex cultures, individuals develop a capacity to adapt their styles of thought and action to the particular values at play in a given circumstance, that is, a capacity for "cognitive and cultural flex."

By the end of Chapter 7, a coherent narrative emerges. The contributions reviewed in Chapters 6 and 7 have different intellectual starting points, yet their conclusions converge. Students of personality architecture and of cognitive/cultural flexibility judge that persons are not merely bundles of inherited traits. People are understood, instead, as thinking beings whose distinctive personality tendencies arise substantially from the enduring beliefs, goals, values, and skills that they acquire through interaction with a social world.

Dr. Gaines concludes Chapter 8, and thus the book, by commenting on this convergence. He does so with optimism about the field's future. Once we treat our subject matter, persons, as self-reflective thinkers who strive toward valued futures, and simultaneously recognize that their diverse thoughts and values reflect the diverse multicultural societies in which they live, insights provided by students of personality architecture intersect with those furnished by ethnic and indigenous psychologists. If one grasps and capitalizes on this intersection, Gaines concludes, there is "potential for this field!"

If the next generation of scholars is informed and inspired by Gaines' text, that potential may well be realized.

Daniel Cervone
University of Illinois Chicago

INTRODUCTION

1

AN INTRODUCTION TO PERSONALITY PSYCHOLOGY

One of the most important lessons that one learns from the history of social psychology (which is covered in *Social Psychology: The Basics*; Frings, 2018) is that interpersonal situations can exert considerable influence on individuals' thoughts, feelings, and behaviour (e.g., G. W. Allport, 1968/1985). By the same token, the history of social psychology acknowledges that not all individuals necessarily think, feel, or behave the same way in a particular interpersonal situation, at a particular point in time (e.g., E. E. Jones, 1985/1998). Indeed, throughout the history of social psychology, individual differences in attitudes (i.e., individuals' positive versus negative thoughts and feelings toward various persons, places, things, and other entities; Blair et al., 2015) have been examined empirically as predictors of interpersonal behaviour (L. Ross et al., 2010).

Gordon W. Allport was a pioneer in the field of social psychology, especially regarding the conceptualisation and measurement of individuals' stereotyped thoughts and prejudiced feelings as potential influences on individuals' behaviour toward members of psychological outgroups (e.g., G. W. Allport, 1954/1979). In addition, G. W. Allport was a pioneer in the field of personality psychology (i.e., the study of the entire, functioning individual; McAdams, 1997), especially concerning the conceptualisation and measurement of traits (i.e., individuals' descriptions of their own psychological characteristics; Paunonen & Hong, 2015) and values (i.e., individuals' priorities in life as reflected in particular

DOI: 10.4324/9781003601777-2

organised sets of beliefs; McAdams & Manczak, 2015) as predictors of individuals' behaviour toward members of psychological ingroups and outgroups alike (e.g., G. W. Allport, 1937/1951, 1955, 1961/1963). Thus, whether viewed from the vantage point of interpersonal relations (e.g., Gaines, 2016/2018) or intergroup relations (e.g., Gaines, 2017/2018), G. W. Allport's psychology of the individual (C. S. Hall & Lindzey, 1970) – including, but not limited to, G. W. Allport's trait theory (Ewen, 1998) – offers a broad, expansive foundation for integrating various theories and results of empirical studies on individual differences in thoughts, feelings, and behaviour within particular social situations (see Funder & Fast, 2010).

In the present book, G. W. Allport's (1937/1951, 1955, 1961/1963) psychology of the individual serves as the primary theoretical framework for our review of the literature in personality psychology. We are aware that, by emphasising G. W. Allport's perspective on personality psychology, we run the risk of ignoring the conceptual road less travelled – most notably, Ross Stagner's *Psychology of Personality*, which presents a comparatively behaviouristic and experimental view of personality psychology across several editions (1937, 1948, 1961, 1974; see McAdams, 1997). However, G. W. Allport's and Stagner's respective orientations share certain basic assumptions about the proper subject matter of personality psychology. For example, G. W. Allport's (1961/1963) definition of personality as "an individual's unique way of perceiving his environment, including himself" (p. 274) – notwithstanding Allport's pre-Women's Rights Era use of masculine pronouns to refer to all of humanity – directly cites Stagner's (1961) third edition of *Psychology of Personality* as a source of inspiration. In any event, with G. W. Allport as our conceptual guide, we shall strive to present a concise (yet comprehensive) review of personality psychology.

OVERVIEW OF THE PRESENT BOOK

One of the most fascinating aspects of personality psychology is the co-existence of several well-defined schools of thought, each of which includes two or more wide-ranging theories that – according to their respective creators – go a long way toward explaining why individuals behave as they do (Funder & Fast, 2010). Certain perspectives (i.e., psychodynamic and behaviourist) consistently are regarded as "classic" (e.g., Benjafield, 2019); other perspectives (i.e., cognitive and biological) consistently are regarded as "current" by comparison (e.g., S. C. Cloninger, 2020); and still other perspectives (i.e., humanistic, existential, and trait) are cast variously as "classic" *or* current, depending upon the viewpoints of respective reviewers (e.g., Funder, 2001; versus Pietikainen, 2019). In Chapters 2 through 6 of the present book, we will learn more about the major schools of thought within personality psychology.

Although the subject matter of the present book obviously fits within the remit of the Society for Personality and Social Psychology (i.e., Division 8 of the American Psychological Association), we would argue that the present subject matter also fits within the remit of the Society for the Psychological Study of Culture, Ethnicity and Race (i.e., Division 45 of the APA; see also A. L. Miller et al., 2019). For instance, in the present introductory chapter, we allude to conceptual and empirical perspectives on individual differences in racial identity (which we shall define for now as individuals' response to the question "Who am I?" as a function of individuals' presumed biological heritage; see also Demanarig et al., 2024). Moreover, at various points in the main text of the present book, we highlight theories that call attention to "coloniality" in mainstream personality psychology (see also Readsura Decolonial Editorial Collective, 2022). An especially distinctive feature of the present book (compared to the first edition of *Personality Psychology: The Basics*; Gaines, 2020) is an all-new version of Chapter 7 on "racial," cultural, and other forms of ethnic diversity as crucial to inclusivity within personality psychology; we shall designate relevant theories (e.g., Mestizo perspectives on personality and mental health; Ramirez, 1983, 1998) as "emerging" perspectives (see also Madowitz & Boutelle, 2014).

EXAMPLES OF CORE CONSTRUCTS IN PERSONALITY PSYCHOLOGY

In order to understand core constructs in personality psychology from the standpoint of G. W. Allport's (1937/1951, 1955, 1961/1963) psychology of the individual, one must begin by examining William James's (1890/2010) seminal version of *self-theory* (see C. S. Hall & Lindzey, 1970). According to James, the *self* is individuals' ongoing awareness that they are distinct from – yet interconnected with – various aspects of the physical and social worlds that they inhabit (see Swann & Bosson, 2010). Having been influenced by Charles Darwin's (1859) theory of natural selection, James (1890/2010) emphasised the biological origins of the self (e.g., the self is a product of the mind – which, in turn, is a product of the brain). However, James (1902) subsequently encouraged readers to decide for themselves whether they believe that the self ultimately is a product of biology or a product of divinity. (Within philosophy and theology, the older term of *soul* historically was used to describe the self as a divinely ordained entity; see Calkins, 1917, for a critique of the pre-psychology literature on the soul.)

In turn, according to James (1890/2010), two major components of the self can be identified – namely, (1) the *pure Ego*, or self-as-knower; and (2) the *empirical* Me, or self-as-known (G. W. Allport, 1955). G. W. Allport contended that the empirical Me – which G. W. Allport preferred to label as the *proprium* – is the aspect of the self that is directly accessible to individuals' consciousness. Having sidestepped the problems that plague James's conceptualisation of the pure Ego (e.g., if the pure Ego reflects upon the self, then what is the entity that presumably reflects upon the pure Ego, and so on; C. S. Hall & Lindzey, 1970), in *Personality: A Psychological Interpretation* (1937/1951), G. W. Allport promoted the empirical Me or proprium in *Pattern and Grown in Personality* (1961/1963) as the component of the self that encompasses and gives order to the wide array of traits, values, and other constructs that are part and parcel of individuals' personalities (Ewen, 1998).

Within the empirical Me or proprium, G. W. Allport (1955) accepted James's (1890/2010) further division into the *material self* (i.e., individuals' physical possessions, including their own bodies), *social self* (i.e., the roles and relationships within which individuals are embedded), and *spiritual self* (i.e., individuals' intelligence and personality characteristics). (The term "spiritual self", which James chose over potentially less soul-evoking terms such as "psychic self," does not appear to have been problematic for G. W. Allport, who shared James's [1902] interest in religion and spirituality; e.g., G. W. Allport, 1950b). G. W. Allport believed that, in everyday life, individuals do not experience components of the proprium as distinct from each other (C. S. Hall & Lindzey, 1970). Nevertheless, G. W. Allport's own programme of research – which included the development of surveys to measure traits (e.g., G. W. Allport, 1928) and values (G. W. Allport, Vernon, & Lindzey, 1960; see also Vernon & G. W. Allport, 1931) – tended to prioritise aspects of the spiritual self (see Ewen, 1998).

With regard to James's (1890/2010) spiritual self, G. W. Allport (1937/1951, 1955, 1961/1963) drew a distinction between individual differences in *intelligence* (i.e., presumed cognitive ability) and individual differences in *personality* (i.e., a variety of psychological attributes that lie outside the domain of presumed cognitive ability; see C. S. Hall & Lindzey, 1970). As it turns out, G. W. Allport's psychology of the individual largely predates the emergence of cognitive psychology, which currently addresses theories and research on intelligence (see Weeks, 2014). In any event, G. W. Allport viewed intelligence as a construct that should be considered separate from the subject matter of personality psychology (a view that is shared by many, but not all, of G. W. Allport's followers; see Ewen, 1998).

Unlike James (1890/2010), G. W. Allport (1937/1951, 1955, 1961/1963) wrote systematically about the relevance of several modern-day personality constructs to the spiritual self (see C. S. Hall & Lindzey, 1970). For example, G. W. Allport's psychology of the individual includes traits, values, attitudes, and motives (the latter of which can be defined as internal forces that direct individuals' behaviour; Sheldon & Schuler, 2015). In principle, one could add *affect* (i.e., individual differences in feelings at a particular point in time; Augustine & Larsen, 2015) – including *emotions* (i.e., feelings that tend to be directed toward particular entities) and *moods* (i.e., feelings that are not necessarily directed toward any particular entity; R. Brown, 1965) – to the list of major personality constructs. Nevertheless, G. W. Allport devoted the bulk of his scholarly efforts toward understanding *traits* in all of their complexity (Ewen, 1998).

Regarding traits, G. W. Allport (1937/1951, 1955, 1961/1963) made a distinction between *common traits* (which can be found in varying degrees among large numbers of individuals and are especially amenable to quantitative research methods) and *personal traits* (which, in principle, might be found only among one individual and are especially amenable to qualitative research methods; C. S. Hall & Lindzey, 1970). G. W. Allport acknowledged that the field of personality psychology in general might gravitate toward studies of common traits (as ultimately proved to be the case during the second half of the twentieth century; McAdams, 1997). However, G. W. Allport's psychology of the individual emphasised personal traits, as the psychological equivalent of fingerprints (i.e., no two individuals possess exactly the same combination of personal traits; Ewen, 1998).

Finally, with respect to personal traits, G. W. Allport (1937/1951, 1955, 1961/1963) distinguished among *cardinal traits* (i.e., single traits that essentially define the entire personalities of some individuals); *central traits* (i.e., five to ten traits that go a long way toward defining the personalities of most individuals); and *secondary traits* (i.e., an unspecified number of traits whose expression in the behaviour of some, if not most, individuals is heavily dependent upon the presence versus absence of situational influences; Ewen, 1998). G. W. Allport's best-known empirical work on traits (i.e., G. W. Allport, 1965) focused on several central traits (e.g., *aggressive, autonomous, sentimental, self-centred*) – or, alternatively, one cardinal trait (i.e., *neurotic*) – of an older woman ("Jenny") with whom a primary correspondent ("Glenn") was acquainted for more than twenty years, via more than 300 letters that the older woman had sent to the correspondent and his wife ("Isabel"), during an interval that spanned more than a decade after the correspondent's stint as a university roommate of the woman's son ("Ross"; see Hall & Lindzey, 1970; for further details on *Letters from Jenny*, see Box 1.1). Compared to cardinal traits and central traits, G. W. Allport de-emphasised secondary traits in practice (Zuroff, 1986).

BOX 1.1 INSIGHT INTO ONE WOMAN'S PERSONALITY: GORDON W. ALLPORT'S *LETTERS FROM JENNY* (1965)

One of the most exhaustive, empirically orientated studies of a particular individual's personality was Gordon W. Allport's

Letters from Jenny (1965; for a review, see Wrightsman, 1981). Although authoritative reviews of *Letters from Jenny* (e.g., Ewen, 1998; C. S. Hall & Lindzey, 1970) have tended to follow G. W. Allport's practice of referring to "Jenny's" main letter-writing correspondent as "Glenn" (and referring to the correspondent's wife as "Isabel"), Winter (1997) revealed that the name "Glenn" was a pseudonym for Gordon Allport himself; and the name "Isabel" was a pseudonym for Gordon Allport's wife, Ada(!). In any event, the letters in question served collectively as a treasure trove of insight into "Jenny's" personality – not just for Gordon Allport, but also for successive generations of personality researchers (O'Dell, 1978).

In the hands of a less-capable researcher, *Letters from Jenny* (G. W. Allport, 1965) might have functioned as a mundane, unenlightening account of the final twelve years of "Jenny's" life, from middle to elderly adulthood. However, G. W. Allport's mastery of entire schools of thought within personality psychology is evident in the ease with which G. W. Allport shifts from an existential perspective to a psychodynamic and, subsequently, trait perspective in fleshing out the unique combination of psychological attributes that comprise "Jenny's" personality (see R. Brown, 1965, for a discussion of laypersons' and scientists' progression from describing individuals' behaviour to drawing conclusions with regard to individuals' personalities). Moreover, despite the increasingly paranoid content of "Jenny's" letters over time (especially in the years following the death of her son, "Ross"), G. W. Allport stopped short of labelling "Jenny" as psychotic. Instead, G. W. Allport opted to emphasise "Jenny's" basic dignity.

Although we will not usually refer to G. W. Allport as a humanist (at least in terms of allegiance to a given school of thought), G. W. Allport's overarching optimism concerning human nature is obvious in the ultimately sympathetic portrait of "Jenny" that one finds in G. W. Allport's book (see also J. F. Brennan, 2003, for a description of G. W. Allport as a humanistic psychologist). Additionally, even though we will not refer to G. W. Allport as a psychodynamic psychologist, we note Wiggins's (2003/2005) description of Allport's *Letters from Jenny* as fitting within a psychodynamic (and, specifically, personological) paradigm in the tradition of Murray (1938). In turn, the eclectic nature of theoretical paradigms that are reflected in *Letters from Jenny* is replicated directly in collaborative assessments of "Madeline G" several decades later, within

Paradigms of Personality Assessment (Wiggins, 2003/2005) and indirectly within *Personality Assessment Paradigms and Methods: A Collaborative Reassessment of Madeline G* (edited by Hopwood & Waugh, 2020), as noted in Chapter 8 of the present book.

We hasten to add that G. W. Allport (1937/1951, 1955, 1961/1963) did not portray traits as the only constructs that were worth studying within personality psychology (C. S. Hall & Lindzey, 1970). Nonetheless, G. W. Allport's psychology of the individual does promote traits as the most relevant constructs for the development of personality psychology as a distinct branch of psychology (Ewen, 1998). By the latter half of the twentieth century, an overwhelming consensus among personality psychologists had emerged such that traits reigned supreme as core constructs within the field (A. H. Buss, 1989).

EXAMPLES OF IMPORTANT (BUT NOT-YET-CORE) CONSTRUCTS IN PERSONALITY PSYCHOLOGY

So far, we have identified core constructs within personality psychology from the perspective of G. W. Allport's (1937/1951, 1955, 1961/1963) psychology of the individual. However, we have not said much about important, but not-yet-core, constructs in personality psychology (notwithstanding their core status in developmental psychology; e.g., C. R. Cooper & Denner, 1998). As a theoretical point of departure, we turn to Erik Erikson's (1959/1980, 1963/1995, 1968/1994) *ego psychology*, which serves as a conceptual bridge between James's (1890/2010) self-theory and G. W. Allport's psychology of the individual (see C. S. Hall & Lindzey, 1970). Erikson is best-known for his writings on *identity*, which Baumeister (1997) – drawing upon Erikson (e.g., Erikson, 1968/1994) – defined as "the [combination or aggregate of] definitions that are created for and superimposed on the self" (p. 682). Identity may be distinguished from the self-concept (i.e., individuals' conscious reflection upon themselves; Baumeister, 1998), such that identity is jointly constructed by self and society; whereas the self-concept ultimately is constructed by one's self (Baumeister, 1997).

In spite of G. W. Allport's (1954/1979) panoramic view regarding intergroup relations (Brewer & R. J. Brown, 1998), G. W. Allport's (1937/1951, 1955, 1961/1963) *psychology of the individual* focused on personal identity (i.e., the aggregate of definitions that are created for the self), rather than social identities (i.e., aggregates of definitions that are superimposed upon the self; see Baumeister, 1997). However, Henri Tajfel's (1981; Tajfel & Turner, 1979) social identity theory incorporated elements of G. W. Allport's (1954/1979) psychology of the individual (and, to a lesser extent, elements of Erikson's [1968/1994] ego psychology), in the process of arguing that self-esteem (i.e., individuals' positive versus negative attitude toward themselves; Blascovich & Tomaka, 1991) reflects the joint influence of individuals' personal and social identities (R. Brown, 1986). Thanks largely to Tajfel's efforts, social identity constructs have become increasingly prominent within the literature on the self (for a review, see Swann & Bosson, 2010).

Returning to Erikson's (1959/1980, 1963/1995, 1968/1994) ego psychology, Erikson's progressively sharp focus on gender identity and (especially) ethnic identity during the 1960s dovetails with the rise of the post-1950s Women's Rights and Civil Rights movements in the United States (see R. Brown, 1986, for a synthesis of the respective literatures on social identities and social movements). On the one hand, research on *gender identity* – exemplified by Janet Spence and Robert Helmreich's studies of individual differences in *gender-related traits* (e.g., Spence et al., 1974, 1979), *gender-role attitudes* (e.g., Spence et al., 1973), and *gender-role compliance* (e.g., Spence et al., 1980), among other gender-related constructs – has not always acknowledged the influence of Erikson's ego psychology (see Frable, 1997). On the other hand, research on *ethnic identity* – exemplified by Jean Phinney's studies of individual differences in *exploration* (i.e., individuals' thoughts about their ethnic groups) and *commitment* (i.e., individuals' feelings about their ethnic groups; e.g., Phinney, 1992; Phinney & Ong, 2007; R. Roberts et al., 1999) – clearly was influenced by Erikson's ego psychology, as interpreted by James Marcia (1966, 1967).

With respect to aspects of individuals' ethnic identity, Erving Goffman's (1963) *interactionist role theory* (see also Goffman, 1959) drew upon Erikson's ego psychology (without citing any specific writings by Erikson) in distinguishing among racial, religious, and national identities (referring to race-based, faith-based, and state-based social identities, respectively; see Verkuyten, 2005). In turn, Stanley Gaines and colleagues (Gaines et al., 2013) acknowledged the influence of Erikson's (1959/1980, 1963/1995, 1968/1994) ego psychology, as well as Goffman's interactionist role theory, on their research concerning individual differences in racial, religious, and national identities. Conceptually speaking, Gaines (2012) has devoted special attention to minority group members' *racial identity*, which might be influenced by intergroup processes such as social perceivers' expressions of stereotyping, prejudice, and discrimination (see also S. T. Fiske, 1998).

Finally, among aspects of individuals' racial identity, Gaines and Reed (1994, 1995; Reed & Gaines, 1997) emphasised *Black identity* (i.e., African-descent persons' psychological attachment toward their racial group; Gaines, 2012) as an especially important type of racial identity within the United States (and, arguably, throughout various Western nations). Drawing upon Gaines and Reed's writings, Robert Sellers and colleagues (Sellers et al., 1998) proposed a multidimensional model of *African American identity* (including racial centrality, racial ideology, racial regard, and racial salience as components). Furthermore, Sellers and colleagues (Sellers et al., 1997) conducted research on individual differences in three of the four components of African American identity (i.e., racial centrality, racial ideology, and racial regard).

Before leaving the topic of important, but not-yet-core, constructs in personality psychology, we note that – in and of themselves – gender and ethnic group *memberships* are *not* personality constructs. If one were to focus exclusively on individuals' birth sex and race (as was common in "differential psychology" during the early twentieth century; for reviews, see Markus, 2008; and Unger, 1979), then one might argue that certain elements of gender and ethnicity comprise part of individuals' material selves (which, in turn, comprise part of the empirical Me or proprium; G. W. Allport, 1955; James, 1890/2010). However, if one were to broaden one's conception of gender and ethnicity beyond individuals' birth sex and race (e.g., Frable, 1997; Howard, 2000), then one might contend that some elements of gender and ethnicity comprise part of individuals' *social selves* (which likewise comprise part of the empirical Me/proprium). In any event, gender and ethnic group memberships per se are best regarded as influences on (but not equivalent to) individuals' gender and ethnic identities, respectively (Swann & Bosson, 2010). In addition, gender and ethnic group memberships are linked to achievement-related motives (e.g., Helmreich & Spence, 1978) and cultural values (e.g., Gaines et al., 1997a), in that order.

PRELUDE TO CHAPTER 2

Perhaps no other school of thought has stimulated as much popular curiosity outside personality psychology, or generated as much scholarly controversy within personality psychology, as has the psychodynamic school (which we mentioned earlier in the present chapter). Representative theories include (in order of appearance) the psychoanalytic theory of Sigmund Freud [1900/1965], which evolved from S. Freud's earlier work with Josef Breuer (e.g., Breuer & S. Freud, 1895/1995); the analytical psychology of Carl Jung [1912/1916]; the individual psychology of Alfred Adler [1927/1957]); the "social-psychological" personality theories of Karen Horney (1922–37/1967) and Harry Stack Sullivan (1953); the ego psychology theories of Anna Freud (1936/1966) and Erik Erikson (1950); and the object relations theory of Melanie Klein (1927), as well as the attachment theory of John Bowlby (1969/1997). In Chapter 2, we shall examine psychodynamic theories, as well as research that addresses those theories.

CLASSIC PERSPECTIVES ON PERSONALITY

2

PSYCHODYNAMIC PERSPECTIVES ON PERSONALITY

In Chapter 1, we learned that William James's (1890/2010) self-theory addresses individuals' consciously experienced mental lives in detail. As it turns out, James also was interested in aspects of individuals' *sub*conscious mental lives (E. Taylor, 1999). Nevertheless, James's self-theory generally is regarded as a theory of consciousness (Poll & T. B. Smith, 2003). In fact, one of the best-known post-Jamesian theories of the self – namely, William Swann's (1983) *self-verification theory* – is based on the assumption that individuals not only are aware of their own self-conceptions but prefer to maintain social and personal relationships with other persons who affirm those self-conceptions, even if those self-conceptions are negative (a prime example of the *Consistency Seeker* mode or metaphor of self-perception, whereby individuals presumably are motivated to seek information that is compatible with prior beliefs about themselves; Robins & John, 1997).

Compared to James's (1890/2010) self-theory, psychodynamic theories historically have tended to prioritise *unconscious* (i.e., not readily accessible via consciousness, and possibly inaccessible) aspects of personality (Poll & T. B. Smith, 2003). Early psychodynamic theorists, such as Josef Breuer and his then-protégé, Sigmund Freud, promoted a "talking cure" that was meant to bring about catharsis or emotional release (e.g., Breuer & S. Freud, 1895/1995) in a manner that James's cognitively orientated psychotherapy was not originally intended to accomplish (E. Taylor, 1999). Despite Breuer's role as a founder of the psychodynamic

DOI: 10.4324/9781003601777-4

school in personality psychology, Sigmund Freud eventually became world-renowned as the standard bearer of the psychodynamic school of thought and the closely associated therapeutic method of psychoanalysis (which involved confronting clients with their own unwanted motives, rather than releasing pent-up emotions *per se*; Tauvon, 2001).

In the present chapter, we will review a variety of psychodynamic theories that owe an intellectual debt to Breuer's (e.g., Breuer & S. Freud, 1895/1995) original conceptualisation and application of the "talking cure" (see Millon, 1996). Also, we will examine the rise of feminist critiques against the psychodynamic school during the 1960s-era Women's Rights Movement in the United States and elsewhere, especially targeting the "masculine psychology" of S. Freud (1900/1965; see Stevens, 2008). Finally, we will consider attempts to reconcile feminism with psychodynamic perspectives from the 1970s onward (Walsh et al., 2014).[1]

BASIC ASSUMPTIONS UNDERLYING PSYCHODYNAMIC PERSPECTIVES

According to psychodynamic perspectives on personality, *motives* (essentially, individuals' answer to the question, "What drives you to do what you do?" – with the caveat that individuals might not be able to answer that question; Gaines, 2016/2018) are stable, unconsciously experienced aspects of personality that may be expressed in different behaviours across different individuals (McClelland, 1985/1987). Exactly which *motives* are the central drivers of individuals' behaviour is a matter of debate among psychodynamic theorists (Ewen, 1998). However, with the notable exception of Henry Murray (developer of a theory in 1938, known as *personology*; C. S. Hall & Lindzey, 1957), psychodynamic theorists generally agree that motives are highly similar across individuals (Millon, 1996).

Most (but not all) of the psychodynamic theorists whom we cover in the present chapter were practising psychotherapists, having been trained in the technique of psychoanalysis (even though most of those theorists eventually rejected the controversial assumption of infant sexuality that was central to the original psychoanalytic theory of S. Freud, 1900/1965; see Buchanan &

Haslam, 2019). The dominance of clinical practitioners within the psychodynamic school helped lead to a close identification of personality psychology with "abnormal" (subsequently re-labelled as clinical) psychology during the early part of the twentieth century (see McAdams, 1997). However, by the latter part of the twentieth century, the American Psychiatric Association removed psychodynamic labels such as "neurosis" from the third (1980) edition of the *Diagnostic and Statistical Manual of Mental Disorders* (DSM) onward (see Buchanan & Haslam, 2019).

During the course of the twentieth century, the psychodynamic school split into various factions (Millon, 1996). For example, Sigmund Freud's (1900/1965) original (and sometimes labelled as "orthodox") version of psychoanalytic theory faced early challenges from two of S. Freud's most prominent former students – namely, Carl Jung's (1912/1916) analytical psychology and Alfred Adler's (1927/1957) individual psychology (not to be confused with G. W. Allport's [1937/1951] psychology of the individual). In turn, Adler's individual psychology inspired challenges from more socially orientated theories by two onetime followers – namely, Karen Horney's (1922–37/1967) feminine psychology and Harry Stack Sullivan's (1953) interpersonal theory (Gaines, 2023). Meanwhile, Anna Freud (1936/1966) – Sigmund Freud's daughter – led a subschool of ego psychologists (such as Erik Erikson, 1950) who retained many elements of orthodox psychoanalytic theory but highlighted the importance of the ego – rather than the id – to personality and social development (Gaines, 2025). Finally, in a direct challenge to Anna Freud and other ego psychologists, Melanie Klein (1927) led a rival subschool of object relations theorists (including John Bowlby, who developed a competing perspective that became known as attachment theory, 1969/1997; Duschinsky, 2020).

THE "BIG THREE" PSYCHODYNAMIC THEORIES

SIGMUND FREUD'S VERSION OF PSYCHOANALYTIC THEORY

Hoping to do for the then-fledgling science of psychology what Charles Darwin's (1859) theory of natural selection had done for the better-established science of biology, Sigmund Freud

(1900/1965) developed the original version of *psychoanalytic theory*, which proposes that humans' behaviour – like the behaviour of (other) animals – is determined largely by the three "master motives" of sex, aggression, and anxiety reduction (McClelland, 1985/1987). S. Freud believed that all motives reside within the *id*, which is present at birth and is an entirely unconscious component of individuals' personality structure (Ewen, 1998). From approximately one to three years of age, according to S. Freud, the *ego* (essentially, the "I" or subjective self in the self-theory of James, 1890/2010) emerges from the id and begins to act on behalf of the id, extending across the unconscious, preconscious, and consciousness (and, thus, protecting individuals from fully comprehending the role of motives in their own behaviour; Schellenberg, 1978). Lastly, from approximately three to five years of age, the *superego* arises from the ego, similarly extending across the unconscious, preconscious, and consciousness (and, thus, competing with the id for attention from the ego by promoting internalised morality; C. S. Hall & Lindzey, 1957).

Following the humanitarian atrocities of World War I, Sigmund Freud (1923/1927) eventually revised his version of psychoanalytic theory so that (1) the sex motive was recast as *eros*, or the "life instinct"; and (2) the aggression motive was recast as *thanatos*, or the "death instinct" (whereas the anxiety-reduction motive was de-emphasised altogether; Ewen, 1998). Nevertheless, S. Freud maintained his belief that all persons possess the same motives and the same personality structure (C. S. Hall & Lindzey, 1957). In one of his final, major revisions to psychoanalytic theory, S. Freud (1933/1990) contended that individual *differences* in personality arise from differences in the degree to which one or two components of personality structure (i.e., id, ego, and superego) become dominant over the other component or components (e.g., dominance by the id leads to an *erotic* type; dominance by the ego leads to a *narcissistic* type; and dominance by the superego leads to a *compulsive* type; Millon, 1996).

S. Freud's (1905/1962) psychoanalytic theory includes a model that identifies five *psychosexual stages* of personality development (summarised in Ewen, 1998, p. 43). First, in the *oral* stage (from birth to approximately 18 months of age), primary erotogenetic zones are the mouth, lips, and tongue (with feeding as the source of conflict); personality characteristics reflecting the enduring influence of the oral stage during adulthood include smoking and eating, as well as passivity and gullibility (and their opposites). Second, during the *anal* stage of psychosexual development (from approximately 1 to 3 years of age), the primary erotogenetic zone is the anus (with toilet training as the source of conflict); personality characteristics reflecting the enduring influence of the anal stage in adulthood include orderliness, parsimoniousness, and obstinacy (and their opposites). Third, during the *urethral* stage (also from approximately 1 to 3 years of age), the primary erotogenetic zone is the urethra (with bedwetting as the source of conflict); personality characteristics reflecting the enduring influence of the urethral stage in adulthood include ambition (and its opposite). Fourth, during the *phallic* stage (from approximately 2 to 5 years of age), the primary erotogenetic zones are the penis and clitoris (with the *Oedipus complex* signifying opposite-sex sexual desires and same-sex aggressive desires in boys, and the *Electra complex* signifying opposite-sex sexual desires and same-sex aggressive desires in girls, as sources of conflict); personality characteristics reflecting the enduring influence of the phallic stage in adulthood include vanity and recklessness (and their opposites). Finally (and following a *latency phase* from approximately 6 to 12 years of age, when no major milestones are experienced in terms of personality development), during the *genital* stage (from adolescence to early adulthood), the primary erotogenetic zones are the penis and vagina (with the inevitable difficulties of life as the sources of conflict); personality characteristics reflecting the enduring influence of the genital stage (the goal of normal development in S. Freud's psychoanalytic theory) include a sincere interest in others, effective sublimations, and realistic enjoyments.

The historical importance of Sigmund Freud's (1900/1965) psychoanalytic theory to personality psychology cannot be overstated, particularly in terms of its impact within popular culture (Benjafield, 2019). Nonetheless, S. Freud's theory does not currently enjoy comparable acceptance within the psychological sciences (Perugini et al., 2020). Suffice it to say that each of the following psychodynamic theories that we cover in the present chapter owes a substantial debt of gratitude toward S. Freud's psychoanalytic theory, even though the subsequent theories have taken issue with S. Freud's theory on one or more key points (see S. C. Cloninger, 2020).

CARL JUNG'S ANALYTICAL PSYCHOLOGY

At one time, Sigmund Freud viewed Carl Jung as the natural successor to lead psychoanalytic theory beyond the early part of the twentieth century (Ewen, 1998). Instead, Jung became the first major defector from psychoanalytic theory, strongly rejecting S. Freud's (1900/1965) emphasis on infant sexuality (C. S. Hall & Lindzey, 1957). Afterward, Jung (1912/1916) developed his own *analytic psychology* as a competing psychodynamic theory of personality (Millon, 1996). Jung placed less emphasis on S. Freud's "master motives" in general and hinted at a different, largely unexplored need to fulfil one's potential; this latter need eventually became known as the *self-actualisation motive* among proponents of humanistic psychology (see Chapter 4 of the present book).

In terms of personality structure, Jung's (1912/1916) analytical psychology retained the constructs of id, ego, and superego from S. Freud's (1900/1965) psychoanalytic theory, although Jung renamed the id as the *personal unconscious*; renamed the ego as the *personal conscious*, and renamed the superego as the *persona* or *collective conscious* (Ewen, 1998). Jung's most original contribution to understanding personality structure was the addition of the *collective unconscious*, which is a repository of unconsciously experienced images that all humans share (and, presumably inherit from pre-human as well as human ancestors; C. S. Hall & Lindzey, 1957). The primary individual-difference construct in Jung's analytical psychology is a de-sexualised version of the *libido* (e.g., Jung, 1921/1971), which can flow inward (thereby leading to *introversion*) or outward (thereby leading to *extraversion*) with regard to a particular individual, at a particular point in time (McClelland, 1985/1987).

Like S. Freud's (1900/1965) version of psychoanalytic theory, Jung's (1912/1916) analytical psychology was promoted as a biologically orientated psychodynamic theory – a claim that is at odds with the lack of any empirical evidence that could trace the existence of a "collective unconscious" that supposedly was passed from pre-human species to *Homo sapiens* (C. S. Hall & Lindzey, 1957). However, Jung's (1921/1971) construct of introversion versus extraversion survives intact as part of a personality typology that is measured via the hugely popular Myers-Briggs Type Indicator (MBTI; I. B. Myers, 1962), and in greatly modified form as one of a relatively small number of major traits that consistently are measured by various comprehensive questionnaires (as we will see in Chapter 5). All things considered, Jung's analytical psychology may be regarded as second only to S. Freud's psychoanalytic theory in terms of influence within personality psychology (Ewen, 1998).

ALFRED ADLER'S INDIVIDUAL PSYCHOLOGY

Like Carl Jung, Alfred Adler initially was a follower of Sigmund Freud's (1900/1965) psychoanalytic theory and rebelled against S. Freud's insistence that human beings act primarily on the basis of sexual urges from birth onward (Millon, 1996). However, Adler's (1925) *individual psychology* differs from Jung's analytical psychology *and* S. Freud's psychoanalytic theory by focusing less on the structure of personality (id, ego, and superego in Jung's and S. Freud's theories; and collective unconscious in Jung's theory), and more on the indivisibility of the individual's psyche (Ewen, 1998). Nevertheless, one can detect influences of Jung's and S. Freud's theories on Adler's theory (e.g., *complexes*, or combinations of unconsciously experienced images that are unique to the id of each individual; and *motives*, or unconsciously experienced psychological needs that exist within the id of all individuals; C. S. Hall & Lindzey, 1957).

Adler's (1925) individual psychology initially proposed that S. Freud's (1900/1965) psychoanalytic theory had placed too little emphasis upon the *aggression* motive (i.e., a need to inflict physical and/or psychological harm to other persons), relative to the *sex* motive (i.e., a need to become physically intimate with other persons; see McClelland, 1985/1987). Subsequently, Adler himself de-emphasised the aggression motive and shifted his attention toward the *power* motive (i.e., a need to exert influence over other persons; Ansbacher, 1978). Finally, Adler de-emphasised the power motive in favour of a *social interest* motive (i.e., a need to act on behalf of the common good; P. R. Peluso et al., 2004) that presumably was the "master motive" for all human beings at birth. Interestingly, Adler believed that individuals' experiences with caregivers form birth until approximately age five or six determined whether individuals' need for social interest would remain high or would wane by adulthood (Ansbacher, 1988).

Adler (1935) proposed a personality typology of "styles of life," based on individuals' combination of need for social interest and activity level by adulthood (Massey, 1988) – a typology that has not been very influential within personality psychology (despite attempts to measure styles of life via surveys by a few of Adler's followers; e.g., Curlette et al., 1996; Wheeler et al., 1986). Nevertheless, Adler's (1932) individual psychology *did* popularise the concepts of *inferiority* and *superiority* complexes via his writings on the presumed effects of birth order on individuals' personality characteristics (Ewen, 1998). In turn, those complexes were central to Adler's "styles of life" typology (i.e., a *ruling* type was characterised by a superiority complex; *getting* and *avoiding* types were characterised by an inferiority complex; and an especially adaptive, *socially useful* type was not characterised by any particular complex; Massey, 1988). All in all, Adler's (1925) individual psychology is widely regarded as a pivotal theory that paved the way for even more overtly "social-psychological" personality theories within the psychodynamic school (C. S. Hall & Lindzey, 1957).

"SOCIAL-PSYCHOLOGICAL" PSYCHODYNAMIC THEORIES

KAREN HORNEY'S FEMININE PSYCHOLOGY

At a time when Sigmund Freud (1923/1927) was writing about women's supposedly arrested development in terms of personality (e.g., unable to progress to the "genital" or highest stage of psychosexual development), Adler (1927/1957) was championing women's rights, such as the right to vote (Ewen, 1998). Furthermore, Adler developed the concept of *masculine protest* to refer to women's (as well as men's) questioning of societal roles and stereotypes that deem women inferior to men (Bitter et al., 2009).

Building upon (yet expanding beyond) Adler's concept of masculine protest, Karen Horney (1922–37/1967) developed her theory of *feminine psychology* as a direct challenge to S. Freud's "masculine psychology" (i.e., psychoanalytic theory; Hirsch, 2005).

Early in her 1922–37 lecture series, Horney did not dispute Sigmund Freud's (1923/1927) controversial contention that women suffer from "penis envy" – though Horney argued that, conversely, men suffer from "womb envy" (O'Connell, 1980). However, later in her 1922–37 lecture series, Horney rejected S. Freud's "anatomy is destiny" argument concerning gender and personality, eventually embracing the view that *societal discrimination* (rather than biology) was the cause of those psychological difficulties that women might experience to a greater degree than did men (C. S. Hall & Lindzey, 1970). Over time, Horney (1937) developed a typology of responses to interpersonal anxiety (i.e., *moving toward others*, resulting in a "compliant" type; *moving against others*, resulting in an "aggressive" type; and *moving away from others*, resulting in a "detached" type; Ewen, 1998) that presumably varied by gender as a function of societal influences (i.e., women were steered in the direction of moving toward others to a greater extent than were men; whereas men were steered in the directions of moving against others and moving away from others to a greater extent than were women; Rendon, 2008).

Despite the intuitive appeal of Horney's (1937) typology of neurotic responses to interpersonal anxiety, no single, agreed-upon measure of those constructs has emerged within personality psychology (although some of Horney's followers have tried to develop such a survey; e.g., Coolidge et al., 2001). However, as the Women's Rights Movement gained momentum within the United States and elsewhere during the late 1960s, Horney's 1922–37 lecture series was (re)published as the book, *Feminine Psychology,* in 1967 (C. S. Hall & Lindzey, 1970). In turn, as Sandra Bem (1994) pointed out, that book helped inspire a re-evaluation of the way that gender-related traits were conceptualised and measured within personality psychology (most obviously in the development of the Bem Sex Role Inventory and gender schema theory by S. Bem, 1974, 1981; for details regarding S. Bem's work, see Chapter 5 of the present book). Horney's theory of feminine psychology was decades ahead of its time in its full-throated affirmation of the basic dignity of human beings, whether male or female (Ewen, 1998).

HARRY STACK SULLIVAN'S INTERPERSONAL THEORY

Like Horney's (1922–37/1967) feminine psychology, Harry Stack Sullivan's (1953) posthumously published *interpersonal theory* highlights the importance of the *anxiety-reduction* motive to a greater degree than do any of the "Big Three" psychodynamic theories (i.e., the psychoanalytic theory of S. Freud, 1900/1965; the analytical psychology of Jung, 1912/1916; and the individual psychology of Adler, 1927/1957; see McClelland, 1985/1987). Moreover, both Horney's feminine psychology and H. S. Sullivan's interpersonal theory cast anxiety as inherently *inter*personal (rather than *intra*personal, as was the case in S. Freud's psychoanalytic theory; C. S. Hall & Lindzey, 1970). However, Horney (1937) was more concerned about the implications of interpersonal anxiety for feelings of helplessness and danger; whereas H. S. Sullivan (1954) was more concerned about the implications of interpersonal anxiety for loss of self-esteem (Zerbe, 1990).

According to H. S. Sullivan's (1953) interpersonal theory, all individuals possess a need for *interpersonal intimacy* – a multifaceted need that is emotionally focused at birth but eventually acquires a sexual dimension as well, once individuals embark on their developmental journey into adolescence (C. S. Hall & Lindzey, 1970). However, given that other persons serve as the primary sources of anxiety in individuals' lives, an especially adaptive process regarding humans' personality development is the emergence of the *self-system* (a structure that serves to reduce anxiety, not unlike the function of the ego in the psychoanalytic theory of S. Freud, 1900/1965; see Westen, 1992). Ideally, the self-system should enable individuals to distinguish among *good-me* (i.e., individuals' acknowledgement of their own socially desirable personality characteristics), *bad-me* (i.e., individuals' acknowledgement of their own socially undesirable personality characteristics), and *not-me* (individuals' acknowledgement of those personality characteristics that they do not possess; Ewen, 1998). However, in practical terms, the self-system might fail to distinguish between bad-me and not-me, thus making it difficult for individuals to identify those aspects of their personalities and corresponding social behaviour that could benefit from therapeutic intervention (H. S. Sullivan, 1954).

Based on his observations of clients in psychotherapy, H. S. Sullivan (1947/1966) developed a list of ten maladaptive personality types (i.e., *nonintegrative*, *self-absorbed*, *incorrigible*, *negativistic*, *stammering*, *ambition-ridden*, *asocial*, *inadequate*, *homosexual*, and *clinically adolescent*) – a list that never attracted much attention within personality psychology (in retrospect, the seemingly arbitrary inclusion of gay men, lesbians, and stutterers within a list of adaptive *or* maladaptive types was not just "politically" incorrect, but also *scientifically* incorrect; Millon, 1996). Nevertheless, H. S. Sullivan's (1953) fundamental premise that all of personality is inherently interpersonal (C. S. Hall & Lindzey, 1970) served as the primary inspiration for a circular or circumplex model of interpersonal traits in particular (T. Leary, 1957) and an interpersonal circumplex theory of personality in general (Wiggins, 1991) that we will examine further in Chapter 5 of the present book. Not only did H. S. Sullivan specifically advocate the establishment of a science of interpersonal relations that would draw upon psychiatry and social psychology; but H. S. Sullivan's interpersonal theory arguably provides a comprehensive framework for conducting programmatic research on personality and close relationship processes within such a science (Gaines, 2007a, b).

EGO PSYCHOLOGY THEORIES

ANNA FREUD'S VERSION OF EGO PSYCHOLOGY

According to Sigmund Freud's (1923/1927) psychoanalytic theory, in the process of navigating between (1) the id's promotion of sexual and aggressive urges toward parents and (2) the superego's prohibition against those same urges toward parents, the ego typically employs one or more *defence mechanisms* to try and reduce individuals' anxiety (Tauvon, 2001). S. Freud focused primarily on the defence mechanism of *repression*, or the ego's attempts to banish unwanted sexual and aggressive urges from consciousness (Baumeister et al., 1998). However, S. Freud mentioned several additional defence mechanisms in his writings, without attempting to provide a single, comprehensive list (even though repression appeared to be insufficient to manage anxiety on its own; Carlin, 2010). Fortunately for psychodynamic theorists and practitioners, Anna Freud (1936/1966) brought together all of the defence mechanisms from S. Freud's varied writings into one coherent list, as part of A. Freud's *ego psychology* (P. F. Kernberg, 1994).

Unlike Sigmund Freud's (1923/1927) psychoanalytic theory, Anna Freud's (1936/1966) ego psychology depicted the ego as highly competent in navigating intrapersonal conflicts that involved conflicting messages from the id and the superego (Millon, 1996). Anna Freud's initial list of defence mechanisms employed by the ego included (1) *denial*, (2) *displacement*, (3) *intellectualisation*, (4) *projection*, (5) *rationalisation*, (6) *reaction formation*, (7) *regression*, (8) *repression*, and (9) *suppression*; A. Freud subsequently added (10) *sublimation*, (11) *identification with the aggressor*, and (12) *altruism* (the latter three of which S. Freud had not explored in detail, P. F. Kernberg, 1994). Westen and Chang (2000) pointed out that A. Freud (1958) was especially concerned with the defence mechanisms that individuals use during adolescence, which is a time of sexual awakening.

Notwithstanding Anna Freud's (1936/1966) efforts toward documenting all of the ways that the ego might reduce (and, perhaps, eliminate) individuals' intrapersonal anxiety, no single, agreed-upon survey exists that could measure most (if not all) of the defence mechanisms (although a small number of A. Freud's followers have attempted to do so; e.g., Joffe & Naditch, 1977). However, to the extent that the relatively new field of *neuropsychoanalysis* has revived academicians' and practitioners' interest in defence mechanisms (including, but not limited to, repression; Boag, 2006), the measurement of A. Freud's complete list of defence mechanisms remains a worthy conceptual and empirical goal within the psychodynamic school of personality psychology (see Davison & MacGregor, 1998). A. Freud's ego psychology functions as a viable alternative to "id psychology" (i.e., the psychoanalytic theory of S. Freud, 1900/1965) without requiring a full-scale rejection of S. Freud's core constructs (Millon, 1996).

ERIK ERIKSON'S VERSION OF EGO PSYCHOLOGY

Erik Erikson (1950) created a version of *ego psychology* that emphasised ego development as occurring in a more adaptive manner than Anna Freud (1936/1966) had assumed (Danzer, 2012). In addition, Erikson's version of ego psychology addressed direct societal influences on individuals' ego development (rather than indirect influences via the superego), to a greater extent than Anna Freud's earlier version of ego psychology had done (Millon, 1996). Lastly, Erikson's version of ego psychology explicitly promoted a *lifespan approach* to ego development, emphasising individuals' potential for psychological growth throughout their lives (Ewen, 1998).

Atalay (2007) contended that Erikson's (1950) version of ego psychology can be considered a "psychology of crisis," because it proposes that individuals either succeed or fail at resolving specific crises during each of Erikson's "Eight Stages of Man." Capps (2012) added that, in a refinement of the "(St)ages of Man," Erikson (1959/1980) identified eight *virtues* or sets of character strengths that emerge from individuals' successful crisis resolution: (1) *Hope* (ideally, during individuals' infancy), (2) *will* (early childhood), (3) *purpose* (preschool age), (4) *competence* (elementary school age), (5) *fidelity* (secondary school age), (6) *love* (young adulthood), (7) *care* (middle adulthood), and (8) *wisdom* (elderly adulthood). Constantinople (1969) devised the 60-item Inventory of Psychosocial Development to measure individual differences in success (5 items) versus failure (5 items) in resolving the first six psychosocial conflicts (i.e., *establishing interpersonal trust, establishing self-control, making further strides toward independence, adjustment to schoolteachers' demands, establishing a sense of who they are as unique persons* [i.e., *identity*], and *establishing a sense of who they are in relation to significant others*) that Erikson (1950) had proposed.

Subsequently, Whitbourne and Waterman (1979) expanded Constantinople's (1969) Inventory of Psychosocial Development to 80 items, adding success versus failure in resolving the final two conflicts (i.e., *mature enactment of societal roles that require caring for other persons*, and *achieving a sense of peace and tranquillity concerning previous successes and failures throughout life*; Ewen, 1998). Results of the respective studies by Constantinople and Whitbourne/Waterman – which were conducted on the same set of participants, ten years apart – revealed that Erikson's (1950) model concerning individuals' progression through the eight stages of psychosocial development was supported for men, but not for women (Ewen, 1998). However, both studies yielded individual differences in crisis resolution at each stage (regardless of gender) as Erikson would have predicted, leading Whitbourne and Waterman to conclude that crisis resolution was influenced by societal change (as distinct from biological maturation) to a greater degree among women than was the case among men.

Furthermore, as we noted in Chapter 1 of the present book, research on *ethnic identity* – a particular aspect of identity that Erikson (1968/1994) discussed at length – has blossomed since the early 1990s (Frable, 1997). When one considers the levels of interest that many cultural psychologists have displayed toward Erikson's construct of ethnic identity as operationalised via the Multigroup Ethnic Identity Measure (MEIM) by Phinney (1992; see Chapter 1 of the present book) and via the Ethnic Identity Scale (EIS) by Umana-Taylor and colleagues (Umana-Taylor, Yazedijan, & Bamaca-Gomez, 2004; see Box 2.1), one realises that Erikson's (1968/1994) ego psychology remains highly relevant to contemporary psychology, outside as well as within personality psychology (see Umana-Taylor, 2012).

BOX 2.1 UMANA-TAYLOR ET AL.'S (2004) ETHNIC IDENTITY SCALE

In Chapter 1 of the present book, we learned that Jean Phinney and colleagues (Phinney, 1992; Phinney & Ong, 2007; R. Roberts et al., 1999) drew heavily upon Erikson's (1959/1980, 1963/1995, 1968/1994) ego psychology as interpreted by Marcia (1966, 1967) in developing their Multigroup Ethnic Identity Measure (MEIM). In a now-classic review article that preceded the wave of research regarding ethnic identity during the 1990s, Phinney (1990) alluded briefly to Henri Tajfel's (1981; Tajfel & Turner, 1979) *social identity theory*, which proposes that individuals' self-esteem is influenced jointly by (1) individuals' unique or personal identity, as well as (2) one or more aspects of individuals' group-related or social identity (Verkuyten, 2005). However, social identity theory was not strongly reflected in the development of Phinney's MEIM (Umana-Taylor, 2012). Indeed, Phinney's conceptualisation of ethnic identity as part and parcel of *acculturation* (i.e., "preservation of one's heritage culture and adaptation to the host society"; Phinney et al., 2001) is more strongly rooted within John Berry's (1990, 1997) model of acculturation, rather than Tajfel's social identity theory.

In order to integrate concepts from Tajfel's (1981; Tajfel & Turner, 1979) social identity theory with concepts from Erikson's (1959/1980, 1963/1995, 1968/1994) ego psychology within one survey, Adriana Umana-Taylor et al. (2004) developed the 17-item Ethnic Identity Scale (EIS; for a review, see Cokley, 2007). Umana-Taylor and colleagues kept Phinney's (1992; Phinney & Ong, 2007; R. Roberts et al., 1999) cognitive construct of *exploration*, added the cognitive construct of *resolution* (i.e., individuals' conscious reflection upon what their ethnicity means to them), and reframed Phinney's affective construct of commitment as *affirmation* (Umana-Taylor, 2012). Results of factor analyses yielded support for Umana-Taylor et al.'s three hypothesised dimensions, although Phinney and Ong (2007) observed an important methodological confound: All of the affirmation items were worded in a *negative* direction; whereas all of the exploration and resolution items were worded in a *positive* direction (thus raising the possibility that Umana-Taylor et al.'s hypothesised distinction between resolution and affirmation should be re-interpreted as a negativity/ positivity distinction; see Kim & Mueller, 1978, concerning valence effects in factor analyses). Perhaps the most balanced appraisal that one can make is that, just as Phinney's own MEIM was designed partly as a rebuttal to perceived problems with pre-existing measures of ethnic identity (particularly racial identity; Helms, 2007), so too was Umana-Taylor et al.'s EIS (as well as the Brief EIS; Douglass & Umana-Taylor, 2015) designed partly as a rebuttal to perceived problems with the MEIM. Further research, ideally conducted outside Umana-Taylor's research programme, will be needed so that personality psychologists can properly evaluate the conceptual and empirical potential of the EIS.

OBJECT RELATIONS AND ATTACHMENT THEORIES

MELANIE KLEIN'S OBJECT RELATIONS THEORY

So far, every psychodynamic theory that we have reviewed in the wake of Sigmund Freud's version of psychoanalytic theory has rejected S. Freud's (1900/1965) initial premise that sexuality was the primary motive underlying infants' behaviour toward their mothers. Melanie Klein's (1927) version of *object relations theory* continues the trend away from an emphasis on infant sexuality, focusing on the quality of the mother–offspring relationship (whereby the mother is cast as the "object" of the offspring's emotions, and the pattern of interaction that develops between the mother and the offspring over time constitutes "relations"; Lubbe, 2008). According to Klein's object relations theory, the mother can simultaneously be the target of her offspring's love, *and* the target of her offspring's hate (with love and hate present in infants at birth; Debbane, 2011). One recurrent (albeit controversial) theme that one might detect from individuals' from childhood to adulthood, from the standpoint of Klein's (1927) theory, is the *splitting* of conflictual pairs of emotions toward a particular object (i.e., individuals' love and hate toward their mothers, such as the distinction between mothers' "good breast" and "bad breast"; Mandin, 2007).

Rusbridger (2012) noted that, in Klein's (1927) version of object relations theory, children may experience anxiety from id-related conflict between (1) the "life instinct" of eros (which gives rise to children's love toward their mothers) and (2) the "death instinct" of thanatos (which gives rise to children's hatred toward their mothers). Klein's (1927) object relations theory emphasises thanatos over eros, unlike Sigmund Freud's (1920/1961) revised psychoanalytic theory (in which eros is at least as important, if not *more* important, in comparison to thanatos; Juni, 2009). Klein believed that thanatos is revealed in the destructiveness that one commonly observes in children's play; such destructiveness presumably reflects unconscious *phantasy* (not to be confused with consciously experienced *fantasy*) on the part of the child (Grotstein, 2008). By the time that individuals reach adulthood, they run the risk of developing the *paranoid-schizoid position* (a mental state in which individuals erroneously perceive other persons as *part-objects*, rather than whole persons); Millon (1996) noted that the modern-day *schizoid personality disorder* (i.e., a psychological disorder that is marked by a sharp break between individuals' perceptions and reality) is a DSM category that bears the influence of Klein's object relations theory.

Klein's (1927) version of object relations theory casts child psychoanalysis (with children's play providing raw data) as analogous to adult psychoanalysis (with free associations providing raw data) – a stance that many of Klein's onetime followers (most notably Bowlby, 1969/1997) found difficult to accept (see H. Steele & M. Steele, 1998). Post-World War II-era research has tended to focus on adults' (as opposed to children's) object relations, such as the development of the Quality of Object Relations Scale (QORS) by Piper and colleagues (e.g., Azim & Piper, 1991; Piper et al., 1984). Nevertheless, van Dijken and colleagues (1998) noted that Klein's (1927) version of object relations theory planted the conceptual seeds of John Bowlby's (1969/1997) attachment theory (which we will cover later in the following subsection). Overall, Klein's object relations theory has been praised for (1) emphasising mother–child relationships and (2) expanding the boundaries of child psychoanalysis beyond free associations and the content of dreams (Millon, 1996).

JOHN BOWLBY'S ATTACHMENT THEORY

Klein's (1927) version of object relations theory eventually competed with Anna Freud's (1927/1975) version of ego psychology for dominance among psychodynamic theorists and practitioners within the UK, after both Klein and Anna Freud emigrated to London in the midst of World War II (and following the death of Sigmund Freud; Chodorow, 2004). In fact, open hostility erupted between Melanie Klein and Anna Freud within the British Psycho-Analytical Society, with many members of the Society feeling that they must choose sides (Prado de Oliviera, 2001). Among those psychodynamic theorists and practitioners who favoured Klein's perspective over A. Freud's perspective but did not wish to be perceived as overtly rejecting A. Freud (which conceivably could make them and their students vulnerable to retaliation from ego psychologists), two relational perspectives emerged within the resulting British Independent or "Middle Group" during the years that followed World War II: (1) Post-Kleinian object relations theories (e.g., Winnicott, 1931; Fairbairn, 1952; Guntrip, 1969); and (2) John Bowlby's (1969/1997, 1973/1998, 1980/1998) *attachment theory* (T. W. Hall, 2007). Unique among the theories that were developed by members of the British Independent Group, Bowlby's attachment theory was influenced jointly by *ethology* (i.e., the science of animal behaviour) and psychoanalysis (S. G. MacDonald, 2001).

In an early version of his attachment theory, Bowlby (1953) rejected Klein's (1927) premise that thanatos (the "death instinct") governed infants' behaviour toward mothers, instead arguing that a *need for emotional intimacy* was the primary motive underlying infants' behaviour – a need that was somewhat akin to eros (the "life instinct") as championed by S. Freud (1920/1961), but without the sexual connotations (H. Steele & M. Steele, 1998). Furthermore, Bowlby rejected Klein's insistence on interpreting children's play behaviour as an expression of children's latent hostility toward their mothers, instead opting to collect large-scale empirical data on the negative effects of long-term separation from mothers on children's personality and social development (van Dijken et al., 1998). Based on the results of observational research with children in hospitals, Bowlby proposed that (1) most caregivers consistently fulfil infants' need for emotional bonding, which leads infants to become *securely attached* to their caregivers; yet (2) some caregivers do *not* consistently meet infants' need for emotional bonding, which leads those infants to become *insecurely attached* to their caregivers (Bretherton, 1992).

Building upon Bowlby's (1953) attachment theory, Mary Salter Ainsworth and colleagues (Ainsworth, 1963, 1967; Ainsworth et al., 1978) developed the "strange situation" experimental paradigm (whereby infants were briefly separated from their mothers and, having been reunited with mothers, displayed different behavioural responses to their mothers) that led to the identification of three *infant attachment styles*: (1) *Secure* (i.e., easily comforted following mothers' return, presumably due to mothers' consistent provision of love and affection toward the infants); (2) *anxious-ambivalent* (i.e., alternating between pulling toward and pushing away from mothers, an insecure style that presumably is due to mothers' inconsistent provision of love and affection); and (3) *avoidant* (i.e., rejecting mothers, an insecure style that presumably is due to mothers' consistent failure to provide love and affection; Hazan & Shaver, 1994a, b). Subsequently, Hazan and Shaver (1987) developed a self-report measure of *adult attachment styles* (i.e., *secure*, or trusting toward romantic partners; *anxious-ambivalent*, or distrustful toward romantic partners because of concerns that their partners will not display as much love or affection toward them, compared to their displays of love and affection toward partners; and *avoidant*, or distrustful toward romantic partners because of concerns that the individuals themselves are unable or unwilling to display love or affection toward their partners; Bartholomew, 1990). Finally, Bartholomew and Horowitz (1991) expanded the scope of adult attachment styles to cover close relationships in general (rather than romantic relationships in particular, which Hazan and Shaver had covered), reconceptualised the anxious-ambivalent attachment style as *preoccupied*, and distinguished between *fearful* and *dismissing* forms of avoidant attachment styles (with the dismissing-avoidant style reflecting an insecure type because of individuals' denial that they possess a need for emotional intimacy, even though all individuals possess such a need; Mikulincer & Shaver, 2016).

Initially, Bowlby's (1953) attachment theory was rejected by other psychodynamic theorists and practitioners – not just by Klein (or, for that matter, A. Freud), but also by Bowlby's fellow members of the so-called "Independent" or "Middle Group" (van Dijken et al., 1998). However, Bowlby's (1969/1997, 1973/1998, 1980/1998) attachment theory has been credited with exerting considerable influence upon contemporary clinicians' diagnoses of *dependent personality disorder* (a dysfunctional, submissive behavioural pattern; Millon, 1996). In addition, Bowlby's theory emerged as the best-known theory of personality development within the field of relationship science (Finkel et al., 2017) and has inspired the development of numerous surveys, most notably the Experiences in Close Relationships (ECR) questionnaire (K. A. Brennan et al., 1998) as a measure of attachment orientations (which we explore further in Box 2.2). Bowlby clearly charted a different conceptual and empirical course than even his fellow

Independent Group members could have imagined concerning personality development (e.g., Ainsworth & Bowlby, 1991).

BOX 2.2 K. A. BRENNAN ET AL.'S (1998) EXPERIENCES IN CLOSE RELATIONSHIPS QUESTIONNAIRE

Earlier in the present chapter, we learned about the typology of secure, anxious-ambivalent, and avoidant attachment styles that Hazan and Shaver (1987) developed concerning adults' personality characteristics, in response to the three-group typology that Ainsworth and colleagues (1978) had created regarding infants' behavioural responses to reunion with their mothers after having been separated for several minutes. Also, we learned about the distinction between fearful-avoidant and dismissing-avoidant attachment styles in adulthood that Bartholomew and Horowitz (1991) proposed, following Bartholomew's (1990) four-category typology. Technically, Bartholomew and Horowitz promoted the measurement of each adult attachment style along a continuum, which yields four separate scores (i.e., secure, anxious-ambivalent/preoccupied, fearful-avoidant, *and* dismissing-avoidant) – rather than the categorical approach of Hazan and Shaver, which yields one score for each individual (see also Bartholomew, 1994, for a critique of then-existing measures of attachment styles).

By the late 1990s, several teams of researchers had concluded that a minimum of two separate dimensions (i.e., *attachment anxiety* and *attachment avoidance*) emerged from factor analyses of various attachment surveys that contained continuous items (Holmes, 2000). Consistent with the movement toward continuous surveys in adult attachment research, Kelly Brennan and colleagues (1998) created the 36-item Experiences in Close Relationships (ECR) Questionnaire, with each item scored along a 7-point range (although the survey has undergone several minor refinements over time; for a review, see Mikulincer & Shaver, 2016). In general, when measured via the ECR and related surveys (e.g., the ECR-Short Form; Wei et al., 2007), attachment avoidance is a significant negative predictor of relationship-promoting behaviour, and a significant positive predictor of relationship-threatening behaviour; whereas attachment anxiety is not consistently related to relationship-promoting or relationship-threatening behaviour (Gaines,

2016/2018). Particularly when one considers the extent to which attachment avoidance undermines aspects of *interdependence* or mutual influence within close relationships (i.e., high attachment avoidance is reflected in low levels of satisfaction with the relationship, high levels of perceived alternatives to the relationship, low levels of investment in the relationship, and low levels of accommodation toward partners' destructive behaviour; Etcheverry et al., 2013), the ECR displays enormous potential in enabling relationship scientists to demonstrate the relevance of attachment orientations to precursors of relationship stability over the long term (see Finkel et al., 2017, for a conceptual rationale that links attachment orientations with interdependence processes).

CRITIQUE OF PSYCHODYNAMIC PERSPECTIVES

Earlier in the present chapter, we learned that Sigmund Freud (1914/1953) held a negative attitude toward gay men, proclaiming that they suffered from "arrested development" when compared to heterosexual men. S. Freud took a similarly dim view toward *all* women, whether lesbian or heterosexual: Women could either (1) admit that they harboured "penis envy" (thus accepting their supposedly inferior status and making the best of a bad situation by attempting to become mothers), or (2) deny that they harboured "penis envy" (thus trying unsuccessfully to become like men and rejecting their own femininity; Margolis, 1984). Obviously, S. Freud's theory placed women in a catch-22 situation (i.e., damned if you do, damned if you don't; Walsh et al., 2014). We have already seen that Karen Horney (1922–37/1967) actively challenged S. Freud's "masculine psychology" by promoting her own, feminine psychology. In addition, Clara Thompson (1953) advocated a "psychology of women" more than a decade before the modern-day Women's Rights Movement in the US and other Western nations sparked widespread interest in such a topic among scholars and students (see Enns, 1989).

One of the more intriguing responses to feminist critiques of Sigmund Freud's (1908/1925) psychoanalytic theory – and, to a large degree, feminist critiques of the psychodynamic school in general – has been the attempt by some writers to seek reconciliation between feminism and psychoanalysis (Walsh et al., 2014). One of the best-known feminist psychoanalysts is Nancy Chodorow (1978), who argued that S. Freud and his followers may have been *right* to call attention to girls' negative feelings toward their mothers and positive feelings toward their fathers, but *wrong* to attribute those sets of feelings to an "Electra complex" (in all fairness, a term that S. Freud did not particularly like; Ewen, 1998). Rather, according to Chodorow, girls might simply respond to well-established connectedness toward their mothers by seeking greater levels of autonomy from their mothers (which, in turn, might result in establishing greater connectedness toward their fathers; Stevens, 2008). Thanks to efforts by Chodorow and other feminist psychoanalysts, members of the psychodynamic school of personality have become increasingly sensitised toward their own gender biases in the post-Women's Rights Era (e.g., emphasising the quality of the mother–child relationship, to the relative exclusion of other caregiver–child relationships; Margolis, 1984).

PRELUDE TO CHAPTER 3

Despite the differences that we have observed between William James's (1890/2010) self-theory and Sigmund Freud's (1900/1965) version of psychoanalytic theory, both theories can be classified as *mentalist*, due to their emphasis on conscious and unconscious within-person influences on individuals' behaviour (Kihlstrom, 2004). Conversely, the *behaviourist* school – which alternatively has been depicted as part of personality psychology (e.g., C. S. Hall & Lindzey, 1978) or as an alternative to personality psychology (e.g., Ewen, 1998) – emphasises *outside*-person influences on individuals' behaviour (Moore, 2013). Representative theories include (in order of appearance) the reflexology of Ivan Pavlov (1926/1928); the connectionism of Edward Thorndike (1911); the classical conditioning theory of John B. Watson (1916); Edward Tolman's (1932) stimulus-stimulus theory; the drive reduction theory of Clark Hull (1943); the operant reinforcement theory of B. F. Skinner (1938); the stimulus-response theory of Neal Miller and John Dollard (1941), and the social learning theories of Julian

Rotter (1954) as well as Albert Bandura and Richard Walters (1963). In Chapter 3, we shall examine behaviourist theories and relevant research in detail.

NOTE

1 Some of the terminology in the present chapter might be objectionable to some readers, especially under-18 readers. Especially when we cover Sigmund Freud's (1900/1965) version of psychoanalytic theory, we will encounter certain sexually charged terms. The authors apologise in advance for any discomfort that readers might experience when such terms appear in the text.

3

BEHAVIOURIST PERSPECTIVES ON PERSONALITY

Many (if not most) historians of science have concluded that Wilhelm Wundt was the founder of modern-day psychology, during the late 1800s (J. F. Brennan, 2003). After all, Wundt published the groundbreaking *Principles of Physiological Psychology* in 1874 (reprinted in 1910) and established the world's first psychological laboratory in 1879 (Wade et al., 2007). However, some historians of science would assert that the *real* founder of modern-day psychology was Ivan Pavlov, during the early 1900s (Walsh et al., 2014). In particular, Pavlov's landmark publication of *Lectures on Conditioned Reflexes: Twenty-Five Years of Objective Study of the Higher Nervous System* in 1926 (reprinted in 1928) documented the evolution of Pavlov's own programme of research from a focus on digestive physiology (for which he won the Nobel Prize in 1904) to an emphasis on classical conditioning (a cornerstone of early behaviourism in psychology; Todes, 1997).

Pavlov (1926/1928) initially viewed his physiologically orientated "reflexology" (which dealt with dogs' *conditioned* responses to environmental cues regarding the imminent availability of food, as built upon dogs' *unconditioned* responses to the food itself) as distinct from psychology (J. F. Brennan, 2003) but eventually aligned his reflexology with psychology (Walsh et al., 2014). Technically speaking, Pavlov's reflexology is a forerunner to the behaviourist school within personality psychology, rather than a behaviourist theory of personality *per se* (Ewen, 1998). Nevertheless, Pavlov's theory and research provided much of the conceptual

DOI: 10.4324/9781003601777-5

and methodological framework that led to the emergence of the behaviourist school (C. S. Hall & Lindzey, 1978).

In the present chapter, we will consider behaviourist perspectives on personality, which are inspired to varying degrees by Pavlov's (1926/1928) reflexology. We will learn that behaviourist theories – especially B. F. Skinner's (1938) operant reinforcement theory, which reflects Skinner's principle of *environmental determinism* (i.e., throughout individuals' lives, behaviour can be explained completely by influences that exist outside the individuals; Schellenberg, 1978) – have been criticised for their relative neglect of within-person influences on behaviour. However, we will also learn about certain neo-behaviourist responses – particularly Daryl Bem's (1972) self-perception theory – that acknowledge the usefulness of personality constructs as related to (but not necessarily causing) individuals' behaviour.

BASIC ASSUMPTIONS UNDERLYING BEHAVIOURIST PERSPECTIVES

A central premise among behaviourist perspectives on personality is the conviction that, in order to understand why persons speak and act as they do, one must consider the impact of the social and physical environments within which persons engage in particular forms of speech and action (Ewen, 1998). At a minimum, behaviourist theories pose important conceptual challenges to Sigmund Freud's principle of *psychic determinism* (i.e., beyond the age of 5 or 6, the speech and action of individuals can be explained completely by influences that exist within those individuals; Schellenberg, 1978). However, behaviourist theories vary in terms of their (de-)emphasis on personality constructs as causes or antecedents of individuals' speech and action (C. S. Hall & Lindzey, 1978).

As noted by J. F. Brennan (2003), behaviourism developed partly as a response to *functionalism* (concerned with the "how" and "why" of consciousness, or individuals' mental processes), which was associated with the self-theory of William James (1890/2010) and the instrumental pragmatism of John Dewey (1909). In turn, functionalism had developed partly as a response to *structuralism* (concerned with the "what" of consciousness, or individuals' mental organisation), which was associated with the content psychology of Edward Titchener (1902) and the content psychology of Titchener's mentor, Wihelm Wundt (1911/1973). Both structuralists and functionalists identify the mind (which, of course, is not directly observable) as the proper object of study for a science of psychology; whereas behaviourists identify observable behaviour as the proper object of study for a science of psychology (Walsh et al., 2014).

One can make a broad distinction between (1) those behaviourist theories that interpret humans' and other organisms' acts in terms of learning principles that can be understood without reference to a social context; versus (2) those behaviourist theories that interpret humans' or other organisms' acts in terms of learning principles that may well depend upon the social context in which organisms' behaviour takes place (see R. M. Ryan et al., 2019). The connectionism of Edward Thorndike (1911), the classical conditioning theory of John B. Watson (1916), the stimulus-stimulus theory of Edward Tolman (1932), and the drive reduction theory of Clark Hull (1943) all invoke asocial learning principles that generalise across species (see Bouton & Boakes, 2019). Conversely, the operant reinforcement theory of B. F. Skinner (1938), the stimulus-response theory of Neal Miller and John Dollard (1941), the social learning theory of Julian Rotter (1954), and the social learning theory of Albert Bandura and Richard Walters (1963) all suggest that – at least for humans – the social context can matter greatly to individuals' learning processes (see S. C. Cloninger, 2020). In the present chapter, we will review all of the aforementioned behaviourist theories from the vantage point of personality psychology.

BEHAVIOURIST THEORIES THAT INVOKE ASOCIAL LEARNING PRINCIPLES

EDWARD THORNDIKE'S CONNECTIONISM

Like Ivan Pavlov's (1926/1928) reflexology, Edward Thorndike's (1911) *connectionism* addresses relatively simple patterns of participants' learning via the associations that they make regarding events that occur close in time to each other, especially among animal participants (Elkind, 1999). However, unlike Pavlov's reflexology (which is concerned primarily with the interval of time that elapses between experimenters' presentation of conditioned and unconditioned *stimuli* to participants), Thorndike's connectionism focuses mainly on the interval of time that elapses between participants' *responses* and the outcomes that those participants experience; Wasserman & R. R. Miller, 1997). Consequently, Thorndike's connectionist theory and related research helped to establish the field of *comparative psychology* (which examines similarities and differences in the capacity for thinking across species; Blaser & Bellizzi, 2014).

John Donahoe (1999) labelled Thorndike (1905) as a "selectionist connectionist" (p. 451), emphasising the impact of Charles Darwin's (1859) theory of natural selection upon Thorndike's theory. To the extent that organisms' response to a particular stimulus is followed closely in time by *reinforcement* (i.e., an event that yields pleasure), one would expect organisms to emit that associated response again if/when the stimulus appears again – a principle that is known as the *law of effect* (Thorndike also proposed, but subsequently dropped the proposal, that *punishment* exerted a similarly strong effect in preventing organisms from emitting an associated response again; J. F. Brennan, 2003). Furthermore, to the extent that response-reinforcement sequences repeatedly occur across time, one would expect organisms' association between those events to be strengthened – a principle that is labelled as the *law of exercise* (Thorndike also proposed, but eventually dropped the proposal, that *lack* of repeated response-reinforcement sequences necessarily would lead to organisms' weakened associations between those events over an extended interval of time; Walsh et al., 2014). Thorndike's law of effect and law of exercise influenced the development of B. F. Skinner's (1938) operant reinforcement theory, which we will cover later in the present chapter (see also Sheehy, 2004).

Thorndike's (1905, 1911) connectionism is *hereditarian* in its assumption that members of certain so-called racial groups (i.e., persons of African descent) generally possessed a lower innate capacity for learning, compared to members of other so-called racial groups (e.g., persons of European descent) – a perspective that has been criticised, not just as "politically incorrect," but (perhaps more importantly) as *scientifically* incorrect (see Popkewitz, 2011). By the same token, Thorndike's (1917) connectionist theory and law of effect have been credited with helping to lay the conceptual foundation for modern-day *educational psychology*, which is concerned with the methods by which teachers can help *all* students learn effectively, regardless of students' racial or other ethnic group memberships (see Chase, 1998). Notwithstanding questions about the status of Thorndike's theory as a *bona fide* behaviourist theory (e.g., J. F. Brennan, 2003), Thorndike's connectionism has been hailed as an important precursor to the behaviourist theories of John B. Watson (1913) and B. F. Skinner (1938), both of which we will cover shortly.

JOHN B. WATSON'S CLASSICAL CONDITIONING THEORY

Rilling (2000) noted that John B. Watson (1916) developed *classical conditioning theory* (which involves the acquisition of *elicited responses* that originally occurred after the introduction of unconditioned stimuli but subsequently occur after the introduction of conditioned stimuli as well; Kirsch et al., 2004) largely as a response to Sigmund Freud's (1900/1965) psychoanalytic theory. J. B. Watson initially admired S. Freud's psychoanalytic theory but believed that individuals' *transference of emotions* (an important process within clinical settings, whereby clients may safely express emotions toward therapists after having been made aware that the emotions in question were originally experienced toward – but never had been expressed toward – their parents or other caregivers earlier in life; T. Davis, 2007) could be explained by appealing to principles of conditioned reflexes (associated with the reflexology of Ivan Pavlov, 1926/1928), rather than defence mechanisms (see Arlow, 2002). J. B. Watson was interested especially in the potential elicitation and generalisation of the "free-floating fear" that is known as anxiety (see Field & Nightingale, 2009).

Guided by classical conditioning theory (e.g., J. B. Watson, 1916), John B. Watson and Rosalie Rayner (1920) conducted one of the most controversial experiments in the history of psychology – namely, their conditioning of the approximately 11-month-old infant known as "Little Albert" to experience anxiety when presented with previously non-anxiety-inducing stimuli (starting with a white rat and adding various white, furry objects thereafter; LeUnes, 1983). As it turns out, J. B. Watson and Rayner were not the first behaviourists to apply classical conditioning techniques to a child (Windholz & Lamal, 1986). However, the ethical lapses in J. B. Watson and Rayner's study (not the least of which was the researchers' apparent use of prior knowledge that "Little Albert" reacted quite negatively to loud noises, which would explain the researchers' subsequent choice of the repeated banging of a gong as their unconditioned stimulus; see Sheehy, 2004) were so egregious – even by pre-World War II standards – that this particular study is a standout because of its precise application of behaviourist principles *and* its problematic methodology (Beck et al., 2009).

Perhaps the most regrettable aspect of J. B. Watson and Rayner's (1920) classical conditioning study was the fact that – having induced anxiety in "Little Albert" regarding several harmless objects – the researchers never attempted to de-condition the infant (who already was suffering from a cognitive impairment at the time of their experiment, as the researchers may have been aware; Fridlund et al., 2012). One of J. B. Watson's students, Mary Cover Jones (1924a), eventually developed a behaviour modification protocol for use with another young child (Kornfeld, 1989); M. C. Jones' pioneering work is profiled in Box 3.1. Perhaps the most neutral evaluation that one can offer concerning J. B. Watson's classical conditioning theory (e.g., J. B. Watson, 1916) and related research (e.g., J. B. Watson & Raynor, 1920) is that J. B. Watson clearly implemented a "behaviourist manifesto" (as originally presented by J. B. Watson, 1913) but offered a version of behaviourism that is questionable in terms of its ultimate benefit to science, especially when one considers the physical and psychological stress that Watson and Raynor inflicted upon "Little Albert" (Walsh et al., 2014).

BOX 3.1 M. C. JONES'S (1924A, B) BEHAVIOUR MODIFICATION PROGRAMME

After hearing John B. Watson give a lecture on classical conditioning theory and practice, Mary Cover Jones set out to remove the "free-floating fear" of anxiety toward particular stimuli in the physical environment (i.e., rabbits) that already had been manifested by a 3-year-old boy who was known as "Little Peter" (Malone, 2014). With the blessing of J. B. Watson, M. C. Jones (1924a) conducted the first known study of *behaviour modification*, whereby M. C. Jones began by bringing a rabbit into same experiment room as "Little Peter" (but without allowing any contact between the rabbit and the child) and subsequently guided "Little Peter" through a series of progressively challenging scenarios (e.g., giving candy to the child while the rabbit was in the room, allowing the rabbit to nibble at the child) that ended with "Little Peter" touching the rabbit without becoming anxious (Gieser, 1993). Over time, M. C. Jones became known for her caring attitude and behaviour toward "Little Peter" and other research participants – a stance that was consistent with her eventual nickname, "the mother of behaviour therapy" (Mussen & Eichorn, 1988).

In a follow-up study, M. C. Jones (1924b) identified anxiety-provoking stimuli in a sample of children and pursued an eclectic range of techniques on a trial-and-error basis, with the effect that some (but not all) techniques proved to be effective at eliminating the children's anxiety levels (see McClelland, 1985/1987). Among the most successful techniques was *systematic desensitisation*, in which other (and increasingly similar) stimuli were paired with the originally anxiety-provoking stimuli across successive trials (Gieser, 1993). Due to the innovative methodology and oft-encouraging outcomes of M. C. Jones's behaviour modification programme, followers have adapted M. C. Jones's techniques for use in measuring behavioural avoidance among children (e.g., Castagna et al., 2017), combining behaviour therapy with electroencephalogram (EEG) feedback in rehabilitating former felons e.g., von Hilsheimer & Quirk, 2006), and combining cognitive-behavioural therapy with drug therapy in treating several personality disorders (e.g., M. Davis et al., 2006), among many applications. Overall, M. C. Jones's behaviour modification programme can be regarded as the logical extension (and impressive complement) to J. B. Watson's classical conditioning programme (Fancher & Rutherford, 2017).

EDWARD TOLMAN'S (1932) STIMULUS-STIMULUS THEORY

Pavlov's (1926/1928) reflexology, Thorndike's (1911) connectionism, and J. B. Watson's (1913) classical conditioning theory collectively served as precursors to Neal Miller and John Dollard's

(1941) stimulus-response theory (to be reviewed later in the present chapter) – a theory that addresses within-organism events that serve as intermediaries between environmental events and organisms' observable behaviour (C. S. Hall & Lindzey, 1978). However, according to Edward Tolman's (1932) *stimulus-stimulus theory*, the environmental events and within-organism events in question are far more complicated than stimulus-response theory and its precursors had realised (Still, 1986). At a minimum, organisms (usually rats in Tolman's research; e.g., Tolman, 1938) routinely encounter a series of environmental events in their daily lives, each of which may trigger within-organism events (and, perhaps, require outward behaviour from the individual along the way; Mackintosh, 1981).

Combining portions of J. B. Watson's (1913) classical conditioning theory with aspects of Kurt Koffka's (1935) *Gestalt psychology* (which posits that the perceptual whole is greater than the sum of its parts; Walsh et al., 2014), Tolman's (1948) stimulus-stimulus theory proposes that various organisms display *purposiveness* (i.e., intentionality) in the process of responding to a series of environmental events as problem-solving exercises (Good & Still, 1986). Tolman's (1932) stimulus-stimulus theory is especially noteworthy for suggesting that rats, humans, and organisms from many other species may construct internal "maps" over time, enabling them to navigate their physical environments in a manner that may or may not be rewarding over the short term but can lead to rewards over the long term (D. E. Leary, 2004). Although the concept of "maps" has led some reviewers to label Tolman's theory as "cognitive behaviourism" (J. F. Brennan, 2003), a more nuanced reading of stimulus-stimulus theory reveals that the concept of *demand* (i.e., internal drive) – which can activated in organisms, via experimenter's manipulation of the environment in a way that creates deprivation (keeping in mind ethical considerations for the species in question) – is as important to Tolman's theory as is cognition (and the cognitive capacity of rats need not be presumed to equal the cognitive capacity of humans; Feest, 2005).

Tolman (1924) selectively bred his laboratory rats in a manner that may have produced an unusually intelligent strain (Dewsbury, 2000) – a practice that has been cited as anticipating the rise of behaviour genetics (e.g., Innis, 1992), for better or worse (we will cover this controversial area of personality psychology in more detail, when we cover biological perspective in Chapter 7). On a more overtly positive note, Tolman's (1932) stimulus-stimulus theory has been credited with anticipating the rise of cognitive perspectives in psychology (J. F. Brennan, 2003). All things considered, Tolman's theory stands as a major contributor to the literature on behaviour and learning, within and beyond personality psychology (C. S. Hall & Lindzey, 1978).

CLARK HULL'S DRIVE REDUCTION THEORY

David McClelland (1985/1987) gave credit to Edward Thorndike's (1911) connectionism and Edward Tolman's (1932) stimulus-stimulus theory for exploring the survival value that biologically based needs might confer to organisms' learning processes across a variety of species. In addition, McClelland cited Clark Hull's (1943) *drive reduction theory* (which argues that potential behaviour is the product of habit strength, inborn needs, learned needs, external stimuli, and incentives; Walsh et al., 2014) as a major advance in behaviourists' attempts to make their learning-orientated research as methodologically precise as possible. Hull's drive reduction theory (also known as *hypotheticodeductive theory*; J. F. Brennan, 2003) is mathematically driven, employing algebraic formulae as testable sets of predictions concerning the interplay between internal and external influences on organisms' behaviour (Sheehy, 2004).

One of the most novel constructs in Hull's (1943) drive reduction theory is *habit strength*, or the degree to which individuals not only have (1) developed and maintained associations between the introduction of external stimuli and individuals' behavioural response but also have (2) received rewards for specific responses to specific stimuli (C. S. Hall & Lindzey, 1978). According to Hull, unless stimuli and responses follow each other closely in time and are rewarded quickly, individuals are unlikely to form a given habit in the first instance (J. F. Brennan, 2003). Once individuals form particular habits, to the extent that individuals experience an increase in rewards over time (following individuals' response to the stimuli in question), individuals' habit strength will tend to rise; to the extent that individuals experience a decrease in rewards over time, individuals' habit strength will tend to fall (Walsh et al., 2014).

Hull's (1943) drive reduction theory has been criticised for assuming (incorrectly, as it turns out) that *all* behaviour in *all* species is as mindless (i.e., completely lacking in forethought and insight) as is the behaviour of laboratory rats in tightly controlled experimental scenarios (J. F. Brennan, 2003). Nevertheless, Hull's theory has received praise for offering a considerably more sophisticated account of learning than John B. Watson's (1913) better-known theory of classical conditioning had offered (Walsh et al., 2014). Especially as elaborated by Kenneth W. Spence (1956) – who addressed many of the empirical shortcomings of Hull's theory in practice – drive reduction theory paved the way for more explicitly social-psychological theories of behaviour, such as Neal Miller and John Dollard's (1941) stimulus-response theory (which we will cover later in the present chapter).

BEHAVIOURIST THEORIES THAT ACKNOWLEDGE THE POTENTIAL IMPACT OF SOCIAL CONTEXT UPON LEARNING PROCESSES

B. F. SKINNER'S OPERANT REINFORCEMENT THEORY

If J. B. Watson (1913) served as the primary proponent of "classical behaviourism" during the early 1900s, then B. F. Skinner (1950) emerged as the main advocate of "radical behaviourism" by the mid-1900s (Ewen, 1998). In contrast to all of the preceding behaviourist theories that we have encountered so far, Skinner's (1938) *operant reinforcement theory* proposes that many (if not most) behaviours that organisms emit are voluntary, even arbitrary – *not* elicited by stimuli (C. S. Hall & Lindzey, 1978). In fact, some behaviours (e.g., a pigeon's pecking a bar) often are emitted *before* stimuli (e.g., birdseed to be released by the bar) are presented to organisms; yet stimuli may reinforce previously occurring behaviour (Clavijo, 2013). Furthermore, to the extent that an organism experiences a stimulus that follows a response as rewarding, the organism will continue to emit the response that yielded the stimulus – an example of *positive reinforcement* (Schellenberg, 1978). Accordingly, Skinner focused on *operant conditioning*, whereby organisms can be guided toward acquiring entirely new sequences of behaviour, depending on the degree to which organisms continue to experience stimuli as rewarding (Sheehy, 2004).

In terms of research, Skinner (1938) was known primarily for his application of operant reinforcement theory to the manipulation of pigeons' and rats' behaviour, (Walsh et al., 2014). However, in *Verbal Behavior*, Skinner (1957) attempted to explain the most uniquely human of all behaviours – namely, *speech* – in terms of operant conditioning principles (Salzinger, 2008). According to Skinner, individuals' speech can be rewarded by audience members (thus making individuals' speech more likely to occur in the future), versus *not* rewarded – or even punished – by audience members (thus making individuals' speech less likely to occur in the future; Goddard, 2012). Thus, regardless of the complexity of the behaviour in question (and regardless of the species whose members' behaviour is under consideration), Skinner believed that the same mechanistic processes can be observed across organisms (J. F. Brennan, 2003).

Not only has Skinner's (1957) operant reinforcement theory been challenged on the grounds that it is inadequate as an explanation for the production of human language in particular (e.g., Chomsky, 1959); but Skinner's theory also has been challenged on the grounds that it dismisses the usefulness of *all* personality constructs (including such consciously experienced constructs as traits, values, and attitudes) as potential predictors of human behaviour in general (a dismissal that arguably helped to fuel the cognitive revolution in psychology; see Haslam et al., 2017). By the same token, even Skinner's critics have acknowledged that operant reinforcement theory seems to explain certain aspects of language production (Goddard, 2012) and does not rule out the possible existence of personality constructs (Clavijo, 2013). Notwithstanding the provocative nature of Skinner's (1974) radical behaviourism, one can commend Skinner for retaining a sense of optimism concerning human behaviour as largely amenable to change via academicians' application of operant reinforcement principles (as distinct from clinicians' and academicians' application of psychodynamic or other "mentalistic" principles; Butt, 2004).

NEAL MILLER AND JOHN DOLLARD'S STIMULUS-RESPONSE THEORY

During the interval between World War I and World War II, the behaviourist school succeeded in prompting psychologists *en masse* to re-define their discipline as the science of behaviour (rather than the science of the mind; Hebb, 1960). However, by the time that World War II had begun to wreak large-scale havoc within and beyond academia, some behaviourists already were seeking to re-incorporate certain "mentalistic" constructs within their theories (Mandler, 2002). One of the earliest examples of the resulting neo-behaviourist perspective on personality was Neil Miller and John Dollard's (1941) *stimulus-response theory*, which drew jointly upon Sigmund Freud's (1900/1965) psychoanalytic theory and Ivan Pavlov's (1927) reflexology (Ewen, 1998). According to stimulus-response theory, behaviours can be understood as direct responses to within-individual influences, which (in turn) can be understood as direct responses to outside-individual influences (thus predicting that within-individual influences will mediate the impact of outside-individual influences on behaviour; C. S. Hall & Lindzey, 1978).

Probably the best-known aspect of Dollard and Miller's (1950) stimulus-response theory was the *frustration-aggression hypothesis*, which holds that – when others are perceived as having prevented individuals from achieving a particular goal – individuals' drive toward aggression (following the drive theory of Hull, 1943) will be activated, leading the individuals to behave in an antisocial manner toward the others in question (Eibl-Eibesfeldt, 1977). Dollard, Miller, and colleagues (Dollard et al., 1939) argued that (1) when one observes individuals behaving in an antisocial manner, one can be reasonably confident that the individuals have already concluded that they were frustrated by others; and (2) when individuals believe that they have been frustrated by others, one can be reasonably confident that individuals subsequently will behave in an antisocial manner toward the others in question (C. S. Hall & Lindzey, 1978). Consistent with the frustration-aggression hypothesis, Hovland and Sears (1940) reported empirical support for the frustration-aggression hypothesis in their secondary analysis of cotton prices and anti-Black lynchings in the US South (i.e., as the price of cotton went down over the years,

Whites' lynchings of Blacks went up in the American South, suggesting that Black Americans appeared to be scapegoats for some White Americans' economic frustration; see J. M. Jones, 1997).

In a re-analysis using modern-day statistical methods, Hepworth and West (1988) found that the magnitude of the correlation between cotton prices at one point in time and anti-Black lynchings at a later point in time was smaller than Hovland and Sears (1940) had initially calculated. In addition, Hepworth and West uncovered a close-to-significant negative correlation between cotton prices and Whites' lynchings of other *Whites* that Hovland and Sears (1940) had neither predicted nor detected (see G. W. Allport, 1954/1979, p. 257, regarding "scapegoats for special occasions"). Nevertheless, Hepworth and West *did* replicate Hovland and Sears's overall finding that regional economic difficulties were a precursor to Whites' subsequent lynching of Blacks, to a significant degree (a testament to the "prejudice problematic," as described by Dixon & Levine, 2012). Overall, Miller and Dollard's (1941; Dollard & Miller, 1950) stimulus-response theory and frustration-aggression hypothesis have (Dollard et al., 1939) received considerable support (for a review, see Marcus-Newhall et al., 2000).

JULIAN ROTTER'S VERSION OF SOCIAL LEARNING THEORY

Miller and Dollard (1941) initially alluded to social learning as a potential influence on individuals' behaviour but did not make social learning a major concept in their subsequent work (e.g., Dollard & Miller, 1950). To a large extent, Miller and Dollard agreed with Hull's (Hull et al., 1940) perspective on social learning as a simple process of association (e.g., "monkey see, monkey do"). In contrast, Julian Rotter's (1954) version of *social learning theory* – which draws partly upon Miller and Dollard's stimulus-response theory – addresses the role that watching other people receive (or fail to receive) reinforcement plays in individuals' formation of beliefs about the likelihood that their own behaviour will be reinforced (C. S. Hall & Lindzey, 1978). Funder (2001) noted that Rotter (1954) identified *expectancy* or expectations about potential, future reinforcement (rather than associations involving past reinforcement) as one major influence on individuals' behaviour.

Weiner (2010) added that the *value* attached by individuals to potential, future reinforcement is the other major influence on individuals' behaviour in Rotter's version of social learning theory. As a result, according to Rotter, expectancy x value = behaviour (i.e., individuals' behaviour reflects individuals' belief about future outcomes, combined with the importance that individuals place upon those outcomes; Strickland, 1989).

Rotter (1966) eventually concluded that individuals differ in their beliefs about causality and control – that is, *locus of control* is assumed to vary across persons (Lefcourt, 1991). Rotter contended that individuals may be *internal* (i.e., perceive their successes or failures in life as due to their own efforts) versus *external* (i.e., perceive their successes or failures on life as due to external factors, such as impersonal fate or powerful others) in their locus of control (Carton & Nowicki, 1994). Accordingly, Rotter (1966) developed the Locus of Control Scale to measure individual differences in this construct, asking participants to answer a series of questions in which they were required to agree with one of a pair of statements (with one statement expressing an internal locus of control, and the other statement expressing an external locus of control; Strickland, 1989). Using a prototype of the Locus of Control Scale, Gore and Rotter (1963) found that persons with an internal locus of control were more likely than were persons with an external locus of control to commit themselves to the US Civil Rights Movement (a finding that is consistent with the view that – having learned about other Americans "making a difference" by getting involved in the struggle for social equality – many individuals apparently decided that they, too, could help to make social change a reality, as would be expected from the social learning theory of Rotter, 1954).

In a critique of Rotter's social learning theory (1954) and conceptualisation of locus of control (1966), Carton and Nowicki (1994) pointed out that the causes or *antecedents* of individual differences in locus of control are not well understood, other than that "external" children report higher levels of stress than do "internals" (possibly because parents of "internals" are more consistent than are parents of "externals," in terms of offering rewards when the children behave well and withholding rewards when the children behave badly). Also, due to concerns about the rigidity of

Rotter's internal–external dichotomy, Levenson (1974) developed an alternative to Rotter's (1966) Locus of Control Scale that did not force participants to choose "external" over "internal" items or vice versa (as we shall see in Box 3.2, a change that allowed Levenson to identify three separate locus of control dimensions). Nevertheless, Rotter's original Locus of Control Scale remains the most popular measure of this construct (Lefcourt, 1991) and has consistently yielded results concerning the *consequences* of internal versus external locus of control (e.g., "internal" adults tend to perform significantly better on academic assessments than do "external" adults; Carton & Nowicki, 1994). All things considered, Rotter's social learning theory has emerged as one of the most influential neo-behaviourist theories of personality (Funder, 2001).

BOX 3.2 LEVENSON'S (1974) INTERNALITY, CHANCE, AND POWERFUL OTHERS SCALES

In spite of the popularity of Julian Rotter's (1966) Locus of Control Scale (undoubtedly owing to the simple, unidimensional nature of the underlying construct), some critics have noted that Rotter never conducted factor analyses of the scale (thus leaving questions unanswered regarding the construct validity of the survey across samples; e.g., West & Finch, 1997). Partly due to questions about Rotter's methodology, subsequent researchers have developed alternatives to the Locus of Control Scale (R. Brown, 1986). One of the best-known alternatives is Hanna Levenson's (1973a) multidimensional version, which measures three distinguishable aspects of locus of control: (1) *Internality*, (2) *control by chance events*, and (3) *control by powerful others* (with the latter two dimensions representing external influences that have originated within individuals' physical and social environments, respectively; Lefcourt, 1991).

In a series of studies, Levenson (e.g., Levenson, 1973a, b; Levenson, 1974) linked internality, control by chance events, and control by powerful others to a variety of behavioural outcomes in the spheres of work, politics, and interpersonal relations (with internality frequently leading to psychologically adaptive outcomes, and control by chance and powerful others frequently leading to psychologically maladaptive outcomes; for a review, see Levenson,

1981). Moreover, Walkey (1979) obtained independent support for Levenson's internality, chance, and powerful others dimensions (scores on chance and powerful others tend to be significantly and positively correlated with each other; whereas scores on internality are not consistently related to scores on the two external dimensions). However, apparently disregarding Levenson's results, Rotter (1975) continued to conceptualise locus of control in terms of opposite (i.e., internal versus external) types. Overall, Rotter's unidimensional perspective emerged as the dominant view regarding locus of control (R. Brown, 1986). Nevertheless, Levenson's multidimensional perspective on locus of control has been praised as a viable alternative to Rotter's view (Lefcourt, 1991).

ALBERT BANDURA AND RICHARD WALTERS' VERSION OF SOCIAL LEARNING THEORY

Compared to Miller and Dollard's (1941) stimulus-response theory, Rotter's (1954) version of social learning theory represents a move away from Sigmund Freud's (1920/1961) version of psychoanalytic theory (C. S. Hall & Lindzey, 1978). As Grusec (1992) noted, Albert Bandura and Richard Walters' version of *social learning theory* (1963) continued the move away from Freudian constructs. W. F. White (1993) added that, according to Bandura and Walters' (1963) social learning theory, most of what individuals learn is acquired from observing other persons' behaviour (along with the rewards versus punishments that those other persons receive). However, Bandura and Walters were not particularly interested in examining the construct of locus of control that Rotter (1966) had popularised (see Funder, 2001). Rather, Bandura and Walters cast their social learning theory as a direct response to Miller and Dollard's (1950) stimulus-response theory – specifically, in testing the frustration-aggression hypothesis (as articulated by Dollard et al., 1939).

Albert Bandura et al.'s (1961) classic study of the effects of modelling on children's displaced aggression (i.e., the "Bobo doll" study) was an important precursor to the development of Bandura and Walters' (1963) social learning theory (Ewen, 1998). Children who not only were prevented from playing with attractive toys (i.e., subjected to frustration, in the terms of Miller &

Dollard, 1941) but also had observed an adult model react to frustration by acting aggressively toward a large Bobo doll were significantly more likely to engage in aggressive behaviour of their own toward the hapless Bobo doll than were children who either (1) saw a model acting *non*aggressively in response to frustration or (2) did not see a model in advance (Sheehy, 2004). Thus, contrary to Miller and Dollard's (1941) stimulus-response theory and frustration-aggression hypothesis (Dollard et al., 1939), Bandura and colleagues found that frustration *did not* lead inevitably to aggression (C. S. Hall & Lindzey, 1978). Indeed, as Markus and Zajonc (1985) pointed out, Bandura and Walters' version of social learning theory has been described as a stimulus-*organism*-response theory, because of the importance that it places upon individuals' capacity for consciously processing information from the environment before deciding on a course of action.

E. E. Jones (1985/1998) criticised Bandura and Walters' (1963) version of social learning theory (among other neo-behaviourist theories) for failing to acknowledge the role that models often play in deliberately seeking to shape observers' behaviour. However, W. F. White (1993) credited Bandura and Walters for attending to individuals' capacity for self-rewards and self-punishments as distinct from the rewards and punishments that they may receive from other persons. Finally, in Bandura and Walters's version of social learning theory, children as well as adults have the capacity to grasp the concepts of rewards and punishments (including self-rewards and self-punishments) – capacities that Hull (1943) and Miller and Dollard (1941) had not anticipated (see C. S. Hall & Lindzey, 1978). All in all, Bandura and Walters's theory helped set the stage for even more overtly cognitive theories of personality (e.g., the social-cognitive theory of Bandura, 1986, which we will cover in Chapter 6) in the aftermath of the cognitive revolution in psychology (see Sheehy, 2004).

A BEHAVIOURIST CHALLENGE TO PREVAILING BEHAVIOURIST THEORIES: EDWIN GUTHRIE'S ONE-TRIAL LEARNING THEORY

Earlier in the present chapter, we noted the role that Ivan Pavlov's (1927) reflexology played in the rise of the behaviourist tradition within psychology, throughout the first half of the twentieth century (see also Posner, 2019). Given the influence of Pavlov's theory and methodology upon the school of behaviourism, one might be surprised to find that at least one historically relevant behaviourist – namely, Edwin Ray Guthrie (1935) – questioned Pavlov's core assumption that the repeated pairing of a single stimulus from the environment with a single response from an organism over time constitutes learning (e.g., Guthrie, 1930; but see also Pavlov, 1932, for a rebuttal of Guthrie's critique). In fact, according to Guthrie's (1942) *one-trial learning theory*, actual "learning" typically involves multiple responses following a given stimulus and consists of the organism's association between the single stimulus and a *subsequent* response – without the need for repeated pairing (Ormond, 2008). The tendency for historians of psychology to cite one-trial learning theory alongside Tolman's (1932) stimulus-stimulus theory and Hull's (1943) drive reduction theory might imply that Guthrie's theory focuses on asocial stimuli (e.g., Clark, 2005). However, some reviewers have alluded to the relevance of Guthrie's theory for social psychology (e.g., Sheffield, 1959).

Following Pavlov's (1932) apparent dismissal of Guthrie's (1930) one-trial learning theory, Guthrie (1934) elaborated upon his view that various forms of conditioning that previously had served as the subject matter for behaviourism – including, but not limited to, classical conditioning as part of Pavlov's reflexology – are best understood as instances of a more general phenomenon that can be described as "the law of simultaneous conditioning or association by contiguity in time" (p. 200), which we shall abbreviate as *contiguous conditioning* (see Escobar & Roca, 2012). Guthrie's theory contends that, just as environments routinely produce a variety of stimuli, so too do organisms produce a variety of responses in everyday life; and organisms may come to associate *some* of the stimuli with *some* of the responses that occur relatively close together in time, even when organisms perceive certain stimuli *after* they perceive their own responses (see Windholz, 1992). Although Guthrie's one-trial learning theory clearly is behaviourist in orientation, Guthrie's theory is sufficiently broad to encompass constructs such as *habits* (e.g., Guthrie & Powers, 1950), which trait theorists such as Allport (1937/1951) cast as precursors to the development of traits (Malone, 2016).

In a direct comparison of Guthrie's (1935) one-trial learning theory (as elaborated by Voeks, 1950) with Hull's (1943) drive reduction theory, David Zeaman and Louis Radner (1953) found that experimenters' presentation of a bright light as a stimulus could lead rats to engage in a natural behavioural response for members of their species (i.e., running) that was sufficient for experimenters to turn *off* the light (thus providing an association between stimulus and response that enabled learning to occur), consistent with both theories. However, Zeaman and Radner also found that rats could not be taught to respond to experimenters' presentation of darkness as a stimulus by running and thus prompting experimenters to turn *on* a light – results that supported Hull's theory (i.e., the type of stimulus mattered; rats find it rewarding to escape bright light, rather than darkness) but not Guthrie's theory (i.e., the type of stimulus should not matter; any stimulus and response that occur closely together should induce rats to associate the two phenomena and thus engage in learning). Bernard Balleine and Sean Ostlund (2007) concluded that (1) Guthrie's theory represented an advance over Tolman's (1932) stimulus-stimulus theory (covered earlier in this chapter); yet (2) Hull's theory represented an advance over Guthrie's theory.

APPLIED BEHAVIOUR ANALYSIS: PRESERVING UNADULTERATED BEHAVIOURISM(?)

According to Funder and Fast (2010), the contemporary practice of *Applied Behaviour Analysis* (ABA) – which draws upon Watsonian classical conditioning and (especially) Skinnerian operant conditioning – stands as an enduring example of unadulterated behaviourism. J. B. Leaf et al. (2017) noted that ABA typically involves clinical intervention that is designed to bring about constructive change in various socially relevant behaviours on the part of individuals across time. However, as J. B. Leaf et al. (2022) pointed out, APA is associated particularly with the treatment of individuals who have been diagnosed with autistic spectrum disorders – not a set of personality disorders *per se*, but rather a set of neurodevelopmental disorders with important implications for individuals' social and psychological functioning beyond clinical and academic settings. T. H. Smith and Eikeseth (2011) specifically credited researcher/practitioner O. Ivar Lovaas (1981, 1987) for popularising ABA as a therapy for managing autistic spectrum disorders among children. Notwithstanding Lovaas's efforts toward promoting ABA, E. K. Morris et al. (2005) observed that B. F. Skinner's (1948/1976) fictitious work *Walden Two* (a utopian account of reinforcement principles as guiding an entire society) anticipates Lovaas's efforts.

One feature of the literature on autism spectrum disorders is that symptoms such as aggressive behaviour are often labelled as "traits," thus lending to the misconception that the underlying psychological problems are manifestations of personality disorders, rather than manifestations of neurodevelopmental disorders (see Matson, 2009). As it happens, the list of personality disorders within the fifth edition of the American Psychiatric Association's (2017) *Diagnostic and Statistical Manual of Mental Disorders* (DSM-V) includes *borderline, antisocial, dependent, narcissistic,* and *schizotypal personality disorders*; autistic spectrum disorders are nowhere to be found within that list (see Widiger & McCabe, 2020). Moreover, even if we put aside the issue of "traits" as implicated in autistic spectrum disorders, the use of ABA in treating symptoms of those particular disorders is controversial in some quarters (e.g., members of neurodiversity communities who have expressed concerns about therapists' violation of autistic persons' rights; J. B. Leaf et al., 2022). The resulting debates over the merits of ABA as directed toward management of autistic spectrum disorders extend beyond the scope of the present book (for an example, see Sandoval-Norton & Shkedy, 2019; versus Gorycki et al., 2020).

Some reviewers have expressed concern that the evidence-based practice (EBP) that traditionally was a core requirement of ABA has become so broadly defined that scientific rigour has been lost within much of the resulting research that purportedly is behaviourist in orientation (e.g., by assigning comparable weight to clinicians' subjective evaluations versus more objective data from clients; Capuano & Killu, 2021). Such a concern might be allayed to the extent that researchers distinguish between (1) ABA (which is designed to address social and psychological issues that transcend the lives of individual clients or other participants in research); and (2) *Clinical Behavioural Analysis*, also known as *CBA* (which is designed to address the social and psychological issues that are experienced by individual clients in therapy; Ferreira et al., 2021). However, that distinction might be blurred by a growing trend toward supplementing quantitative research with more qualitative research, even within ABA (for an example of advocacy regarding the use of qualitative methods within ABA, see Burney et al., 2023). In the meantime, even proponents of ABA have begun to ask whether the impact of their research should be judged primarily on the basis of real-world influence, rather than academic publications and citations (e.g., Malott, 2018).

CRITIQUE OF BEHAVIOURIST PERSPECTIVES

Is it as easy for psychologists to banish the self and its contents (e.g., all of the personality constructs that one will find in the present book) from empirical consideration as some behaviourists (especially Skinner, 1938) would have us believe? By and large, personality psychologists would respond with an emphatic "No!" to such a question (see Ewen, 1998). Surely human beings possess selves (James, 1890/2010), however unaware individuals might be regarding particular contents of their selves at a particular point in time (S. Freud, 1900/1965). Surely the self and its contents are linked to individuals' behaviour (G. W. Allport, 1961/1963), however dependent individuals' behaviour might be upon situational influences (G. W. Allport, 1937/1951).

One of the most creative attempts to reconcile behaviourism (most notably operant conditioning theory; Skinner, 1938) with "mentalism" (most notably self-theory; James, 1890/2010) is Daryl Bem's (1965, 1967, 1972) *self-perception theory* (which proposes that individuals infer their attitudes partly by speculating on the reasons why they behave as they do toward specific physical and social stimuli; Schellenberg, 1978). In practice, D. Bem's self-perception theory does not explain the formation of *all* attitudes (or the consequences of *all* behaviours; S. T. Fiske & S. E. Taylor, 1991). Nonetheless, D. Bem's theory complements Leon

Festinger's (1957) *cognitive dissonance theory* (which posits that discrepancies between individuals' attitudes and behaviour result in anxiety, which individuals may seek to reduce by changing their attitudes over time; Petty & Brinol, 2015) by explaining that no presumption of prior discrepancy-generated anxiety is necessary for one to understand how particular attitudes are formed (Molouki & Pronin, 2015). More generally, D. Bem's self-perception theory embodies the *Scientist* mode or metaphor of self-perception (which is based on the assumption that individuals are motivated to acquire the most accurate information that they can acquire about themselves; Robins & John, 1997) and might ultimately be applied to other aspects of the self.

PRELUDE TO CHAPTER 4

In *Societal Structures of the Mind*, Uriel G. Foa and Edna B. Foa (1974) contended that psychodynamic therapists (in the tradition of S. Freud, 1900/1965) tend to deny respect (if not affection) to their clients; whereas it is not clear whether behaviourist therapists (in the tradition of Skinner, 1938) give or deny the interpersonal resources of affection and respect to their clients. In stark contrast, according to U. G. Foa and E. B. Foa, *humanistic* therapists (in the tradition of Rogers, 1961) tend to give affection as well as respect to their clients – a testament to the "Third Force" that Abraham Maslow (1954) envisioned for humanism as a counterpoint to the psychodynamic and behaviourist schools in personality psychology (Sappington, 1989). Within the school of humanism, representative theories include (in order of appearance) the love-oriented aspects of Erich Fromm's (1955, 1956) existential humanism (as distinct from the hate-orientated aspects for which Fromm may be better known; e.g., Fromm, 1941); Kurt Goldstein's (1939) organismic psychology, Charlotte Buhler's (1968) version of humanistic psychology, Abraham Maslow's (1968) version of self-actualisation theory, and Carl Rogers' (1961) version of self-actualisation theory. [In addition, within the related school of *existentialism*, representative theories include (in order of appearance) Jean-Paul Sartre's (1943/1956) version of existential philosophy, Simone de Beauvoir's (1947) version of existential philosophy, Frantz Fanon's

(1952/1967) version of existential psychology, and Rollo May's (1953) version of existential psychology.] In Chapter 4, we will examine these theories and associated research – alongside alternative perspectives from the emergent *positive psychology* movement (i.e., Diener et al., 1985; Ryan & Deci, 2000b; Ryff, 1989) – in greater detail.

4

HUMANISTIC AND EXISTENTIAL PERSPECTIVES ON PERSONALITY

In Chapter 2 of the present book, we covered various psychodynamic theories that placed greater emphasis upon social-psychological influences on individuals' personality development than Sigmund Freud's (1900/1965) version of psychoanalytic theory had addressed (see also S. C. Cloninger, 2020). However, we neglected to mention Erich Fromm's (1941, 1955) *existential humanism*, which maintains that the degree to which entire societies are functional versus dysfunctional will tend to be reflected in the personalities and corresponding behaviours of individuals who inhabit those societies (see Pietikainen, 2019). For examples, in *The Art of Loving*, Fromm (1956) contended that – despite the allure of *authoritarianism* as a means toward escaping the demands of freedom (with the negative consequence of succumbing to hatred toward entire groups of stigmatised persons) – individuals ideally should embrace *freedom* by choosing to enter and maintain particular close relationships (Cortina, 2015).

Fromm's (1956) resulting typology of *ways of loving* (i.e., individuals' attitudes toward various types of close relationships) is reflected in John Alan Lee's (1973) typology of *colours of love* (i.e., *brotherly love*, or friendship love; *motherly love*, or selfless love; *erotic love*, or passionate love; *self-love*, or love turned inward; and *love of one's Creator*, or religious love). In turn, J. A. Lee's typology is reflected in Clyde Hendrick and Susan Hendrick's (1986; C. Hendrick et al., 1984, 1998) typology of *love styles*, or attitudes toward love (i.e., *eros*, or passionate love; *agape*, or selfless

DOI: 10.4324/9781003601777-6

love; *pragma*, or practical love; *storge*, or friendship love; *mania*, or obsessive love; and *ludus*, or game-playing love; see Djikic & Oatley, 2004). With the exception of ludus (which clearly undermines pro-relationship behaviour), love styles either promote pro-relationship behaviour (i.e., eros, possibly agape) or – at a minimum – do not work against individuals' relationship-maintaining behaviour (i.e., pragma, storge, and mania; Gaines, 2016/2018).

Fromm's (1941, 1955) existential humanism ultimately emerged as a seminal influence on theories, research, and practice in humanistic as well as existential psychology (D. Hoffman, 2003). Accordingly, in the present chapter, we shall examine personality theories from the separate yet related perspectives of humanistic psychology and existential psychology. Notwithstanding the differences between humanistic and existential perspectives (most notably concerning humans' awareness of their own mortality, which is emphasised more prominently within existential psychology than it is emphasised within humanistic psychology; C. S. Hall & Lindzey, 1970), we shall refer to "humanistic/existential psychology" as a school of thought that is unified by the belief that human nature essentially is positive or constructive (see Ewen, 1998). Along the way, we shall also consider contributions from the modern-day positive psychology movement, which has been cast as more empirically rigorous than humanistic/existential psychology (e.g., Seligman & Csikszentmihalyi, 2000) but nonetheless owes a considerable intellectual debt to humanistic/existential psychology (e.g., K. J. Schneider, 2011b).

BASIC ASSUMPTIONS UNDERLYING HUMANISTIC AND EXISTENTIAL PERSPECTIVES

According to humanistic/existential psychology, the whole person – not the gene, cell, or even brain of the person – is the proper unit of analysis for personality psychology (E. Taylor, 2000). Implicit in this core belief is the assumption that human behaviour cannot be reduced entirely to mechanistic processes involving individuals' brains working in isolation from individuals' physical and social environments (the latter of which typically includes interaction with other human beings; see E. Taylor, 1991). Rather, in order to understand why humans behave as they to, one must begin with the individual person and subsequently consider information about the person's behaviour as a function of various forces within the person *and* various forces outside the person (E. Taylor, 2010).

Furthermore, just as the human mind is integral to the body (especially the brain) within which it resides, according to humanistic/existential psychology, so too is human consciousness an essential aspect of the mind that gave rise to it (a stance that distinguishes the humanistic/existential school from the psychodynamic and behaviouristic schools of thought within personality psychology; K. J. Schneider, 2011a). Like freedom, consciousness is never absolute; human beings operate within physical and psychological constraints that necessarily place limits on their awareness of the world (Greening, 1992). Nevertheless, among mortal entities on Earth, humans' capacity for awareness of their physical and social environments seems to be unrivalled (although some critics might contend that human beings are not sufficiently aware of [other] animals' awareness to claim outright superiority in this regard; e.g., Adams, 2010).

Finally, just as human consciousness is part and parcel of the mind from which it arose, in the view of humanistic/existential psychology, so too is the self a vital aspect of the consciousness from which it was derived (a perspective that likewise distinguishes the humanistic/existential school from the psychodynamic and behaviourist schools; Slife & Barnard, 1988). Among human beings, it is not just the case that individuals are aware of their physical and social environments; individuals are aware that *they* are the ones who possess such awareness (although the self may be far more elusive than any other aspect of individuals' daily experience; Puhakka, 2000). If any of the constructs that we have covered so far in the present chapter qualifies as uniquely human, then the self (and its by-product, the self-concept) would seem to be such a candidate (Sleeth, 2006).

Before covering specific theories in detail, we acknowledge that some critics (e.g., DeCarvalho, 1990) have distinguished between (1) the process of "becoming" (part of the being versus becoming dichotomy) as determined by a self-actualisation motive, from the standpoint of humanistic personality theories (e.g., Buhler, 1968; Goldstein, 1939, 1940; Maslow, 1962, 1968; Rogers, 1951, 1961);

and (2) the process of "becoming" as freely sought by individuals, from the standpoint of existential personality theories (e.g., de Beauvoir, 1947, 1949/2009; Fanon, 1952/1967, 1961/1963; May, 1953, 1969; Sartre, 1943/1956, 1953/1996). However, other critics (e.g., McDonald & Wearing, 2013) do not draw such a distinction between humanistic and existential theories. In any event, throughout the present chapter, we will pay close attention to the manner in which "becoming" is described within various humanistic and existential theories.

HUMANISTIC THEORIES OF PERSONALITY

KKURT GGOLDSTEIN'S ORGANISMIC PSYCHOLOGY

According to Kurt Goldstein's (1939) *organismic psychology*, unity among the mind, body, and soul promotes individuals' physical and mental health; whereas discord among mind, body, and soul places individuals' physical and mental health at risk (Noppeney, 2001). Goldstein overtly drew upon William James's (1890/2010) self-theory – not just in promoting mind–body unity, but also in emphasising the construct of soul (a controversial construct throughout the history of psychology, as we observed in Chapter 1 of the present book). Having specialised in the rehabilitation of former World War I-era German soldiers whose brain injuries had resulted in *aphasia* (i.e., severe impairment in spoken and/or written language; York, 2009), Goldstein (1940) proposed that all human beings – whether brain-damaged or not – possess a motive or psychological need toward *self-actualisation* (i.e., the need to achieve or fulfil one's own potential; Fisher, 1949).

Notwithstanding the universality of self-actualisation as a psychological need among human beings, Goldstein's (1939, 1940) organismic psychology does *not* assume that all humans are equally successful in meeting that need (C. S. Hall et al., 1998). Various aspects of individuals' *environment* (which Goldstein conceived as the objective world; C. S. Hall et al., 1985) can enable or impede individuals' quest for self-actualisation. Details regarding the ways in which the environment can influence individuals' success versus failure in striving to fulfil their innate potential are provided by C. S. Hall and Lindzey (1978).

Goldstein (1939, 1940) has been criticised for basing an entire theory of personality on the physical and psychological experiences of a highly atypical group of individuals (i.e., former soldiers who suffered from aphasia; C. S. Hall et al., 1985). By the same token, Goldstein's organismic psychology in general (and construct of the self-actualisation motive in particular) is reflected directly in the subsequent self-actualisation theories of Maslow (1968) and Rogers (1961) – both of which have been applied to studies of non-clinical populations (see C. S. Hall et al., 1998). Furthermore, Goldstein's theory helped to revive psychologists' interest in James's (1890/2010) self-theory at a time when James's influence was in decline (e.g., James's focus on conscious experience had been criticised by psychodynamic theorists and behaviourists alike; see E. Taylor, 1999).

CHARLOTTE BUHLER'S VERSION OF HUMANISTIC PSYCHOLOGY

From the standpoint of Charlotte Buhler's (1968) version of *humanistic psychology*, the entire self is amenable to development, throughout individuals' life span (DeRobertis, 2015). Although Buhler (e.g., Buhler & M. Allen, 1972) acknowledged the influence of Goldstein's (1939) organismic psychology (DeRobertis, 2006), Buhler's version of humanistic psychology did not propose the existence of a single, all-encompassing master motive (i.e., self-actualisation). Compared to Goldstein, Buhler was more concerned with individuals' *intentionality* (i.e., the set of ideas that individuals possess regarding the goals that they embrace, combined with the set of ideas that individuals possess regarding the ways that they might go about fulfilling those goals) – rather than any particular motive – as a guiding force in individuals' self-development (see Jacobsen, 2007).

At first glance, one might detect a passing similarity between Buhler's (1968; Buhler & M. Allen, 1972) version of humanistic psychology and Erikson's (1959/1980, 1963/1995, 1968/1994) ego psychology in terms of a shared concern with individuals' lifelong personality development. Indeed, given the greater prominence of Erikson's ego psychology (e.g., Ewen, 1998; C. S. Hall & Lindzey, 1970), one might ask what (if any) unique insight Buhler's version of humanistic psychology has to offer regarding the self, beyond the insight that Erikson's ego psychology already offers. In response, one is struck by Buhler's attention to the entire, unified self – not the oft-fragmented personality structure of id, ego, and superego that appears so often in Erikson's theory (DeRobertis, 2006).

Buhler's (1968; Buhler & Allen, 1972) version of humanistic psychology has been neglected, relative to other humanistic theories of personality (DeRobertis, 2006) – a situation that might lead one to question the importance of Buhler's theory. However, it may be more plausible for one to speculate that Buhler's status as one of the few prominent women in humanistic psychology (see E. Taylor, 2000) may have been responsible for personality psychologists' tendency to overlook Buhler's conceptual contributions to the field. Taken in its proper historical context, Buhler's version of humanistic theory serves as a solid bridge between humanistic and existential perspectives on personality (DeRobertis, 2006).

ABRAHAM MASLOW'S VERSION OF SELF-ACTUALISATION THEORY

Abraham Maslow's (1962, 1968) version of *self-actualisation theory* proposes that the self-actualisation motive is the most prized, yet least often fulfilled, of all human needs (Ewen, 1998). Unlike Goldstein's (1939, 1940) organismic psychology, Maslow's version of self-actualisation theory postulates the existence of several needs (i.e., physiological, safety, love/belonging, esteem/respect, and self-actualisation) that individuals typically experience as hierarchical (e.g., before one can satisfy one's safety needs for shelter and protection, one must attend to one's needs for food and water). Nevertheless, Maslow's version of self-actualisation theory clearly bears the influence of Goldstein's organismic psychology (C. S. Hall & Lindzey, 1970).

Guided by Abraham Maslow's (1954) version of self-actualisation theory, Everett Shostrom (1964) developed the Personal Orientation Inventory (POI) to measure individual differences in achieved self-actualisation. As Tosi and Lindamood (1975) observed, the POI consists of 150 items, with 127 of those items belong to one subscale, termed *inner-directedness* (i.e., the degree to which individuals live in a manner that reflects their beliefs, even if it means placing individuals at odds with significant others); the remaining 23 items belong to a second subscale, termed *time competence* (i.e., the extent to which individuals live in the here and now, rather than the past or the future; but see Forest and Sicz, 1981, concerning errors in the scoring manual of Shostrom, 1974, regarding time competence). Criticisms regarding forced-choice format and high intercorrelations among supposedly independent subscales of Shostrom's POI were so frequent and so consistent that Shostrom eventually developed a new survey, the Personal Orientation Dimensions (POD; Shostrom, 1975). Nevertheless, H. Friedman (2008) noted that (despite its psychometric problems) Shostrom's original POI remains the best-known measure of individual differences in achieved self-actualisation.

More recently, Robert Taormina and Jennifer Gao (2013) developed a 72-item inventory to measure individual differences in satisfaction of all five of the needs within Maslow's (1962) hierarchy (12 items measuring satisfaction of the self-actualisation need, 15 items apiece measuring satisfaction of the physiological, safety, love/belonging, and esteem/respect needs). All five of Taormina and Gao's scales proved to be valid (in terms of construct validity) and reliable (in terms of internal consistency) within a large sample of individuals in China, even though the scales initially were written in English. Taormina and Gao obtained significant positive correlations among scores on all five of the need satisfaction scales, with the highest correlations emerging among pairs of needs that were closest to each other conceptually within Maslow's need hierarchy. In addition, Taormina and Gao reported that scores on family support, traditional values, and life satisfaction were significantly and positively correlated with satisfaction of all five of the needs within Maslow's hierarchy. Finally, Taormina and Gao found that *neuroticism* or emotional instability was significantly and negatively correlated with satisfaction of all five needs within Maslow's hierarchy. (We will learn more about neuroticism when we cover the trait school of thought in Chapter 5.)

Guest (2014) noted that Maslow (1969) had described a sixth set of needs –that is, *ego-transcendent* needs that are spiritual, not self-interested – in order to understand what might motivate those lucky few individuals who had become self-actualised. Unfortunately, Maslow died in 1970, before having a chance to develop the concept of self-transcendent needs more fully. Few humanistic psychologists seem to be aware of Maslow's (1969) concept of ego-transcendent needs, which could explain the lack of systematic research on these latter needs. However, Koltko-Rivera (2006) pointed out that Maslow's evolving thoughts concerning ego-transcendent needs (also known as *metaneeds*) led him to serve as one of the founders of the Journal of Transpersonal Psychology. At any rate, Maslow's version of self-actualisation theory (including the original hierarchy of needs) arguably is the best-known and most influential of all theories within the humanistic/existential school of personality psychology (see Moss, 2015).

CARL ROGERS' VERSION OF SELF-ACTUALISATION THEORY

In Carl Rogers' (1951, 1961) version of *self-actualisation theory*, the need for self-actualisation is the only master motive that individuals possess at birth (Ewen, 1998). Unlike Goldstein's (1939, 1940) organismic psychology, Rogers' version of self-actualisation theory also proposes that individuals acquire the *need for positive regard from others* and the *need for self-regard* in the years following infancy (C. S. Hall & Lindzey, 1970). Nonetheless, like Maslow's (1962, 1968) version, Rogers' version of self-actualisation theory pays homage to Goldstein's organismic theory (McClelland, 1985/1987).

Rogers' (1951, 1961) version of self-actualisation theory arose from Rogers' experience as a counselling psychologist (Warner, 2009). Based on his work with clients who were facing everyday problems (as distinct from the clients whose cases involving moderate-to-severe psychological impairment provided much of the source material for psychiatrists and clinicians, especially within the psychodynamic tradition; Millon, 1996), Rogers concluded that most individuals already possess the social and psychological tools that they need to resolve their own problems (C. S. Hall & Lindzey, 1970). Moreover, Rogers became convinced that – above all else – counsellors should provide *unconditional positive regard* to their clients (thus helping clients meet their needs for positive regard from others, self-regard, and self-actualisation; Ewen, 1998). Consistent with Rogers' belief in clients' ability to work through their difficulties with little to no overt guidance from counsellors, Rogers used terms such as *client-centred therapy*, *person-centred therapy*, and *nondirective therapy* to describe his approach to psychotherapy (Kensit, 2000).

One problem that arises for students of Rogers' (1951, 1961) version of self-actualisation theory is the lack of precision that characterises some of Rogers' writings (Tudor, 2010). For example, the terms *self* and *self-concept* – which, as we learned in Chapter 1 of the present book, are not identical (i.e., the self-concept is individuals' reflection on the self; Baumeister, 1997) – often are used as if they *are* identical (see Ewen, 1998). However, among all of the major theories within the humanistic/existential school of personality psychology, Rogers' version of self-actualisation theory may have exerted the greatest influence on quantitative research regarding self-esteem (undoubtedly due to Rogers' leading role as a "guardian of the self"; Morf & Mischel, 2012, p. 23). In Box 4.1, we review the Rosenberg Self-Esteem Scale (variously labelled as the SES or the RSES; Rosenberg, 1965), which was inspired partly by Rogers' version of self-actualisation theory (Funder & Fast, 2010).

BOX 4.1 ROSENBERG'S (1965) SELF-ESTEEM SCALE

In their chapter on modes or metaphors of self-perception, Robins and John (1997) contended that the *Egoist* metaphor is evident in certain proto-humanist personality theories, especially James's (1890/2010) self-theory and G. W. Allport's (1937/1951) psychology of the individual; certain humanist personality theories, especially Rogers' (1959) version of self-actualisation theory; and Rosenberg's (1965) empirical research on self-esteem. Although the Egoist metaphor might lead one to assume that self-enhancement *per se* is maladaptive (e.g., unhealthy whether expressed via high self-esteem or via high narcissism; Baumeister, 1998), it is worth distinguishing between genuinely high self-esteem and the inflated view of self that is properly termed as *narcissism* (which we covered in Chapter 2 of the present book). The Rosenberg Self-Esteem Scale (SES, also known as the RSES), developed by Morris Rosenberg in 1965, has emerged as the most widely used measure of individuals' realistically high (versus low) levels of self-esteem within personality and social psychology (G. MacDonald & M. R. Leary, 2012).

Funder and Fast (2010) identified a direct conceptual link between Rogers' (1951, 1961) concept of unconditional positive regard (which therapists ideally should display toward clients; Walsh et al., 2014) and Rosenberg's (1965) construct of self-esteem as measured by the Self-Esteem Scale. Possibly the best-documented result regarding the impact of self-esteem on other personality constructs is the tendency for self-esteem to act as a significant negative predictor of depression (Blascovich & Tomaka, 1991). In addition, self-esteem is a significant positive predictor of life satisfaction and a significant negative predictor of anxiety (Rosenberg, 1989). All of these results can be explained by Rogers' version of self-actualisation theory, which identifies a variety of adaptive functions of the self (Morf & Mischel, 2012).

Of course, self-esteem is not a panacea for all that ails individuals (Baumeister, 1998). Nevertheless, the Self-Esteem Scale (Rosenberg, 1965) measures self-esteem in a manner that allows researchers to propose and test a large assortment of hypotheses regarding the effects of self-esteem on other personality variables (Blascovich & Tomaka, 1991). In fact, G. MacDonald and M. R. Leary (2012) credited the Rosenberg Self-Esteem Scale with fuelling the enormous rise in studies of self-esteem that occurred within personality and social psychology during the 1960s and 1970s.

EXISTENTIAL THEORIES OF PERSONALITY

JEAN-PAUL SARTRE'S VERSION OF EXISTENTIAL PHILOSOPHY

Looming large over humanistic psychology in general is Aristotelian philosophy (e.g., *The Ethics of Aristotle: The Nicomachean Ethics*; Thomson, 1955), which defined the human *mind* as a set of psychological attributes that includes *nutritive* (i.e., appetite-orientated), *sensitive* (i.e., emotion-orientated), and *rational* (i.e., reason-orientated) "*souls*" (Garcia-Valdecasas, 2005). Despite the historical importance of Aristotelian philosophy to humanistic psychology (Moss, 2015), philosopher Jean-Paul Sartre (1943/1956) rejected Aristotle's basic premise that human beings possess "souls" at birth (or ever; Qizilbash, 1998). Instead, Sartre developed a version of *existential philosophy* that depicts individuals' *existence* (i.e., the ongoing process by which individuals make something of themselves) as necessarily preceding and giving rise to individuals' *essence* (i.e., that which individuals have made of themselves at any given point in time; L. Hoffman et al., 2015).

In general, Sartre (1943/1956) cast his version of existential philosophy as orientated toward human consciousness (Dolezal, 2012). However, Sartre (1953/1996) eventually attempted to combine elements of his theory with Sigmund Freud's (1900/1965) version of psychoanalytic theory to produce *existential psychoanalysis* (emphasising unconscious aspects of individuals' existence via the content of psychobiographies; Churchill & Wertz, 2015). According to Sartre's existential psychoanalysis, an important task of self-development is the excavation of personal material out of the unconscious and into consciousness (Gilliam, 2017). As it turns out, the existential psychoanalytic therapies of Medard Boss (1963) and R. D. Laing (1960), among others, were influenced by the psychoanalytic component of Sartre's existential philosophy (A. Jones, 2001).

Sartre's (1943/1956) version of existential philosophy has been criticised for logical inconsistencies concerning existence and essence (e.g., Sartre considers the philosophical and theological construct of human nature to be part of individuals' essence, yet human nature surely must exist at the time of individuals' birth; Dolezal, 2012). However, if Sartre's theory is applied narrowly to psychological constructs such as self and identity (e.g., the individual self exists at birth and subsequently gives rise to identity development; see Gilliam, 2017), then Sartre's version of existential philosophy – or, perhaps more correctly, the component of Sartre's theory that is known as *existential phenomenology* (emphasising individuals' subjective, conscious experience of themselves as existing in the world; Churchill & Wertz, 2015) – may qualify as logically consistent after all (especially if one acknowledges the role of other persons in co-creating individuals' identities over time; L. Hoffman et al., 2015). To sum it up, Sartre's version of existential philosophy – like Aristotle's philosophy (as we will learn later in the present chapter, when we examine the positive psychology movement) – offers important insight into individuals' responsibility for their own character development (Qizilbash, 1998).

SIMONE DE BEAUVOIR'S VERSION OF EXISTENTIAL PHILOSOPHY

From the standpoint of Simone de Beauvoir's (1947, 1949/2009) version of *existential philosophy*, although human beings in general possess the *capacity* for expression of their will (and, hence, seek freedom as well as morality), not all groups of individuals are in an equally advantaged position to *act* on the basis of their will (Hekman, 2015). Unlike Sartre's (1943/1956, 1953/1996) version of existential philosophy, de Beauvoir's version highlights the additional societal-level as well as individual-level difficulties that women (compared to men) must overcome in order to express free will (Tantam, 2015). Nevertheless, de Beauvoir's version of existential philosophy reflects the joint influence of Sigmund Freud's (1900/1965) version of psychoanalytic theory and Sartre's version of existential philosophy (particularly Sartre's [1953/1996] existential psychoanalysis; Adkins, 2013).

Like Sartre, de Beauvoir was not a trained psychotherapist (Tantam, 2015). However, unlike Sartre, de Beauvoir served as an unofficial counsellor for many female students. Moreover, de Beauvoir's (1947, 1949/2009) version of existential philosophy has been credited with helping psychotherapists offer practical advice to those women whose (frequently male) partners expect them to serve as relationship managers (e.g., Barker, 2010). Finally, lest we give the impression that de Beauvoir's version of existential philosophy is relevant only to women's social-psychological functioning, de Beauvoir's theory has been cited for its insight into the roots of *narcissistic personality disorder* among men as well as women (e.g., even individuals who possess unusually high levels of self-love need relationship partners who are willing to affirm individuals' emotions; Gildersleeve, 2015).

A key criticism of de Beauvoir's (1947, 1949/2009) version of existential philosophy is the lack of a clear explanation regarding ways that individual women can exercise their free will (e.g., Hekman, 1999). Nonetheless, de Beauvoir's theory does suggest that groups of women (as well as some men) should band together to seek societal change that, in turn, would enable individual women to express their will and seek freedom and morality (Hekman, 2015). Perhaps the most obvious evidence concerning the lingering impact of de Beauvoir's version of existential philosophy (outside, if not necessarily within, the male-dominated school of humanistic/existential psychology during the mid-twentieth century; Tantam, 2015) is feminist Betty Friedan's acknowledgement that de Beauvoir's *The Second Sex* (1953/2009) had influenced Friedan's own classic, *The Feminine Mystique* (1963).

FRANTZ FANON'S VERSION OF EXISTENTIAL PSYCHOLOGY

According to Frantz Fanon's (1952/1967, 1961/1963) version of *existential psychology*, the existence (and, consequently, the essence) of victims of colonialism is fundamentally different from the existence (and essence) of perpetrators of colonialism throughout the world (Omar, 2009). Like de Beauvoir's (1947, 1949/2009) version of existential philosophy – and unlike Sartre's (1943/1956, 1953/1996) version of existential philosophy – Fanon's version of existential psychology directly addresses the dehumanising effects of slavery on enslaved persons and slave masters alike (as well as the descendants of slaves and masters; Adkins, 2013). However, unlike either de Beauvoir's or Sartre's versions of existential philosophy, Fanon's version of existential psychology focused on ethnicity (and especially race) as the primary construct for viewing the role of society in promoting or hindering individuals' expression of free will (Bernasconi, 2000). Despite the differences between Fanon's version of existential psychology and the existential philosophies of de Beauvoir and Sartre, Fanon's construct of the "White gaze" (literally and figuratively, a means by which persons of European descent may objectify persons of African descent; Zeiler, 2013) was derived from Sartre's construct of "the Look" (a means by which any individual may objectify another person; see Pearce, 2011).

After World War II, Fanon was trained as a psychiatrist (Clarke, 2000). Given that Fanon was well-versed in the methods of psychoanalysis (e.g., free association, probing clients' unconscious via examination of the content of dreams), Fanon's (1952/1967, 1961/1963) version of existential psychology deals primarily with the *interpersonal anxiety* that victims of colonialism experience on a daily basis (e.g., African-descent persons' negative affective or emotional reaction to the "White gaze"; see Maldonado-Torres, 2017). Thus, Fanon's version of existential psychology offers a unique, practitioner-based twist on the existential psychoanalysis that both Sartre (1943/1956, 1953/1996) and de Beauvoir (1947, 1949/2009) had advocated (Adkins, 2013).

Fanon's (1952/1967, 1961/1963) version of existential psychology – particularly as presented in *Black Skin, White Masks* (1952) – has been criticised as sexist, due to its objectification of women (Adkins, 2013). By the same token, in *The Wretched of the Earth* (1961/1963), Fanon's personal experience as a freedom fighter in Algeria sensitised Fanon to the negative effects of colonialism on men and women alike (Omar, 2009). All in all, Fanon's version of existential psychology has been credited with influencing the development of Black/African psychology as an interdisciplinary field, within and beyond the United States (Jamison, 2010).

ROLLO MAY'S VERSION OF EXISTENTIAL PSYCHOLOGY

In Rollo May's (1953, 1969) version of *existential psychology*, the dread that accompanies human beings' awareness of their own mortality – that is, their *existential anxiety* – emerges as a central construct (Craig, 2008). Perhaps to a greater extent than does any other theory within the humanistic/existential school, May's version of existential psychology challenges individuals to directly confront (if not conquer) their existential anxiety over the short term, because such confrontation is essential to individuals' success in achieving and maintaining well-being over the long term (Kiser, 2007). Nevertheless, May's version of existential psychology clearly owes an intellectual debt to Sartre's (1952/1963, 1943/1956) version of existential philosophy (Churchill & Wertz, 2015).

Following Sartre's (1943/1956, 1953/1996) lead, May's (1953, 1969) version of existential psychology casts *love* – which May famously defined as "*a delight in the presence of the other person and an affirming of [the other person's] value and development as much as one's own [value and development]*" (1953, p. 206, emphasis in original) – as an emotion that is sufficiently powerful to enable individuals to face their existential anxiety in an authentic manner (Kiser, 2007). As a trained clinician, May applied his version of existential psychology to clients' dual concerns with (1) being versus nonbeing (manifested in clients' existential anxiety toward the spectre of death) and (2) being versus becoming (manifested in clients' love toward significant others; Medina, 2008). Subsequently, Pitchford (2009) – having been influenced by May's best-selling classic, *Love and Will* (1969) – reported the successful treatment of a former soldier who had suffered from post-traumatic stress disorder (PTSD), via a direct appeal to the client's love for his former comrades (alongside the client's love for himself).

May's (1953, 1969) version of existential psychology has been criticised for failing to stimulate quantitative research in humanistic or existential psychology (a critique that has been directed toward the existential psychology theories of Binswanger, 1963; and Boss, 1963; see C. S. Hall & Lindzey, 1970). However, May's "kinds of love" (i.e., *sex*, or lustful love; *eros*, or passionate love; *philia*, or friendship love; and *agape*, or selfless love) – described most explicitly in May's *Love and Will* (1969) – directly influenced Lee's (1976) qualitative research on "colours of love" (described earlier in the present chapter), which subsequently influenced C. Hendrick and S. S. Hendrick's (1986; C. Hendrick et al., 1984, 1998) aforementioned quantitative research on love styles (Gaines, 2016/2018). Overall, May's version of existential psychology arguably stands as the best-known theory of personality within the existential tradition (Ewen, 1998).

POSITIVE PSYCHOLOGY: A PREFERRED ALTERNATIVE TO HUMANISTIC/EXISTENTIAL PSYCHOLOGY(?)

In the preceding section, we noted that May's (1953, 1969) version of existential psychology elaborated upon love as a basis for individuals' ability to come to terms with a search for meaning in their all-too-finite lives. In some of his later work, May (1981/1999) distinguished between *happiness* (an emotion that is relatively static, associated with contentment) and *joy* (an emotion that is relatively dynamic, associated with excitement) as building blocks for romantic love (Bradford, 2015). May was concerned that, over time, individuals in romantic relationships may put considerable effort into holding onto happiness but do not put comparable effort into maintaining joy – a situation that might help explain why the current "happiness craze" in the biological and social sciences has been embraced more wholeheartedly within the modern-day positive psychology movement (following Seligman & Csikszentmihalyi, 2000) than it has been embraced within the older humanistic/existential school of personality psychology (see K. J. Schneider, 2015).

To some extent, the positive psychology movement covers the same conceptual ground regarding happiness and other constructs (e.g., the self, positive aspects of human nature) that the humanistic/existential school previously covered, although positive psychologists do not consistently give due credit to their humanistic/existential predecessors (Montuori & Purser, 2015). In fact, some of the comments from positive psychologists (e.g., Seligman & Csikszentmihalyi, 2000) toward the contributions of humanistic and existential psychologists have been overtly dismissive (K. J. Schneider, 2011b). Nonetheless, the positive psychology movement may ultimately serve to complement, rather than denigrate or supplant, the humanistic/existential tradition. In the present section, we shall review those perspectives from the positive psychology movement (i.e., Diener et al., 2003; Ryan & Deci, 2001; Ryff & Singer, 2008) that show exceptional promise regarding integration with the humanistic/existential school of personality psychology.

ED DIENER'S CONSTRUCT OF SUBJECTIVE WELL-BEING

Ed Diener and colleagues (e.g., Diener et al., 2003) define *subjective well-being* as individuals' cognitive (i.e., thought-based) and affective (i.e., feeling-based) evaluation of their lives – basically, individuals' positive versus negative attitude toward their lives (see S. C. White et al., 2012). Diener and colleagues contend that the cognitive component of subjective well-being is *life satisfaction* (measured via the Satisfaction With Life Scale, or SWLS; Diener et al., 1985); whereas the affective components of subjective well-being are *positive moods* and *negative moods* (measured via the Positive and Negative Affect Schedule, or PANAS; D. Watson et al., 1988). Thus, according to Diener and colleagues, high subjective well-being represents a combination of high levels of life satisfaction, high levels of positive moods, and low levels of negative moods (e.g., D. G. Myers & Diener, 1995).

One of the most noteworthy sets of findings from Diener and colleagues' programme of research on subjective well-being (e.g., D. G. Myers & Diener, 1995) is that (1) on average, individuals in economically rich nations report significantly higher levels of subjective well-being than do individuals in economically not-rich nations; yet (2) within the economically richest nation on Earth (i.e., the United States), the positive effect of income on individuals' subjective well-being is statistically significant but practically negligible (see Peterson & Seligman, 2004). Actually, within the US, it appears that the impact of income on subjective well-being is best understood as *curvilinear* (i.e., highest levels of subjective well-being among individuals within the $100,000 to $250,000 bracket, lower scores of subjective well-being among individuals whose incomes either fall below or fall above that range; D. G. Myers & Diener, 2018), rather than linear. All things considered, Diener's conceptualisation and measurement of subjective well-being have largely defined the literature on well-being within the positive psychology movement (see S. C. White et al., 2012).

CAROL RYFF'S CONSTRUCT OF PSYCHOLOGICAL WELL-BEING

Drawing partly upon Marie Jahoda's (1958) *theory of positive mental health* (a conceptual precursor to the contemporary positive psychology movement, focusing on the presence of mental wellness, not just the absence of mental illness; Peterson & Seligman, 2004), Carol Ryff and colleagues (e.g., Ryff & Singer, 1998a, b) define *psychological well-being* as individuals' achievement of fulfilment and self-realisation in their lives (see S. C. White et al., 2012). Ryff and colleagues (e.g., Ryff, 1989; Ryff & Keyes, 1995) have identified six dimensions of psychological well-being on conceptual and empirical grounds (i.e., *self-acceptance*, *positive relations with others*, *autonomy*, *environmental mastery*, *purpose in life*, and *personal growth*). In Ryff's view, psychological well-being reflects a combination of high levels of all six dimensions (possibly exemplifying individuals' fundamental values and ideals; e.g., Ryff, 1995).

A major problem with Ryff's (1989; Ryff & Keyes, 1995) psychological well-being survey is the absence of published empirical support for the internal consistency of her six scales, as assessed via Cronbach's alpha (a problem that also characterised Jahoda's

[1958] prototypical measures of processes that promote positive mental health; see Peterson & Seligman, 2004). In fact, Ryff and colleagues have tended to publish descriptions of hypothetical low-scorers and high-scorers on the six dimensions, rather than the actual items that comprise the scales. Although Ryff and colleagues (e.g., Ryff & Singer, 1998a, b) have offered a spirited defence of their conceptualisation and measurement of psychological well-being, the long-term success or failure of their survey will depend heavily upon empirical demonstrations of the internal consistency of the six scales (see Nunnally & Bernstein, 1994, concerning the importance of Cronbach's alpha as an index of reliability in psychometric analyses of scales). In the meantime, Ryff's construct of psychological well-being has emerged as the primary counterpoint to Diener's (e.g., Diener et al., 1985) construct of subjective well-being (S. C. White et al., 2012) – though Diener and colleagues (i.e., Diener, et al., 2010) have developed alternative measures of well-being, in response to Ryff and colleagues' critiques (see Box 4.2 concerning Diener et al.'s newer measures of flourishing, positive emotions, and negative emotions).

BOX 4.2 DIENER ET AL.'S (2010) FLOURISHING, POSITIVE EMOTION, AND NEGATIVE EMOTION SCALES

In an edition of *Psychological Inquiry* that was constructed around a target article by Ryff and Singer (1998b) on "The Contours of Positive Human Health," Diener and colleagues (Diener et al., 1998, rebuttal) and Ryff and Singer (1998a, rejoinder) clashed verbally over the adequacy of subjective well-being (emphasising an hedonic or optimal-experience perspective; Diener et al., 1985) versus psychological well-being (emphasising an eudaimonic or optimal-functioning perspective; Ryff, 1989; Ryff & Keyes, 1995) as mental health constructs. Ryan and Deci (2001) tactfully described the clash as "an engaging and instructive debate" (p. 146). Although Ryan and Deci implied that Ryff and Singer (1998b) had struck the first verbal blow, a careful reading of that target article reveals that Ryff and Singer (1998b) had *omitted* (i.e., failed to cite) Diener and colleagues' prior work on subjective well-being. In response to that omission, Diener et al. (1998) not only promoted their construct of subjective well-being but also claimed that their construct was a better reflection of the content of everyday persons' daily lives than was Ryff and colleagues' construct of psychological well-being. Subsequently, Ryff and Singer (1998a) directly challenged Diener's hedonic construct by pointing to the ostensibly superior real-world utility of their eudaimonic construct. At any rate, Diener and Ryff clearly opposed each other's views concerning the conceptual operationalisation of well-being (although the differences may have been overstated; see Lucas & Diener, 2015).

Diener et al. (2010) have attempted to reconcile their hedonic perspective with Ryff's (1989; Ryff & Singer, 1998b) eudemonic perspective on well-being, which Diener et al. labelled as "humanistic" (an overly restrictive label, considering that Ryff drew on several theories across the psychodynamic, humanistic/existential, and trait schools of personality; e.g., Ryff & Singer, 2008). Diener et al. developed the Flourishing Scale as a measure of psychological well-being (consistent with Ryff and colleagues' eudaimonic view of well-being), as well as the Scale of Positive and Negative Experience as a measure of the affective component of subjective well-being (consistent with Diener and colleagues' hedonic view of well-being). Diener et al. found that flourishing was significantly and positively correlated with all six of Ryff's (1989; Ryff & Keyes, 1995) psychological well-being dimensions (Diener et al. did not say whether positive or negative feelings were significantly correlated with Ryff's dimensions). In retrospect, perhaps the Diener–Ryff debate has been "engaging and instructive" after all(!).

RICHARD RYAN AND EDWARD DECI'S CONSTRUCT OF SUBJECTIVE VITALITY

Finally, within their *self-determination theory* (e.g., Ryan & Deci, 2001), Richard Ryan and Edward Deci (e.g., Deci & Ryan, 2000; Ryan & Deci, 2000b) define *subjective vitality* as individuals' sense that they are *functioning* in an optimal manner, not just *experiencing* their lives in an optimal manner (S. C. White et al., 2012). Consistent with self-determination theory, Ryan and Frederick (1997) developed short-term and long-term versions of a scale that measures individuals' subjective vitality (Peterson & Seligman, 2004). According to Ryan and Deci, individuals' subjective vitality is high when three particular needs – specifically, *autonomy*, *competence*, and *relatedness* – have been fulfilled; whereas individuals' subjective vitality is low when those needs have been blocked or thwarted (e.g., Ryan & Deci, 2000a).

Results of studies by Ryan, Deci, and colleagues (e.g., Reis et al., 2000) indicate that individuals' fulfilment of all three human needs (i.e., autonomy, competence, and relatedness) are significant positive predictors of subjective vitality (Peterson & Seligman, 2004). Ryan and Deci (2001) interpret the results of their studies concerning human needs and subjective vitality as affirming the same *eudaimonic* view of well-being (i.e., emphasis on optimal functioning) that Ryff and colleagues (e.g., Ryff & Singer, 1998a, b) have endorsed, as distinct from the *hedonic* view of well-being (i.e., emphasis on optimal experience) that Diener and colleagues (e.g., Diener et al., 2003) have endorsed. Summing it up, Ryan and Deci's construct of subjective vitality shows promise as one of the most theoretically driven and empirically verifiable constructs within the literature on well-being (see S. C. White et al., 2012).

[*ADDENDUM*: In *Wellbeing: Science and Policy*, economists Richard Layard and Jan-Emmanuel De Neve (2023) promoted a *well-being science* that presumably is broader in scope than are the humanistic psychology *or* positive psychology movements. However, Layard and De Neve operationalised well-being in terms of Diener's (1984) construct of subjective well-being, without mentioning the hedonic nature of Diener's construct. Unfortunately, the debate that ensued between Diener (e.g., Diener et al., 1998) and Ryff (e.g., Ryff & Singer, 1998a, b) regarding the usefulness of hedonically orientated subjective well-being versus eudaimonically orientated psychological well-being as key constructs was not documented in Layard and De Neve's book. Especially when one realises that the generalisability of results concerning studies of subjective well-being beyond persons from so-called Western, Educated, Industrialised, Rich, and Democratic (WEIRD) populations has been questioned implicitly or explicitly (e.g., Sanches de Oliviera & Baggs, 2023), one might find it prudent to acknowledge multiple approaches toward conceptualising and measuring well-being-related constructs within an emerging science of well-being. It remains to be seen whether well-being science expands or constricts the boundaries of current constructs.]

CRITIQUE OF HUMANISTIC AND EXISTENTIAL PERSPECTIVES

From the first edition (C. S. Hall & Lindzey, 1957) through the third edition (C. S. Hall & Lindzey, 1978) of their classic book, *Theories of Personality*, Calvin S. Hall and Gardner Lindzey covered humanistic and existential personality theories across three separate chapters (two chapters on humanistic theories, one chapter on existential theories). However, in *Introduction to Theories of Personality*, C. S. Hall and Lindzey (C. S. Hall et al., 1985) reduced the number of chapters to two (one chapter apiece on humanistic and existential theories, respectively). Afterward, in the fourth edition of *Theories of Personality*, C. S. Hall and Lindzey (C. S. Hall et al., 1998) offered a single chapter on humanistic theories (and no chapters on existential theories). Given the diminished coverage that C. S. Hall and Lindzey gave to humanistic and existential theories over the course of the late twentieth century, one might reasonably conclude that the influence of humanistic and existential theories within personality psychology is in the midst of an irreversible decline (see E. Taylor, 2010).

In spite of the decreased coverage that C. S. Hall and Lindzey (1957, 1970, 1978; C. S. Hall et al., 1985, 1998) have afforded to the humanistic/existential school over the years, it may be premature for personality psychologists to give up studying humanistic and existential perspectives. Looking backward, one can find precursors to the humanistic/ existential school in various theories that we have considered so far, including William James's (1890/2010) self-theory, Gordon Allport's (1937/1951) psychology of the individual, and Henry Murray's (1938) personology, among other sources (for details, see E. Taylor, 2010). Looking forward, one can detect the influence of the humanistic/existential school on later cognitive theories, most notably George Kelly's (1955) psychology of personal constructs (which arguably could be classified as a humanistic theory; Benjafield, 2008). All in all, the humanistic/existential school has established itself firmly as a "third force" in challenging the onetime dominance of psychodynamic and behaviourist theories within and outside personality psychology (E. Taylor, 2000).

PRELUDE TO CHAPTER 5

During the latter half of the twentieth century, the *trait* school (which, unlike the humanistic/existential school, emphasises individuals' striving for accuracy – rather than positivity – in gathering information about themselves; see Robins & John, 1997) gradually attained the status of a fourth major perspective in personality psychology (Funder 2001). The trait school (which is based on the belief that individuals are fully aware of those aspects of their personalities that are most relevant to their everyday behaviour; Digman, 1990) currently is the most influential perspective within personality psychology and has been championed primarily by academicians (in contrast to the practitioners who largely have promoted the humanistic and existentialist perspectives; see McAdams, 1997). Representative theories within the trait school include (in order of appearance) G. W. Allport's (1961/1963) trait theory; the factor-analytic trait theories of Cattell (1946), H. J. Eysenck (1947), Costa and McCrae (1985), J. P. Guilford (1975), and Ashton and Lee (2001); Sandra Bem's (1981) gender schema theory; Spence's (1993) multifactorial gender identity theory; and Wiggins's (1991) interpersonal circumplex theory. In Chapter 5, we cover these theories and accompanying research in detail.

CURRENT AND EMERGING PERSPECTIVES ON PERSONALITY

5

TRAIT PERSPECTIVES ON PERSONALITY

In Chapter 1, we learned about Gordon Allport's (1937/1951, 1961/1963) psychology of the individual, including G. W. Allport's pioneering version of *trait theory*. Legend has it that G. W. Allport developed trait theory largely as the result of an uncomfortable encounter that he experienced with Sigmund Freud, who apparently responded to G. W. Allport's recounting of an incident that he had just witnessed on a train ride (in which a little boy and the boy's mother seemed to be excessively concerned with keeping dirt off the boy's clothing) with the none-too-rhetorical question, "And was that little boy you?" (Ewen, 1998, p. 283). From that day onward, G. W. Allport allegedly had little use for Freud's "depth psychology," opting instead for a direct approach to learning about the core aspects of individuals' personalities: Just ask individuals what they are like (C. S. Hall & Lindzey, 1957).

In principle, G. W. Allport and Odbert's (1936) exhaustive reading of an unabridged English-language dictionary yielded a list of approximately 18,000 trait terms, which could be narrowed to "only" 4,500 or so terms after synonyms and antonyms are taken into account (Ewen, 1998). However, in practice, G. W. Allport (1928) developed a survey to measure only one trait – specifically, "ascendance/submission," which corresponds roughly to *dominance* (i.e., individuals' tendency to behave in a manner that is intended to benefit themselves; Wiggins, 1979). In retrospect, G. W. Allport chose his construct well; every trait survey that we will review in the present chapter includes either "pure"

DOI: 10.4324/9781003601777-8

dominance or, arguably, a blend of dominance with another trait (typically *nurturance*, or individuals' tendency to behave in a manner that is intended to benefit persons other than, or in addition to, themselves; see Gaines, 2016/2018).

In the present chapter, we will consider trait perspectives on personality, in the tradition of G. W. Allport (1937/1951, 1961/1963). As we will see, trait perspectives were subjected to withering criticism during the 1960s – most notably from Walter Mischel (1968), who contended that a particular trait usually explains no more than 9–10% of variance in behaviour across individuals (M. Snyder & Ickes, 1985). By the same token, we will learn about various strategies that trait theorists have pursued in order to address (and, in some instances, to overtly refute) challenges from Mischel and other critics concerning the traditional (i.e., *dispositional*) approach to personality and social behaviour (Ickes et al., 1997; Snyder & Cantor, 1998). Along the way, we revisit the controversial topic of trait "heritability," which offers surprisingly little substantive evidence concerning those genes or (at least) chromosomes that supposedly are implicated in individual differences regarding traits or accompanying behaviour.

BASIC ASSUMPTIONS UNDERLYING TRAIT PERSPECTIVES

According to trait perspectives on personality, one can regard *traits* (essentially, individuals' answer to the question, "How would you describe yourself"; Gaines, 2016/2018) as stable, consciously experienced aspects of personality that tend to be reflected in cross-situational consistency in individuals' behaviour across time (although the concepts of stability, consistency, and length of time as applied to trait-behaviour covariance are not absolute; M. Snyder & Ickes, 1985). Compared to motives (which, as we learned in Chapters 2 and 4, are emphasised in psychodynamic and humanistic/existential perspectives), traits presumably are more accessible to consciousness and are more likely to be manifested consistently across a variety of situations (McClelland, 1985/1987). Nevertheless, both motives and traits appear to be relatively stable, at least throughout individuals' adult years (McAdams, 1997).

G. W. Allport defined traits as "neuropsychic structure[s] having the capacity to render many stimuli functionally equivalent, and to initiate and guide equivalent (meaningfully consistent) forms of aptitude and expressive behaviour" (1961/1963, p. 347). Does the term "neuropsychic structure" imply that G. W. Allport viewed traits as biologically given (i.e., inherited) within individuals? Not necessarily: In G. W. Allport's view, the building blocks of traits are *habits* (i.e., repeated sequences of behaviour that eventually may characterise individuals over time; e.g., G. W. Allport, 1927), rather than genes. Unlike genes, habits tend to be learned (see F. H. Allport & G. W. Allport, 1921). However, the relative influence of "nature versus nurture" on the development of individuals' traits *en utero* and across the life span has been debated throughout the history of personality psychology (Deary, 2009).

Broadly speaking, those trait perspectives that have been concerned with identifying all of the major traits along which individuals differ (e.g., the factor-analytic trait theories of Cattell, 1946; H. J. Eysenck, 1947; J. P. Guilford, 1975; and Costa & McCrae, 1985) have been especially receptive to appeals toward *nature* as a primary influence on trait development (but see the factor-analytic trait theory of Ashton & K. Lee, 2001, for a notable exception); whereas those trait perspectives that have been concerned with identifying a limited set of salient traits along which individuals differ (e.g., the gender schema theory of Sandra Bem, 1981; the multifactorial gender identity theory of Spence, 1993; and the interpersonal circumplex theory of Wiggins, 1991) have been especially receptive to appeals toward *nurture* as a primary influence on trait development (see Gaines, 2016/2018). Given the lack of solid genetic evidence outside the realm of modern-day psychiatry (where, for example, specific chromosomes have been repeatedly implicated in the development of the "abnormal" trait of *schizophrenia*, which formerly was known as "madness"; see Walker et al., 2004; but see also Wahlsten, 1999, regarding a re-evaluation of results concerning schizophrenia), we do not attempt to resolve the thorny issue of nature versus nurture (following Deary, 2009). Instead, we will keep this issue in mind as we review major theories and relevant studies among trait perspectives on personality.

THEORIES PROPOSING COMPREHENSIVE LISTS OF TRAITS

RAYMOND CATTELL'S VERSION OF FACTOR-ANALYTIC TRAIT THEORY

As we noted earlier in the present chapter, G. W. Allport and Odbert (1936) tried valiantly to reduce their 18,000-term trait taxonomy to a more manageable size. Unfortunately, their remaining list of roughly 4,500 trait terms was still too unwieldy for empirical or conceptual purposes (e.g., conducting research, achieving parsimony; Wiggins & Trapnell, 1997). Thus, Raymond Cattell (1946) took it upon himself to apply the then-new technique of *factor analysis* (a psychometric analysis that examines correlations among scores on measured variables within a particular sample, with the intention of uncovering a smaller number of latent or unmeasured variables that presumably explain individual differences in the scores; Nunnally & Bernstein, 1994) to data from an already-reduced taxonomy of 160 trait terms (Ewen, 1998). Cattell's resulting trait perspective is known as a version of *factor-analytic trait theory* (or factor theory, for short; C. S. Hall & Lindzey, 1957).

On the basis of results from factor analyses, Cattell (1950) eventually condensed G. W. Allport and Odbert's (1936) trait taxonomy to 16 terms (perhaps rising to 23 terms, if data from clinical samples were included alongside data from more commonly used, nonclinical samples; C. S. Hall & Lindzey, 1957). Although Cattell was fond of creating his own, somewhat idiosyncratic terminology, Ewen (1998) noted that Cattell's list of traits could be interpreted as *intellect*, *warmth*, *emotional stability*, *dominance*, *liveliness*, *rule-consciousness*, *social boldness*, *sensitivity*, *vigilance*, *abstractedness*, *privateness*, *apprehension*, *openness to change*, *self-reliance*, *perfectionism*, and *tension*. From the outset, Cattell's inclusion of "intellect" or intelligence (which usually is regarded as individuals' presumed cognitive ability; C. S. Hall & Lindzey, 1957) as a trait was controversial. Even more controversially, Cattell assumed that approximately half of the variance in "intellect" and (other) traits across individuals was a function of heredity – an assumption that was commonplace throughout World War II-era differential psychology but was undermined largely by the revelation that Cyril Burt (one of the earliest and best-known proponents of the

50%-heritability dictum concerning psychological attributes; e.g., Burt, 1966) had fabricated individual-differences data (Fairchild et al., 1995; Yee et al., 1993). Nevertheless, Cattell succeeded in creating a taxonomy (as well as a survey, the Sixteen Personality Factor Questionnaire, or 16PF; Cattell, 1970) that was empirically and conceptually viable as a means toward measuring individual differences in all of the major traits (Digman, 1990).

Notwithstanding the controversial aspects of Cattell's (1946) factor-analytic trait theory, some of Cattell's psychometric choices are questionable. For example, with regard to *construct validity* (i.e., the extent to which a survey actually measures the construct[s] that the survey was designed to measure; Nunnally & Bernstein, 1994), Cattell's use of a particular type of factor analysis that tends to produce a large number of interrelated latent variables (i.e., *oblique factor analysis*) probably led him to overestimate the minimum number of traits that should be identified (Digman, 1990). In addition, Cattell himself (e.g., Cattell, 1973) raised the possibility that the subscales underlying the 16PF lacked *internal consistency* (i.e., lack of measurement error; Nunnally & Bernstein, 1994) as measured by Cronbach's alpha reliability coefficient (although Cattell might have been unduly critical of his own survey in that regard; see Saville & Blinkhorn, 1981). Then again, G. W. Allport (1961/1963) – whose taxonomy (G. W. Allport & Odbert, 1936) had served as the inspiration for Cattell's 16PF – credited Cattell with helping to bring the statistical analysis of trait data into the then-fledgling computer era (see also Digman, 1990).

HANS EYSENCK'S VERSION OF FACTOR-ANALYTIC TRAIT THEORY

Just as Cattell (1946) had argued that G. W. Allport and Odbert's (1936) list of 4,500 traits was too large for practical purposes, so too did Hans J. Eysenck (1947) contend that Cattell's own list of 16 traits was too unwieldy (Ewen, 1998). Like Cattell, H. J. Eysenck believed that factor analysis was the optimal means toward identifying a minimum number of major traits – hence, the labelling of Eysenck's trait as another version of *factor-analytic trait theory*. However, unlike Cattell (who drew upon the trait theory of G. W. Allport, 1937/1951), H. J. Eysenck was influenced primarily by behaviourist theories (i.e., the classical conditioning theory of Pavlov, 1927; and the drive reduction theory of Hull, 1943) that suggested as few as two traits that needed to be measured – namely, *extraversion* (i.e., outgoingness) and *neuroticism* (i.e., emotional instability), respectively (C. S. Hall & Lindzey, 1957).

Using the psychometric technique of *orthogonal factor analysis* (which tends to identify a relatively small number of latent variables that are independent of each other; Nunnally & Bernstein, 1994), H. J. Eysenck and S. B. G. Eysenck (1968) eventually obtained evidence from their 57-item Eysenck Personality Inventory (EPI) that yielded evidence for extraversion and neuroticism as the two major traits (McCrae & Costa, 2003/2006). In addition to reducing Cattell's (1946) trait list considerably, H. J. Eysenck and S. B. G. Eysenck omitted "intellect" or intelligence from Cattell's list – a change that was consistent with the view that intelligence really constituted part of the subject matter for the emerging field of cognitive psychology, rather than personality psychology (Ewen, 1998). However, like Cattell, H. J. Eysenck and S. B. G. Eysenck agreed with Cattell that the major traits were likely to be 50% heritable (C. S. Hall & Lindzey, 1970)

Even if we set aside H. J. Eysenck and S. B. G. Eysenck's (1968) controversial assertions regarding the heritability of extraversion and neuroticism, one might challenge the empirical evidence for the biological systems (i.e., limbic system and ascending reticular activation system, in that order) that, according to H. J. Eysenck (1967), gave rise to the respective traits (although Gray, 1981, offered plausible alternatives to the biological systems that H. J. Eysenck had proposed; Pickering et al., 2013). Also, despite H. J. Eysenck and S. B. G. Eysenck's (1975) assertion that their newer, 100-item Eysenck Personality Questionnaire (EPI) included a third scale that measured *psychoticism* (i.e., severe psychological impairment), H. J. Eysenck did not offer any detailed description of a specific biological system that might have been responsible for individual differences in that trait (and "psychoticism" actually seems to represent a combination of low levels of the "Big Five" traits of friendliness and conscientiousness, as noted by Digman, 1990; see the next subsection of the present chapter regarding the "Big Five"). Nevertheless, H. J. Eysenck's success in extracting extraversion and neuroticism as major traits foreshadowed findings of all subsequent studies on comprehensive lists of traits (Ewen, 1998).

PAUL COSTA AND ROBERT MCCRAE'S VERSION OF FACTOR-ANALYTIC TRAIT THEORY

By the 1970s, several independent teams of researchers (e.g., Banks, 1948; Borgatta, 1964; D. W. Fiske, 1949; G. M. Smith, 1967; Tupes & Christal, 1961) had concluded that Cattell's (1946) 16PF Questionnaire – which, as the name implies, supposedly measured 16 traits (if one counts "intellect") – actually measured no more than five major traits (Digman, 1990). The five resulting traits – which Paul Costa and Robert McCrae (1985) subsequently labelled as *openness to experience* (i.e., broad-mindedness; formerly known as Cattell's "intellect" factor), *conscientiousness* (i.e., reliability), *extraversion* (i.e., outgoingness), *agreeableness* (i.e., friendliness), and *neuroticism* (i.e., emotional instability) – included, yet were extended beyond, H. J. Eysenck's (1947) "Big Two" traits of extraversion and neuroticism (Wiggins & Pincus, 1992). Costa and McCrae's version of *factor-analytic trait theory* (i.e., the "enduring dispositional view of the Big Five," according to Wiggins & Trapnell, 1997, p. 745) proposes that those particular five traits consistently emerge for a reason: Human beings want to know where potential comrades or adversaries stand on those particular traits (and we humans are aware that other persons want to know where we stand on those particular traits; see Funder & Fast, 2010).

Like H. J. Eysenck and S. B. G. Eysenck (1968), Costa and McCrae (1985) used orthogonal factor analysis to extract latent variables (thus optimising the likelihood of extracting truly independent dimensions; Digman, 1990). However, unlike H. J. Eysenck or S. B. G. Eysenck, Costa and McCrae essentially performed second-order factor analyses (e.g., taking an initial, lower-order set of factors and then conducting another, higher-order factor analysis) on the scales from the Neuroticism-Extraversion-Openness Personality Inventory, Revised Version (NEO-PI-R; conscientiousness and agreeableness emerged as two unexpected dimensions; Wiggins & Trapnell, 1997). In any event, Costa and McCrae developed a version of factor-analytic trait theory that provided an acceptable middle ground between Cattell's (1946) insistence on a minimum of 16 traits and H. J. Eysenck's (1947) insistence on a minimum of two traits (Ewen, 1998).

Costa and McCrae (e.g., McCrae & Costa, 1986) did not originally claim that the "Big Five" traits (which can be memorised via the acronym, *OCEAN*) were largely inherited (Cervone, 2005). However, with the passage of time, Costa and McCrae (e.g., McCrae, 2009; McCrae & Costa, 1989) increasingly have made such a claim – a problematic stance, given that the evidence at hand does not identify *which* particular genes supposedly are linked to individual differences in scores on the "Big Five" traits (Deary, 2009). Nevertheless, unlike Cattell (1946) or H. J. Eysenck (1947), Costa and McCrae have *not* asserted that individuals' trait scores are linked to the same genes that are implicated in individuals' racial group membership (e.g., McCrae & Costa, 1997). Overall, Costa and McCrae's version of factor-analytic trait theory has emerged as the dominant view among trait perspectives on personality (Ewen, 1998). Given that the NEO-PI-R (Costa & McCrae, 1985, 1989, 1992) is only available commercially, we shall comment at greater length upon a freely available measure of the "Big Five" traits (i.e., the Big Five Inventory, or BFI; John et al., 1991) in Box 5.1.

BOX 5.1 JOHN ET AL.'S (1991) BIG FIVE INVENTORY

The current (i.e., 240-item) version of Costa and McCrae's (1992) NEO-PI-Revised Edition is not available within the public domain. Thus, in order to gain access to the NEO-PI-R, we would need to purchase Costa and McCrae's survey. Alternatively, we could obtain freely available copies of various versions of the Big Five Inventory (BFI), which was developed by Oliver John and colleagues (e.g., John et al., 1991; Soto & John, 2017b). Like the NEO-PI in its multiple forms, all versions of the BFI were designed to measure the "Big Five" traits of openness to experience, conscientiousness, extraversion, agreeableness, and neuroticism (Cervone, 2005).

The original, 44-item BFI (John et al., 1991) was published commercially in English but subsequently was published within the public domain by Benet-Martínez and John (1998), in Spanish as well as English versions (see Kwan & Herrmann, 2015). Afterward, the 60-item Next Big Five Inventory (BFI-2; Soto & John, 2017b) was published within the public domain, in English (Ashton et al., 2019). Unlike the original BFI (which retained the same labels for the "Big Five" traits as Costa & McCrae, 1985, 1989, 1992 had used in their versions of the NEO-PI), the BFI-2 relabelled neuroticism as negative emotionality and openness to experience as open-mindedness (see also Soto & John, 2017a). Nevertheless, the original and revised versions of the BFI apparently yield comparable levels of construct validity (as established via orthogonal factor analyses) and internal consistency (as established via reliability analysis; see Nunnally & Bernstein, 1994).

Whether measured by versions of the BFI (John et al., 1991; Soto & John, 2017b) or by versions of the NEO-PI (Costa & McCrae, 1985, 1989, 1992), two of the "Big Five" traits consistently have been linked to individuals' behaviour within the context of close relationships (see Simpson & Campbell, 2013a, b). Specifically, extraversion tends to promote individuals' relationship-maintaining behaviour; whereas neuroticism tends to undermine individuals' relationship-maintaining behaviour (for a review, see McNulty, 2013). The other "Big Five" traits are not consistently reflected in individuals' relationship-maintaining behaviour, although agreeableness occasionally has emerged as a significant positive predictor (see Gaines, 2016/2018). Overall, more research is needed concerning the predictive ability (i.e., ability to explain individual differences in behaviour; Nunnally & Bernstein, 1994) of the "Big Five" traits (for a broader critique of predictive ability within personality psychology, see Funder, 2001).

JOY PAUL GUILFORD'S VERSION OF FACTOR-ANALYTIC TRAIT THEORY

The rise of the "Big Five" trait perspective in personality (especially as proposed and measured by Costa & McCrae, 1985) brought renewed attention to Joy Paul Guilford's (1975) earlier version of *factor-analytic trait theory*, which could be interpreted as generating research findings in support of four of the "Big Five" traits (i.e., conscientiousness, extraversion, agreeableness, and neuroticism; Digman, 1990). It turns out that J. P. Guilford had developed one of the earliest factor-analytic approaches to studying traits (specifically, when examining the trait of extraversion; J. P. Guilford & R. B. Guilford, 1934). However, J. P. Guilford (1975) identified at least ten first-order traits: (1) *general activity vs. slowness and lacking in energy*; (2) *restraint and seriousness vs. rhathymia and impulsiveness*; (3) *ascendance and social boldness vs. submissiveness and timidity*; (4) *sociability and social interest vs. seclusiveness and shyness*; (5) *emotional stability and optimism vs. instability and depression*; (6) *objectivity vs. subjectivity and hypersensitivity*; (7) *friendliness and agreeableness vs. hostility and belligerence*; (8) *thoughtfulness or reflectiveness vs. unreflectiveness*; (9) *good personal relations and cooperativeness vs. criticalness and intolerance*; and (10) *masculinity of interests and emotions vs. femininity*. Amelang and Borkenau (1982) suggested reinterpreting and re-analysing J. P. Guilford's data in such a way that the equivalents of conscientiousness, extraversion, agreeableness, and neuroticism could be extracted as higher-level dimensions via orthogonal factor analyses (Digman, 1990).

J. P. Guilford and Wayne S. Zimmerman (1949) developed the Guilford-Zimmerman Temperament Survey to measure the ten aforementioned, lower-order traits that eventually would become the core dimensions in Guilford's (1975) version of factor-analytic trait theory (Digman, 1990). The term "temperament" in the Guilford-Zimmerman Temperament Survey reflects the belief that certain biologically hardwired precursors to traits are present at birth, manifested in individual differences in behaviour from infancy onward (see Shiner, 2015) – a belief that also is reflected in the term "temperamental traits," as promoted by Cattell (1965; see also Rutter & Silberg, 2002). Putting aside the question of temperamental precursors to traits, Goldberg (1981) – who apparently coined the term "Big Five," prior to Costa and McCrae's (1985 1989, 1992) popularisation of the term (Digman, 1990) – concluded that J. P. Guilford and Zimmerman had not measured more than five traits (and, as we have seen, four factors were extracted by Amelang & Borkenau, 1982). Thus, as a measure of ten distinct traits, the Guilford-Zimmerman Temperament Survey is questionable in terms of construct validity (for a discussion of the extent to which acceptance of J. P. Guilford's ten factors is based upon the persuasiveness of theoretical arguments rather than scientific data, see C. S. Hall & Lindzey, 1978). As for internal consistency, independent reviewers rarely (if ever) comment upon the reliability of the scales that underlie the Guilford-Zimmerman Temperament Survey (as assessed via Cronbach's alpha; e.g., Schuerger et al., 1989).

Unlike the other factor-analytic trait theories and relevant surveys that we have covered so far, one will not find any acknowledgement of J. P. Guilford's (1975) version of factor-analytic trait theory or the Guilford-Zimmerman Temperament Survey (J. P. Guilford & Zimmerman, 1949) in Ozer and Reise's (1994) review of the literature on personality assessment (which, in turn was designed to complement the emphasis on personality structure in an earlier review by Wiggins & Pincus, 1992). Similarly, one will not find any mention of J. P. Guilford's factor theory and trait survey within the fifth edition of Ewen's *An Introduction to Theories of* Personality (1998). Nevertheless, in the third edition of *Theories of Personality*, C. S. Hall and Lindzey (1978) regard the influence of J. P. Guilford's theory and survey upon the field of personality psychology as comparable to the influence of H. J. Eysenck's factor theory (e.g., H. J. Eysenck, 1947) and trait survey (e.g., H. J. Eysenck & S. B. G. Eysenck, 1968). Perhaps J. P. Guilford's contributions to personality psychology are best summarised as (1) pioneering the use of factor analysis to identify a manageable set of major traits, (2) developing a coherent theory to account for those theories, and (3) creating a trait survey that has stood the test of time a set of accomplishments that, at a minimum, support the inclusion of J. P. Guilford's theory and survey in historical overviews of trait perspectives in personality (Digman, 1990).

MICHAEL ASHTON AND KIBEOM LEE'S VERSION OF FACTOR-ANALYTIC TRAIT THEORY

So far, we have regarded the "Big Five" trait approach (especially as reflected in the factor-analytic trait theory and survey of Costa & McCrae, 1985, 1989 1992) as invariant across cultural groups (currently the consensus view within personality psychology; e.g., Draguns & Tanaka-Matsumi, 2020). However, in 2000, A. Timothy Church concluded that – if one broadens one's conceptual and methodological focus from participants in

European-language (typically, but not always, English-language) nations to participants in Asian-language nations – then a trait that Church labelled as "Chinese tradition" is conspicuously missing from ostensibly comprehensive surveys (Kwan & Herrmann, 2015). In turn, drawing partly upon the results of studies by Church and colleagues (e.g., Church et al., 1997, 1998; see also Church & Lonner, 1998) and the results of their own studies (e.g., Ashton, 1998; Ashton et al., 1998a, b; Ashton et al., 2000), among other sources, Michael Ashton and Kibeom Lee (2001) proposed that the often-omitted trait of "Chinese tradition" is best interpreted as *honesty/humility* (Gaughan et al., 2012). In the process of incorporating honesty/humility into their version of *factor-analytic trait theory*, Ashton and K. Lee proposed a six-factor model with the acronym of HEXACO (i.e., *H*onesty/humility, *E*motionality/neuroticism, e*X*traversion, *A*greeableness, *C*onscientiousness, and *O*penness to experience; Hough et al., 2015).

K. Lee and Ashton (2004) developed the original, 192-item HEXACO Personality Inventory (HEXACO-PI) to measure the six dimensions within their (Ashton & K. Lee, 2001) version of factor-analytic trait theory (see DeYoung, 2015). Subsequently, K. Lee and Ashton (2006) published a 200-item version of their survey, labelled as the HEXACO Personality Inventory-Revised Version (HEXACO-PI-R; Gaughan et al., 2012). Both the HEXACO-PI and HEXACO-PI-R yield acceptable levels of construct validity (as assessed via orthogonal factor analyses) and internal consistency (as assessed via reliability analyses; see Nunnally & Bernstein, 1994). Moreover, results of a direct comparison between the psychometric properties of the HEXACO-PI-R (K. Lee & Ashton, 2004) and the most recent version of the NEO-PI-R (Costa & McCrae, 1992) indicate that the two surveys are similarly high in construct validity and internal consistency, with the six HEXACO traits combining to explain significantly more variance in individuals' levels of psychopathology than do the "Big Five" traits (primarily because of the inclusion of honesty/humility within the HEXACO-PI-R; Gaughan et al., 2012).

Certain problems have arisen regarding comparisons between the content of the six HEXACO traits (as measured by K. Lee & Ashton, 2004, 2006) and the content of the "Big Five" traits (as measured by Costa & McCrae, 1985, 1989, 1992). For example, K. Lee and Ashton's emotionality trait is limited to internally directed negative emotions (whereas Costa and McCrae's neuroticism trait included externally as well as internally directed negative emotions); and K. Lee and Ashton's honesty/humility trait overlaps substantially with their own agreeableness trait (whereas Costa and McCrae likely would subsume honesty/humility within their agreeableness trait; Gaughan et al., 2012). However, it is worth noting that Costa and McCrae's own "Big Five" traits are not as empirically distinct from each other as their version of factor-analytic trait theory would suggest (see Funder, 2001). In any event, Ashton and K. Lee's factor theory and survey have emerged as viable alternatives to Costa and McCrae's earlier factor theory and survey (Paunonen & Hong, 2015).

THEORIES PROPOSING LIMITED SETS OF SALIENT TRAITS

Sandra Bem's gender schema theory. In a review of the literature on gender and personality, Anne Constantinople (1973) concluded that then-existing measures of gender-related personality traits (most notably Terman & Miles, 1936) tended to constrain individuals to score *either* as "masculine" (i.e., possessing psychological attributes that stereotypically are associated with males in a particular society) *or* as "feminine" (i.e., possessing psychological attributes that stereotypically are associated with females in a given society), possibly leading to an exaggeration of gender differences in those traits. Subsequently (though not specifically mentioning Constantinople's review), Sandra Bem (1974) published the appropriately-named Bem Sex Role Inventory (BSRI), which contained separate scales measuring "masculinity" (20 items) and "femininity" (20 items). Finally, having shown that some (but not most) men and women are "androgynous" (i.e., possess "masculine" as well as "feminine" personality characteristics), S. Bem (1981) proposed a *gender schema theory* that promoted the ideal of "androgyny" (reflecting individuals' refusal to create mental constructions of themselves and the world in rigid, "masculine" versus "feminine" terms) as an index of mental well-being (Lenney, 1991).

In terms of psychometric analyses, S. Bem (1974) reported that the internal consistency of the masculinity and femininity scales was satisfactory (i.e., Cronbach's alphas consistently > .70; see Nunnally & Bernstein, 1994). However, S. Bem did *not* report results of factor analyses, which would have allowed readers to evaluate the construct validity of the masculinity and femininity scales. As it turns out, results of orthogonal factor analyses by subsequent researchers revealed that (1) the term "masculine" does *not* fit with the rest of the items (e.g., "acts as a leader," "self-sufficient") within the so-called "masculinity" scale; and (2) the term "feminine" does *not* fit with the rest of the items (e.g., "affectionate," "gentle") within the so-called "femininity" scale (R. Brown, 1986). Thus, some critics (most notably Spence, 1985) have concluded that – despite S. Bem's (e.g., S. Bem, 1985) assertions to the contrary – the BSRI does not measure general "sex role orientations" but, rather, measures the specific, gender-related traits of *instrumentality* (essentially, dominance as defined earlier in the present chapter) and *expressivity* (basically, nurturance as defined in the present chapter; see Wiggins, 1991).

Perhaps the most controversial assertion within S. Bem's (1981) gender schema theory is the claim that individuals' *psychological* "androgyny" (i.e., simultaneous possession of instrumental and expressive traits) covaries with individuals' *sexual* "androgyny" (i.e., *bisexuality*, or attraction toward both men and women as potential sexual partners; Spence & Helmreich, 1978). The available evidence does not support S. Bem's assumption that individuals' personality traits and sexual orientation are empirically linked (R. Brown, 1986). Nevertheless, S. Bem's gender schema theory and BRSI have emerged as the most influential theory and gender-related trait survey, respectively, in the post-1960s literature on gender and personality (Lenney, 1991).

JANET SPENCE'S MULTIFACTORIAL GENDER IDENTITY THEORY

During the same year that S. Bem (1974) published the aforementioned BSRI, Janet Spence and colleagues (Spence et al., 1974) released their own survey – namely, the 24-item Personal Attributes Questionnaire (PAQ) – that was designed to measure "masculinity" and "femininity" as separate dimensions (Lenney,

1991). Like S. Bem, Spence et al. concluded that some men and some women are psychologically "androgynous" (i.e., score relatively high in "masculine" and "feminine" traits). However, unlike S. Bem, Spence and colleagues never assumed that the PAQ (or the BSRI, for that matter) measured individuals' sexual orientation (R. Brown, 1986). Indeed (as noted in Chapter 1 of the present book), Spence et al. eventually developed surveys that not only measured gender-related traits (e.g., Spence et al., 1979) but also gender-related attitudes (e.g., Spence et al., 1973) and achievement-related motives that have been linked empirically to gender (e.g., Helmreich & Spence, 1978) – an eclectic approach that led to the development of Spence's (1993) *multifactorial gender identity theory* (Frable, 1997).

Having reflected upon the content of S. Bem's (1974) BSRI and their own PAQ (Spence et al., 1974), Spence and Helmreich (1978) concluded that they (and S. Bem) had primarily (and, in the case of the PAQ, exclusively) measured socially desirable or positive aspects of "masculinity" and "femininity." Afterward, Spence and colleagues (Spence et al., 1979) developed the 40-item Extended Personal Attributes Questionnaire (EPAQ) to measure negative as well as positive aspects of "masculinity" and "femininity." Finally, Spence and colleagues (Helmreich et al., 1981) published results regarding the psychometric properties of the original PAQ and the EPAQ. Not only did oblique factor analyses identify positive and negative aspects of "masculinity" and "femininity" as distinct dimensions; but – with the notable exception of negative "femininity" in the EPAQ (i.e., Cronbach's alphas below .50) – the internal consistency of the PAQ and EPAQ scales proved to be satisfactory (i.e., Cronbach's alphas near or above .70; Nunnally & Bernstein, 1994).

Spence's (1993) multifactorial gender identity theory and two versions of the PAQ (Spence et al., 1974, 1979) have not enjoyed quite the same popularity that S. Bem's (1981) gender schema theory and BSRI (Bem, 1974) have enjoyed within the literature on gender and personality (see Wood & Eagly, 2010). However, both Spence and S. Bem have made major contributions to the literature, consistently obtaining modest-but-significant gender differences on scores on the separate dimensions of "masculinity" (with men scoring higher than women) and "femininity" (with women scoring higher than men; Helgeson, 2015). Moreover, Spence and colleagues (e.g., Spence et al., 1985) have led the way toward replacing the overloaded trait terms of "masculinity" and "femininity" with the more limited (and arguably more accurate) trait terms of instrumentality and expressivity (R. Brown, 1986). All in all, Spence's multifactorial gender identity theory and relevant research clearly are reflected in Deaux and LaFrance's (1998) conclusion that – where personality is concerned – gender is "part of the 'air [that] we breathe'" (p. 788).

JERRY WIGGINS'S INTERPERSONAL CIRCUMPLEX THEORY

In Chapter 2 of the present book, we learned that Harry Stack Sullivan's (1953) interpersonal theory (a "social-psychological" theory of personality; C. S. Hall & Lindzey, 1957) emphasised the importance of target persons' behaviour toward significant others (with therapists potentially qualifying as clients' "significant others"; see also Sullivan, 1954) as the data that ideally serve as bases for social perceivers' attributions concerning target persons' personality characteristics (Ewen, 1998). Subsequently, based on his interpretation of Sullivan's interpersonal theory and his own analysis of clinical data via the Kaiser Foundation, Timothy Leary (1957) concluded that *dominance* and *nurturance* (described earlier in the present chapter) are the two major interpersonal traits along which individuals differ (Millon, 1996). In turn, building upon T. Leary's circumplex model of interpersonal traits, Maurice Lorr and Douglas McNair (1965) obtained reports from clinicians regarding clients' behaviour, extracting T. Leary's constructs of dominance and nurturance as interpersonal traits. Finally, Jerry Wiggins and Ana Holzmuller (1978) collected self-reported data from non-clinical samples and (like T. Leary, 1957; as well as Lorr & McNair, 1963) identified dominance and nurturance as the two major interpersonal traits that differ across individuals. Wiggins (1991) ultimately developed a wide-ranging *interpersonal circumplex theory* that identifies *agency* as an intrapersonally directed aspect of the human condition (including, but not limited to, the trait of dominance) and *communion* as an interpersonally directed aspect of the human condition (including, but not limited to, the trait of nurturance; Gaines, 2016/2018).

In an effort to measure interpersonal traits in all of their complexity, Wiggins (1979) developed the 128-item Interpersonal Adjective Scales (IAS), which included eight lower-order traits (i.e., *assured-dominant*, *arrogant-calculating*, *cold-quarrelsome*, *aloof-introverted*, *unassured-submissive*, *unassuming-ingenuous*, *warm-agreeable*, and *gregarious-extraverted*) with intercorrelations that allowed researchers to plot those traits in a circular or circumplex order around the underlying, higher-order traits of dominance (the Y axis) and nurturance (the X axis; Millon, 1996). Afterward, Wiggins and colleagues (Wiggins et al., 1988) published the 64-item Revised Interpersonal Adjective Scales (IAS-R), which preserved the statistical properties of the original IAS (i.e., starting at the 12 o'clock position and working one's way anticlockwise through the set of lower-order traits that are listed above, at approximately 45-degree angles, one begins with the assured-dominant trait and ends with the gregarious-extraverted trait; Gaines, 2016/2018). Using an independent or orthogonal version of principal components analyses (which are similar, though not identical to, factor analyses; Tabachnick & Fidell, 2007), Wiggins et al. consistently obtained support for dominance and nurturance as underlying dimensions (Fabrigar et al., 1997). Although some critics (e.g., Gaines, Panter et al., 1997) have questioned the precision by which the IAS and IAS-R measure interpersonal traits within a two-dimensional grid, the consensus view (e.g., Gurtman & Pincus, 2000) is that the IAS and IAS-R provide optimal measures of interpersonal traits (Acton & Revelle, 2002).

The most persistent criticism of the original and revised versions of the IAS (Wiggins, 1979; Wiggins et al., 1988) may be that – despite high levels of construct validity (at least when using scores on the eight lower-order traits to extract dominance and nurturance as higher-order dimensions via principal components analyses) and high levels of internal consistency (as assessed via Cronbach's alpha; e.g., Wiggins, 1995; Wiggins et al., 1981) – Wiggins and colleagues have relied too heavily upon obscure synonyms and antonyms (e.g., "unbold," "ironhearted") in order to generate nearly-perfect circumplex patterns of lower-order trait correlations (e.g., Benjamin, 2011). In an effort to resolve the linguistic problems that underlie the IAS and IAS-R, Patrick M. Markey and Charlotte N. Markey (2009) have developed the everyday-language International Personality Item Pool-Interpersonal Circumplex (IPIP-IPC) survey (which is profiled in Box 5.2). Notwithstanding empirical issues concerning Wiggins et al.'s measurement of interpersonal traits, Wiggins's (1991) interpersonal circumplex theory has gained prominence due to the ease with which it allows researchers to incorporate the gender-related traits of positive "masculinity" (i.e., high end of the dominance axis), positive "femininity" (high end of the nurturance axis), negative "femininity" (low end of the dominance axis), and negative "masculinity" (low end of the nurturance axis) – as well as the "Big Five" traits of extraversion (combination of high dominance and high nurturance) and agreeableness (combination of low dominance and high nurturance) – within one circular model of interpersonal traits (Helgeson, 2015).

BOX 5.2 P. M. MARKEY AND C. N. MARKEY'S (2009) INTERNATIONAL PERSONALITY ITEM POOL-INTERPERSONAL CIRCUMPLEX INVENTORY

Notwithstanding its widespread popularity (Locke, 2011), the IAS (Wiggins, 1979; Wiggins et al., 1988) has been criticised for its use of terms that are so infrequently used that Wiggins and colleagues have found it necessary to make English-language dictionaries available to their participants (see Benjamin, 2011). Influenced by Wiggins's (1991) interpersonal circumplex theory, Patrick M. Markey and Charlotte N. Markey (2009) published the 32-item International Personality Item Pool-Interpersonal Circumplex (IPIP-IPC). However, unlike Wiggins and colleagues (who drew largely upon the 4,500-word, dictionary-driven taxonomy of Allport & Odbert (1936) when constructing the IAS; e.g., Wiggins, 1979), P. M. Markey and C. N. Markey used commonly used words and phrases from the general IPIP, as developed by Goldberg (1999).

Relying primarily (though not exclusively) upon orthogonal versions of principal components analyses of scores from the eight lower-order traits of assured-dominant, arrogant-calculating, cold-quarrelsome, aloof-introverted, unassured-submissive, unassuming-ingenuous, warm-agreeable, and gregarious-extraverted, P. M. Markey and C. N. Markey concluded that the IPIP-IPC possessed satisfactory construct validity as a measure of the higher-order traits of dominance and nurturance. However, internal consistency across the eight subscales within the IPIP-IPC varied dramatically, with Cronbach's alphas ranging from highs of nearly .80 (highly impressive, especially for 4-item subscales) to lows of .50 (not impressive, even for subscales with only four items; see Cortina, 1993). Thus, the measurement error for certain subscales of the IPIP-IPC is potentially problematic (see Nunnally & Bernstein, 1994).

Despite obtaining lower-than-optimal reliabilities for P. M. Markey and C. N. Markey's (2009) interpersonal trait subscales, Gaines (2023) found that dominance and nurturance were significant predictors of *accommodation* (i.e., individuals' refraining from reciprocating partners' anger or criticism over the short term, instead responding in ways that are intended to maintain their close relationships over the long term; see Rusbult et al., 1991, for details regarding the conceptualisation and measurement of accommodation) across two large samples in the UK. Specifically, Gaines reported that (1) nurturance was *positively* related to accommodation; whereas (2) dominance was *negatively* related to accommodation – a set of results that clarified the destructive role that dominance can play within close relationships (for a discussion of questions that have arisen within the field of relationship science concerning the usefulness of dominance and other agentic aspects of personality as predictors of relationship processes, see Gaines, 2016/2018). The predictive validity of the IPIP-IPC subscales in Gaines's study likely benefitted from the use of *covariance structure analysis*, which enables researchers to control statistically for measurement error (see Kline, 2023). At any rate, Gaines's results indicate that the IPIP-IPC is a viable survey.

ON THE RECURRENT ISSUE OF "HERITABILITY": UPDATE FOR THE PRESENT EDITION

During the same year that the first edition of *Personality Psychology: The Basics* (Gaines, 2020) was published, the second edition of the *Cambridge Handbook of Personality Psychology* (edited by Corr & Matthews, 2020) likewise was published. We note that, within that *Handbook*, Alexander Weiss and Ian J. Deary (2020) substantially revised Deary's (2009) previously stated views on the "heritability" of traits. We highlight this point because much of our rationale for maintaining scepticism regarding claims about "heritability," given the lack of substantive evidence for specific genes (or even specific chromosomes) that supposedly exert so much influence upon the incidence of specific traits, has drawn upon Deary's (2009) original statement. We do not know why Weiss and Deary's (2020) more recent chapter is relatively uncritical about trait "heritability"; having sifted through every instance in which they used the term "trait," we cannot find a single instance in which Weiss and Deary identified specific genes (or, at least, specific chromosomes) that presumably would be needed in order to verify such claims. Afterward, we sifted through the entire second edition of the *Cambridge Handbook of Personality Psychology*; again, we did not find any substantive evidence for trait "heritability" from specific genes or chromosomes.

Our exhaustive search for substantiated claims of genetic or chromosomal inheritance as expressed via personality traits was aided greatly by our possession of an e-book version of the second edition of the *Cambridge Handbook of Personality Psychology* (edited by Corr & Matthews, 2020). Consequently, our search was even more extensive than was Gaines's (2023) spot-check of the term "trait" across several chapters from the print edition of the *Oxford Handbook of the Five Factor Model* (edited by Widiger, 2017), with regard to trait "heritability." Nonetheless, we reached the same conclusion that Gaines had reached in *The Self in Relationships: Social-Personality Theory, Research, and New Directions* (2023) – namely, the biological basis for broad claims about the "heritability" of personality traits is shockingly slim. The results of our literature search (as well as the search that was undertaken by Gaines, 2023) lend support to Gaines's decision in *Personality and Close Relationship Processes* (2016/2018) to relegate trait "heritability" to a side issue. In the interest of scientific correctness (as distinct from "political correctness"), we believe that the current lack of evidence warrants scepticism, as far as claims about genetic or chromosomal precursors to traits within the "normal" range of personality are concerned.

To the extent that personality psychologists continue to invoke the concept of trait "heritability" in the absence of solid genetic of chromosomal evidence, the circumstances will be ripe for laypersons and scientists alike to misconstrue the meaning of statistics such as correlations between identical versus fraternal twins on specific personality traits (Gaines, 2025). For instance, McCrae and Costa (2003/2006) – whose version of factor-analytic trait theory currently stands as the definitive trait theory (as we have observed in the present chapter) – have found it necessary to correct journalists who have interpreted the Five-Factor Model as suggesting that individuals' traits are set in stone. Moreover, Wiggins (2003/2005) – whose interpersonal circumplex theory complements McCrae and Costa's trait theory (again, as we have learned in the present chapter) – took pains to distance the entire trait school of personality psychology from the taint of scientific racism that had accompanied the eugenics movement throughout the twentieth century. Especially as gender-informed theories of personality (e.g., the gender schema theory of S. L. Bem, 1981; and the multifactorial gender identity theory of J. T. Spence, 1993) lose currency, we must wonder whether the adage "biology is destiny" will persist implicitly or explicitly within behavioural genetics.

CRITIQUE OF TRAIT PERSPECTIVES

Given the current pre-eminence of trait perspectives within personality psychology (Funder & Fast, 2010), one might be surprised to learn that the practical (if not statistical) significance of trait measurement was a point of contention during the late 1960s, particularly for Walter Mischel (1968). However, Mischel helped to instigate a crisis throughout personality psychology by asserting that traits did not explain nearly as much variance in individuals' behaviour as trait theories (going as far back as Allport, 1937/1951, 1961/1963) would suggest (for an analogous critique concerning attitudes as predictors of behaviour within social psychology, see Wicker, 1969). Although some trait theorists may find it tempting to cast Mischel as the "bad guy" in contrast to Allport as the "good guy" in the debate over the practical value of traits (Wiggins & Pincus, 1992), Mischel *did* have a point regarding the possibility that personality psychologists generally had placed excessive emphasis on construct validity, as opposed to predictive validity (M. Snyder & Ickes, 1985).

According to Ickes et al. (1997), constructive responses on the part of personality psychologists regarding challenges to the traditional, *"dispositional" approach* to personality and social behaviour (exemplified by the trait theory of Allport, 1937/1951, 1961/1963) include the development of a *statistical version of an interactionist approach* (whereby greater attention was paid to specifying *which* traits, behaviours, persons, and situations would be more versus less likely to yield trait-behaviour covariance that was practically as well as statistically significant) as well as a *dynamic version of an interactionist approach* (whereby greater attention was paid to individuals' relative freedom to choose the situations within which their traits and behaviour are examined; see also Funder, 1991). Furthermore, according to M. Snyder and Cantor (1998), personality psychologists increasingly have articulated a *functionalist approach* to personality and social behaviour (whereby features of persons and features of situations are conceptualised as influences on intrapersonal, social, relational, and group agendas; see Gaines, 2016/2018). Overall, personality psychologists have succeeded in defending trait perspectives from conceptual and empirical challenges by Mischel (1968) and other critics (for a review, see Zuroff, 1986).

PRELUDE TO CHAPTER 6

By the end of the twentieth century, two additional perspectives had gained prominence within personality psychology – specifically, (1) the *cognitive* perspective (which emphasises individuals' information-processing and other higher-order thought processes as influences on behaviour) and (2) the *biological* perspective (which emphasises "organic" influences on individuals' behaviour; S. C. Cloninger, 2020). In the previous edition of *Personality Psychology: The Basics* (Gaines, 2020), we regarded the cognitive and biological perspectives as separate schools of thought (following Funder & Fast, 2010). However, in that edition, we chose not to highlight the overlap that exists between the cognitive and biological perspectives with regard to modern-day constructs such as *emotions* (i.e., affective experiences that reflect individuals' feeling toward someone or something; see Devonis, 2019).

In Chapter 6 of the present edition, we shall treat the cognitive and biological perspectives as subschools within one increasingly unified school of thought in personality psychology (see Reisenzein et al., 2020). Representative theories within the cognitive subschool include (in order of appearance) Mischel's (1973) version of social-cognitive theory, Bandura's (1986) recasting of his earlier social learning theory (Bandura & Walters, 1963) as a separate version of social-cognitive theory, Higgins's (1987) self-discrepancy theory, and Baldwin's (1992) relational schema theory. Afterward, representative theories within the biological subschool include (in order of appearance) Darwin's (1859) theory of natural selection; Galton's (1869) theory of eugenics; J. A. Gray's (1970) reinforcement sensitivity theory; Depue's (1995) version of neurotransmitter theory; A. H. Buss and Plomin's (1975) temperament theory of personality development; and D. M. Buss and Schmitt's (1993) sexual strategy theory.

6

COGNITIVE AND BIOLOGICAL PERSPECTIVES ON PERSONALITY

When we covered Hans J. Eysenck's (1967) version of factor-analytic trait theory in Chapter 5, we noted the degree to which Eysenck's theory reflected the influence of behaviourist (and, specifically, classical conditioning) perspectives within personality psychology (Bouton & Boakes, 2019). However, given H. J. Eysenck's proposal that specific processes within the brain include a type of "conceptual nervous system" that is responsible for covariance between traits and behaviour, Eysenck's theory can be interpreted as partly cognitive and partly biological as well (Matthews & Gilliland, 1999). On the one hand, H. J. Eysenck's version of factor theory has been criticised for placing unwarranted emphasis upon arousal as facilitating poor performance (1) among low-extravert individuals (a) in interpersonal situations (which inherently are experienced as demanding), and possibly (b) work contexts (which may or may not be demanding); and (2) among high-neurotic individuals when exposed to external stressors in general (e.g., Matthews, 2016). On the other hand, H. J. Eysenck's theory has been praised for offering a psychophysiological account of arousal (especially *emotional* arousal as a moderator of the link between neuroticism and quality of performance) as implicated in individuals' behaviour (Geen, 1997).

We do not wish to overstate the relevance of H. J. Eysenck's (1967) version of factor-analytic theory for cognitive (as distinct from biological) theories of personality; for instance, Gerald Matthews (2020b) noted that H. J. Eysenck's theory addresses

DOI: 10.4324/9781003601777-9

presumed neurological mechanisms but does not attempt to explain which higher-order thought processes (if any) might be linked to the neurological mechanisms. By the same token, James Szalma (2020) pointed out that various cognitive-science approaches to studying traits and behaviour propose that traits mediate the impact of arousal (which itself reflects the influence of neurological variables) upon individuals' behaviour. Boele de Raad and Dick Barelds (2020) surmised that – *if* one accepts H. J. Eysenck's premise that traits within his factor theory (i.e., neuroticism and extraversion, if not "psychoticism") are largely heritable – then cognitive as well as biological processes are well-represented within Eysenck's theory (although the cognitive nature and genetic endowment of traits are left implicit, not articulated in a direct manner). Finally, Rachel Mitchell and Veena Kumari (2016) concluded that H. J. Eysenck's theory has yielded empirical support from a few studies within cognitive neuroscience, although further research is needed regarding the development of individual differences.

Particularly among those psychologists who adopt a *biopsychosocial* approach toward understanding individual-difference influences on health-related behaviours, the prospect that cognitive and biological theories of personality can be integrated into one unified perspective seems plausible (Heilmayr & H. S. Friedman, 2020). Nonetheless, even within the field of *health psychology* (which draws upon medicine and psychology), it is clear that biological precursors to individuals' behaviour tend not to be as direct (or as impactful) as some personality psychologists might assume (Matthews, 2013). At any rate, personality psychologists might do well to examine the myriad ways that cognitive and biological constructs may be implicated separately and together (along with additional variables) in associations between personality and behaviour, within and outside health-related domains (see Ferguson, 2013). In the present chapter, we shall proceed with the assumption that a discernible school encompassing cognitive as well as biological perspectives has begun to coalesce within modern-day personality psychology (e.g., as exemplified by the emerging research area of cognitive and personality functioning across humans' lifespan; see Staudinger, 2020).

BASIC ASSUMPTIONS UNDERLYING COGNITIVE AND BIOLOGICAL PERSPECTIVES

In Chapter 4 of the present book, we highlighted the emphasis on the whole person within the humanistic/existential school of personality psychology (see also Wong, 2005). Some reviewers have noted that cognitive and biological perspectives on personality likewise offer important contributions toward psychologists' understanding of the entire functioning person (e.g., S. C. Cloninger, 2020). However, other reviewers have described cognitive and (especially) biological perspectives as providing insight into infrahuman *and* human personality (e.g., Delval et al., 2024; but see also Cervone, 2027, for a discussion of controversies surrounding the subject area of "animal personality"). Perhaps the most balanced appraisal that we can make regarding the utility of cognitive and biological perspectives for understanding the whole person is that conceptual and empirical advances emanating from those perspectives can be put to use by contemporary humanistic and existential psychologists in the process of examining the complexities of human selfhood (see also Bland & DeRobertis, 2019). Indeed, the literature on neural plasticity suggests that cognitive and biological influences may promote stability *and* change in human personality (Kostromina & Grishina, 2023).

It is commonplace for personality psychologists to depict the evolutionary development of human personality as proceeding from (1) the emotion-generating neurobiological structures that characterise humans' animal ancestry in general, to (2) the cognition-generating neurobiological structures that characterise humans' mammalian ancestry in particular (with special emphasis generally placed upon humans' primate heritage; e.g., Montag & Panksepp, 2017). However, results from contemporary studies in neurobiology indicate that humans' limbic system (associated with the "emotional brain") as well as humans' cerebellum (integral to the "cognitive brain") are involved in the production and moderation of emotions and cognitions alike (Y. Liu et al., 2009). Therefore, it would be more accurate for personality psychologists to refer to a unified human brain that is responsible for a variety of emotion–cognition interactions that may be manifested as individual differences in adaptive versus maladaptive behaviour within particular physical and social environments (Okon-Singer et al., 2015). Furthermore, interactions between emotions and cognitions may be reflected in a range of adaptive behaviours *and* a range of maladaptive behaviours among humans (Tyng et al., 2017).

Throughout the present book, we have made several passing references to Charles Darwin's (1859) theory of natural selection. At this point in the present chapter, we shall add a few details about Darwin's theory of natural selection as a forerunner to modern-day theories and research within the cognitive/biological school of personality (consistent with Burghardt, 2009). According to Darwin's theory, to the extent that organisms within any species possess biological (and, at least among humans and [other] great apes, cognitive) characteristics that enable them to survive long enough to reproduce within a particular environment, the descendants of those organisms will tend to possess characteristics that are comparable – yet not necessarily identical – to the organisms in question (see Gross, 2010). Especially relevant to the present chapter is Darwin's belief that the emotion of *shame*, if displayed by humans and by (other) animals alike, would serve as evidence of a common experience of self-consciousness (P. Snyder et al., 2010). However, Darwin's own programme of research did not identify shame as a basic emotion, among humans or other species (see Denis & B. Young, 2019). At any rate, we shall revisit Darwin's theory later in the current chapter.

COGNITIVE THEORIES OF PERSONALITY

WALTER MISCHEL'S VERSION OF SOCIAL-COGNITIVE THEORY

In Chapter 5 of the present book, we learned that Walter Mischel (1968) helped to bring about a crisis throughout personality psychology by questioning the practical significance of covariance between individuals' scores on traits and behaviour (M. Snyder & Ickes, 1985). As Mischel (2004) acknowledged in later years, one of the most promising responses within the field was personality psychologists' collective adoption of a statistical version of an interactionist approach to personality and social behaviour (e.g., taking into account joint effects of individual-difference and social-psychological variables on individuals' behaviour) – an approach that Mischel credited to Magnusson and Endler (1977) in particular. However, Mischel also identified an alternative approach that he had advocated as early as 1973 – specifically, the adoption of an early version of *social-cognitive theory* that acknowledged the impact of individual differences in the construal of social situations (e.g., through specific encoding and appraisal processes) on individual differences in behaviour (see Funder & Fast, 2010).

As Funder (2001) observed, Mischel and Shoda (1995) developed the *cognitive-affective personality system*, or CAPS, model as an extension of Mischel's (1973) version of social-cognitive theory. In particular, "if-then" behavioural profiles or *behavioural signatures* are key concepts in Mischel and Shoda's CAPS model (Holmes, 2002). These behavioural profiles or signatures specify what a given individual will do in each particular situation that he or she encounters (Endler, 2000). In the process of elaborating upon the CAPS model, Mischel (2004) alluded to one hypothetical example of behavioural signatures in action – specifically, considering two children who score equally high on a trait measure of aggressiveness, but who show different behaviours across different social situations (i.e., Child A might display aggressive tendencies on the playground, but not in the classroom; whereas the reverse might be true for Child B).

In a critique of Mischel's (1973) version of social cognitive theory in general and Mischel and Shoda's (1995) CAPS model in particular, Funder (2001) argued that the usefulness of Mischel's model is limited by the fact that no clear, simple system exists for classifying those situations that will yield particular if-then profiles. By the same token, Funder and Fast (2010) concluded that Mischel's (1973) version of social-cognitive theory successfully incorporates the diverse array of models and studies that reflect cognitive approaches to personality. Furthermore, as we note in Box 6.1, John Holmes (2002) used Mischel and Shoda's CAPS model as the conceptual framework for his own *s*ituation-Partner *A*–Partner *B*-*i*nteraction (SABI) model of interdependence between individuals in close relationships (see also Gaines, 2016/2018). Thus, it may be safe to say that Mischel is no longer a "villain" in personality psychology (to the extent that he ever deserved that dis-honour; McAdams, 1997).

BOX 6.1 HOLMES'S (2002) SABI MODEL

Prior to the cognitive revolution within psychology, Kurt Lewin (1936) developed *field theory*, which argues that a given person's behaviour (*B*) can be understood as a joint function of the person (*P*) and the environment (*E*; for a review, see Schellenberg, 1978). Although field theory is an individual-differences theory (C. S. Hall & Lindzey, 1957), Lewin's theory served as a basis for John Thibaut and Harold Kelley's (1959; Kelley, 1979; Kelley & Thibaut, 1978) social-psychological *interdependence theory* (which contends that close relationships are defined by the extent to which partners influence each other's thoughts, feelings, and behaviour; Van Lange & Balliet, 2015). Subsequently, John Holmes (2002) combined elements of field theory and interdependence theory with elements of Mischel's (1973) version of social-cognitive theory (especially the aforementioned CAPS model of Mischel & Shoda, 1995) and Baldwin's (1992) relational schema theory (which we shall encounter later in the present chapter) to produce the SABI model (see Rusbult & Van Lange, 2003).

According to Holmes (2002), interpersonal situations vary in the degree to which they make particular aspects of individuals' personalities relevant to individuals' interactions with relationship partners (see also Holmes, 2000). Furthermore, Holmes's SABI model suggests that certain interpersonal situations may reveal the extent to which particular personality constructs are manifested in individuals' interpersonal behaviour (see Reis, Capobianco, & Tsai, 2002). Holmes's model identifies six dimensions of situations (i.e., *degree of interdependence*, *mutuality of interdependence*, *correspondence of outcomes*, *basis of control*, *temporal structure*, and *degree of uncertainty*), each of which logically calls for the expression of one or two relevant interpersonal dispositions (thus affirming the role of cognition in activating certain aspects of individuals' personality repertoire within close relationships; Rusbult & Van Lange, 2003).

Holmes's (2002) SABI model was instrumental to the development of a taxonomy of twenty interpersonal situations by Kelley et al. (2003) – an accomplishment that, so far, has not been accompanied by a corresponding taxonomy of interpersonal dispositions (Gaines, 2016/2018). However, as the field of relationship science progresses from "greening" (Berscheid, 1999) to "ripening" (Reis, 2007) to "blossoming" (Simpson & Campbell, 2013a, b), researchers increasingly seek to identify those personality constructs and interpersonal goals that are most relevant to particular relationship contexts (see Finkel et al., 2017). Overall, Holmes's SABI model demonstrates potential as a cognitive account of personality and behaviour in close relationships (Rusbult & Van Lange, 2003).

ALBERT BANDURA'S VERSION OF SOCIAL-COGNITIVE THEORY

As we learned in Chapter 3 of the present book, Albert Bandura and Richard Walters's (1963) version of social learning theory followed the lead of Julian Rotter's (1954) earlier version of social learning theory in moving away from neo-Freudian perspectives on drives as presumed predictors of behaviour (see also C. S. Hall & Lindzey, 1970). As it happens, Bandura (1978) elaborated upon Bandura and Walters's (1963) version of social learning theory, noting that factors within individuals, together with factors within the environment, were reflected in individuals' behaviour at one point in time (indeed, one can conceive of individuals' personalities, situational contexts, and behaviour influencing each other; Ewen, 1998). Subsequently, Bandura (1986) introduced his version of *social-cognitive theory* (which is concerned explicitly with humans' capacity to reflect on their own personalities, their own behaviour, and the environment that they inhabit) as an extension of Bandura and Walters's version of social learning theory (Funder, 2001).

In his version of social-cognitive theory, Bandura (1986) explained that because of their capacity for active reflection, humans possess *agency* (i.e., individuals' ability to exert control over their personalities, behaviour, and environment; Ewen, 1998). Furthermore, Bandura identified *self-efficacy* (i.e., the belief that one can exert control over the events that affect one's life, with the caveat that individuals differ in this belief) as a key personality construct within his social-cognitive theory (Funder, 2001). Some followers of Bandura (e.g., Kihlstrom & Harackiewicz, 1990) have argued that self-efficacy is best understood as a *state* (i.e., unstable, dependent upon the situation); whereas other followers of Bandura (e.g., Schunk, 1991) have contended that self-efficacy is best understood as a *trait* (i.e., stable, independent of the situation). In any event, at least when one considers the academic domain, individuals' academic self-efficacy is a significant positive predictor of individuals' academic performance over time (Funder & Fast, 2010).

Lefcourt (1991) questioned whether Bandura's (1986) construct of self-efficacy is different from Rotter's (1966) construct of locus of control (which we covered in Chapter 3) or Rosenberg's (1965) construct of self-esteem (which we covered in Chapter 4). However, unlike locus of control, self-efficacy does not address individuals' expectations regarding success or failure (see Eccles & Wigfield, 2002). Also, unlike self-esteem, self-efficacy does not address individuals' feelings about themselves (see Brewin, 1996). Overall, the construct of self-efficacy is central to Bandura's version of social-cognitive theory, which (like Mischel's [1973] version of social-cognitive theory) provides a useful conceptual bridge between personality psychology and other areas of psychology (e.g., cognitive, social; Kihlstrom & Harackiewicz, 1990).

E. TORY HIGGINS'S SELF-DISCREPANCY THEORY

Cognitive consistency theories (invoking the Consistency Seeker mode/metaphor which assumes that individuals are motivated to seek self-relevant information that fits their pre-existing conceptions of themselves) have tended to (1) ignore individuals' specific affective states for the most part (e.g., the balance theory of Heider, 1958) or (2) acknowledge the conceptual importance of specific affective states (e.g., anxiety) to individuals' consistency-seeking processes, yet fail to generate empirical research that directly assesses those affective states (e.g., the cognitive dissonance theory of Festinger, 1957; for a review, see Robins & John, 1997). In contrast to most cognitive consistency theories (and, we would add, in contrast to the other cognitive theories of personality that are highlighted in the present chapter), E. Tory Higgins's (1987) *self-discrepancy theory* places individuals' particular affective states at the forefront of a conceptual framework that lends itself readily to empirical research (Funder, 2001). Specifically, Higgins's self-discrepancy theory predicts that individuals' failure to be whom they *should* be (i.e., ought-self discrepancy) can place individuals at risk for anxiety and "agitation emotions"; whereas individuals' failure to be whom they *want* to be (i.e., ideal-self discrepancy) can place individuals at risk for depression and "dejection emotions" (Silvia & Eddington, 2012).

As Karniol and M. Ross (1996) pointed out, Higgins's (1987) self-discrepancy theory proposes that individuals possess (1) an *ought-self regulatory system* that directs individuals to avoid situations in which they anticipate negative outcomes, and (2) an *ideal-self regulatory system* that directs individuals to approach situations in which they anticipate positive outcomes, during the course of their daily lives. Over time, according to Higgins's theory, individuals develop and pursue goals that enable individuals to act in accordance with their regulatory systems (Cervone, 2005). Furthermore, Higgins has conducted a programme of research that documents a variety of negative versus positive cognitive, affective, and behavioural consequences of individuals' resulting avoidance-related versus approach-related activities (Funder, 2001). Higgins's self-discrepancy theory and related research represent marked departures from much of the conceptual and empirical literature on social cognition that characterised the mid-1980s (during which emotions were commonly regarded as "hot cognitions"; Markus & Zajonc, 1985).

In a critique of Higgins's (1987) self-discrepancy theory, Silvia and Eddington (2012) noted that scores on ought-self and ideal-self discrepancies are so highly correlated (sometimes exceeding +.70 in value, which would suggest that the two forms of self-discrepancy share 50% or more of their variance across individuals, especially if measurement error is taken into account; see Nunnally & Bernstein, 1994). Such high intercorrelations between the independent variables make it difficult (though not necessarily impossible) for researchers to confidently state how much variance in depression, anxiety, and other specific affective states can be explained separately by ought-self versus ideal-self discrepancies (see J. Cohen et al., 2003). Nevertheless, Higgins's conceptual distinction between ought-self and ideal-self regulatory systems has proven to be useful within Daniel Cervone's (2004b) knowledge-and-appraisal personality architecture (KAPA) model, comprising within-individual personality structures and processes, that is based largely upon the assumption that individuals possess separate-yet-interrelated cognitive structures or schemas about ought, ideal, and actual selves (e.g., Shadel et al., 2004). We will cover Cervone's KAPA model later in the present chapter.

MARK BALDWIN'S RELATIONAL SCHEMA THEORY

In Chapter 2 of the present book, we learned that Bowlby's (1969/1997, 1973/1998, 1980/1998) attachment theory made a broad distinction between secure and insecure forms of attachment – a distinction that is reflected in Bartholomew and Horowitz's (1991) measurement of one secure attachment style and three insecure attachment styles (i.e., preoccupied/anxious-ambivalent, fearful-avoidant, and dismissing-avoidant). However, Bartholomew and Horowitz's research also reflects Bowlby's concept of *internal working models of self and other* (i.e., individuals' internal representation of themselves, as well as individuals' internal representation of their significant others in general, in relation to each other; Bartholomew, 1990). Drawing partly upon Bowlby's attachment theory, Mark Baldwin (1992) proposed a *relational schema theory* in which (1) Bowlby's internal working model of self was reconceptualised as a *self-schema*; (2) Bowlby's internal working model of other was reconceptualised as a partner-specific *other-schema*; and (3) a script for anticipated sequences of interaction between self and partner was added and conceptualised as an *event schema* (Berscheid, 1994).

According to Baldwin (1992), the cognitive structures of self-schema, other-schema, and event schema are incorporated into an overarching cognitive structure or relational schema for each close relationship in which a particular individual is involved (Holmes, 2000). To the extent that relational schemas reflect individuals' inferences concerning the auses of their own behaviour, relational schemas can be interpreted as individual-difference variables (Funder, 2001). However, to the extent that relational schemas reflect individuals' inferences regarding the causes of particular significant others' behaviour, relational schemas also can be interpreted as social-psychological variables (Berscheid, 1994). Finally, to the extent that both partners in a given relationship bring their separate relational schemas to bear upon their behaviour toward each other, the potential for conflict can be considerable – an interpersonal scenario that can provide important challenges for clinical and counselling psychologists who seek to reduce (if not eliminate) conflict among distressed couples (Fincham & Beach, 1999).

Just as Charles Horton Cooley's (1902) version of self-theory has been criticised for fragmenting William James's (1890/2010) construct of the self beyond recognition (i.e., by championing a "looking-glass self" that adds a new vantage point for every new member who joins the target person's audience; Swann & Bosson, 2010), so too has Baldwin's (1992) relational schema theory been criticised for fragmenting Allport's (1937/1951, 1961/1963) construct of personality beyond recognition (see Funder, 2001). Nevertheless, John Holmes has pointed out areas of compatibility between Baldwin's relational schema theory and the aforementioned CAPS model of Mischel and Shoda (1995), as well as areas of compatibility between Baldwin's relational schema theory and Holmes's own SABI model (Holmes, 2002). All in all, Baldwin's relational schema theory serves as a consciously orientated counterpoint to Bowlby's (1969/1997, 1973/1998, 1980/1998) attachment theory (the latter of which relies heavily upon nonconscious, if not overtly *un*conscious, personality processes; Bugental & Johnston, 2000).

BIOLOGICAL THEORIES OF PERSONALITY

JEFFREY GRAY'S REINFORCEMENT SENSITIVITY THEORY

One of the more curious theories from pre-Scientific Revolution Era medicine was *humourism* (i.e., the belief that imbalances among the proportions of individuals' bodily fluids give rise to various mental and physical disorders; J. F. Brennan, 2003). Dating as far back as ancient Greece (if not earlier), practitioners of humourism pointed to an internal balance among (1) "*black bile*" (which, in excessive amounts, leads to a melancholic or depressive temperament); (2) "*yellow bile*" (which, in excessive amounts, leads to a choleric or quick-tempered temperament); (3) *phlegm* (which, in excessive amounts, leads to a "phlegmatic" or calm-yet-sluggish temperament); and (4) *blood* (which, in excessive amounts, leads to a sanguine or cheerful temperament) as essential to individuals' physical and mental health (Walsh et al., 2014). One might be surprised to learn that echoes of humourism reverberate through Pavlov's (1927) reflexology (which we covered in Chapter 3, though we did not refer to humourism in that chapter), via Pavlov's typology of individuals' nervous systems: (1) *Weak* (analogous to melancholic temperament); (2) *strong, yet unbalanced* (analogous to choleric temperament); (3) *strong and balanced, yet slow* (analogous to phlegmatic temperament); and (4) *strong, balanced, and mobile* (analogous to sanguine temperament; Haslam et al., 2017). Furthermore (and especially relevant to the present chapter), one can detect traces of humourism in H. J. Eysenck's (1967) version of factor-analytic trait theory, in the form of Eysenck's typology of personality traits: (1) *Neurotic introversion* (analogous to melancholic temperament); (2) *neurotic extraversion* (analogous to choleric temperament); *stable introversion* (analogous to phlegmatic temperament); and (4) *stable extraversion* (analogous to sanguine temperament; Sheehy, 2004).

In his *reinforcement sensitivity theory*, Jeffrey A. Gray (1970) – a former student of H. J. Eysenck – literally overhauled Eysenck's (1967) version of factor-analytic trait theory from top-bottom to bottom-up (Corr, 2009). Rather than begin with *a priori* hypotheses concerning the existence of particular traits (i.e., neuroticism and extraversion) and then develop *a posteriori* hypotheses concerning the brain structures that might give rise to those traits, J. A. Gray (1972, 1981) began by postulating three brain structures (i.e., the *Fight/Flight/Freeze System*, or FFFS, that is associated with individuals' specific emotion of fear; the *Behavioural Inhibition System*, or BIS, that is associated with individuals' generalized emotion of anxiety; and the *Behavioural Approach System*, or BAS, that is associated with individuals' motivation toward fulfilling their desires) that are most likely to be implicated in personality traits (Haslam, et al., 2017). Having identified specific brain structures, J. A. Gray (e.g., J. A. Gray & McNaughton, 2000) settled on *punishment sensitivity* (reflecting the chronic activation of individuals' FFFS and/or BIS) and *reward sensitivity* (reflecting the chronic activation of individuals' BAS) as the resulting traits, which in principle can be measured by existing inventories of *anxiety* and *impulsivity*, respectively (although, in practice, anxiety is not empirically separable from neuroticism; and impulsivity is not empirically separable from extraversion; DeYoung & J. R. Gray, 2009).

Notwithstanding critiques about the oversimplified nature of theories of arousability, such as J. A. Gray's reinforcement stimulus theory (as well as the version of factor-analytic theory by H. J. Eysenck, 1967; see Geen, 1997), J. A. Gray's theory arguably has breathed new life into an area of research that had been in decline (partly due to the inconsistency of results from previous studies that had been driven by H. J. Eysenck's theory; see Sheehy, 2004). Moreover, J. A. Gray's theory (alongside H. J. Eysenck's theory) helped to pave the way for Marvin Zuckerman's (1971) model and research concerning *sensation-seeking* as a trait. We shall review Zuckerman's model in Box 6.2.

BOX 6.2 ZUCKERMAN'S (1971) SENSATION-SEEKING MODEL

As we noted in Chapter 1 of the present book, despite the considerable influence that social situations can exert upon individuals' behaviour, not all individuals behave the same way in the same situation (see also Funder & Fast, 2010). A case in point involves research on individuals' responses to sensory deprivation: Not all persons are equally likely to pursue physical or psychological stimulation in a particular situation (Zuckerman, 1969). After reviewing results from previous sensory deprivation studies, Marvin Zuckerman (1971) developed the trait construct of *sensation-seeking* (Geen, 1997). Both the name and the content of Zuckerman's sensation-seeking trait are similar (though not identical) to C. Robert Cloninger's (1987) *novelty-seeking* temperament (e.g., Zuckerman & Cloninger, 1996), the latter of which we will cover shortly in the present chapter.

As measured by the Sensation-Seeking Scale (SSS; Zuckerman et al., 1978), sensation-seeking comprises four interrelated dimensions: (1) *Thrill/adventure-seeking*, (2) *experience-seeking*, (3) *boredom susceptibility*, and (4) *disinhibition* (Geen, 1997). The thrill/adventure-seeking and disinhibition dimensions have been studied most intensively, with scores on those two dimensions correlating significantly and positively with individuals' skin conductance responses to sensory stimuli (e.g., Feji et al., 1985; T. N. Robinson & Zahn, 1983). Some researchers have obtained similar results with total scores on sensation-seeking (e.g., Neary &

Zuckerman, 1976; but see also Ridgeway & Hare, 1981, for nonsignificant results regarding total scores on sensation-seeking).

Zuckerman (1984, 1990) proposed an elaborate model concerning the biological origins and functions of sensation-seeking that is beyond the scope of the present book (see also DeYoung & J. R. Gray, 2009). Suffice it to say that – within limits – Zuckerman viewed sensation-seeking as an adaptive trait that presumably enabled humans' ancestors to explore a wide variety of often-challenging environments (with the effect – though not necessarily the intent – of dispersing members of the species across the globe and, thus, maximizing access to food and other resources; see Geen, 1997). Zuckerman's model of sensation-seeking (like the factor-analytic trait theory of H. J. Eysenck, 1967; and the reinforcement sensitivity theory of J. A. Gray, 1970) has been criticised as unduly simplistic in its depiction of arousal (with some of Zuckerman's own results failing to support the hypothesis that chronic under-arousal leads to sensation-seeking; e.g., Carroll et al., 1982). However, some independent results (e.g., individuals who score high on sensation-seeking tend to possess low levels of *cortisol*, a key "fight-or-flight" hormone; e.g., Beaton et al., 2006) indicate that Zuckerman's original predictions may have been correct after all (see Funder & Fast, 2010).

RICHARD DEPUE'S VERSION OF NEUROTRANSMITTER THEORY

In the wake of J. A. Gray's (1970, 1972, 1981) reinforcement stimulus theory, C. Robert Cloninger (1987) developed a version of *neurotransmitter theory* that essentially retained two of the brain structures (i.e., the BIS and the BAS) from Gray's theory, dropped the third brain structure (i.e., the FFFS) from Gray's theory, and added a new brain structure (i.e., the *Reward Dependence System*, or RDS; Haslam et al., 2017). According to Cloninger's theory, (1) the BIS promotes the production of *serotonin* (involved in emotion regulation) as a neurotransmitter, which in turn promotes the chronic expression of *harm avoidance* as a temperament; (2) the BAS promotes the production of *dopamine* (involved in the experience of reward) as a neurotransmitter, which consequently promotes the chronic expression of *novelty seeking* as a temperament; and (3) the RDS promotes the production of *norepinephrine* (also known as *noradrenaline*, involved in the "fight or flight" response) as a neurotransmitter, which subsequently promotes the chronic expression of *reward dependence* as a temperament (Yarkoni, 2015). However, not only is the predicted one-to-one correspondence between neurotransmitters and temperaments unsupported by evidence; but C. R. Cloninger et al.'s (1993) own Temperament and Character Inventory (TCI) apparently measures the Big Five traits of openness to experience, conscientiousness, extraversion, agreeableness, and neuroticism – *not* the three temperaments of harm avoidance, novelty seeking, or reward dependence (or, for that matter, the additional temperament of *persistence*; let alone the "character dimensions" of *self-directedness*, *cooperativeness*, or *self-transcendence*; DeYoung & J. R. Gray, 2009).

Following the publication of C. R. Cloninger's (1987) version of neurotransmitter theory, Richard Depue (1995) offered his own version of *neurotransmitter theory* that deals primarily with the traits of "*agentic extraversion*" (akin to the Big Five trait of extraversion), *affiliation* (akin to agreeableness), and *constraint* (akin to conscientiousness; Haslam et al., 2017). Depue generally has used the Multidimensional Personality Questionnaire (MPQ; Tellegen, 1982) in measuring the three traits in question (S. T. Smith & Guller, 2015). At the heart of Depue's theory is the premise (e.g., Depue & Collins, 1999) that individual differences regarding activities of the *mesolimbic dopamine pathway* (which promotes reward-seeking behaviour) are reflected in individual differences regarding the expression of agentic extraversion – a premise that has received substantial empirical support (Yarkoni, 2015). Depue's theory is not nearly as detailed regarding links between specific neurotransmitters and the other traits that he has measured (although serotonin has been associated with constraint; Carver, 2015). Nevertheless, Depue's version of neurotransmitter theory has emerged as the best-known alternative to C. R. Cloninger's version (DeYoung & J. R. Gray, 2009).

ARNOLD BUSS AND ROBERT PLOMIN'S TEMPERAMENT THEORY OF PERSONALITY DEVELOPMENT

At the time that he published his theory of natural selection, Darwin (1859) was not aware that an unassuming monk, Gregor

Johann Mendel, already had begun a programme of then-unpublished botanical research that eventually would serve as the cornerstone of modern-day genetics (Walsh et al., 2014). Although Darwin had referred to hypothetical "*pangens*" (the term that would be recast as *genes*) as "factors" that somehow must be passed from parents to offspring, it was Mendel's work that would provide the definitive account of biological inheritance (Gangestad, 2012). Indeed, Mendel's results helped to reinforce the empirical foundation underlying Darwin's theory (J. F. Brennan, 2003).

Following the establishment of genetics within the discipline of biology, several biologically orientated psychologists contributed to the development of *behaviour genetics* – a misnomer, since "behaviour geneticists" typically are *not* trained in genetics (Cervone, 2005) and tend to study trait correlations, *not* behaviour (Funder, 2001). At any rate, one of the best-known theories within behaviour genetics is Arnold H. Buss and Robert Plomin's (1984) *temperament theory of personality development* (Rowe, 1997). According to A. H. Buss and Plomin, *temperament* refers to individual differences in stable traits that are observable from birth onward (although one could argue that "temperament" might be defined more precisely as individual differences in unstable *emotions* at birth that, if experienced repeatedly over time, may serve as the bases for the development of individual differences in stable traits; e.g., Goldsmith et al., 1987).

A. H. Buss and Plomin (1975) originally proposed four temperaments (i.e., *emotionality*, *activity*, *sociability*, and *impulsivity*) but subsequently dropped impulsivity after concluding (on the basis of scores that mothers gave to identical versus fraternal twins on the Emotionality, Activity, Sociability, and Impulsivity [EASI] Temperament Inventory; A. H. Buss et al., 1973) that twins' heritability estimates across all temperaments except impulsivity exceeded 50% (although some behaviour geneticists have advocated re-inclusion of impulsivity, on the grounds that A. H. Buss and Plomin's criteria for inclusion were overly restrictive; e.g., Shiner et al., 2012). Like other theories within behaviour genetics, A. H. Buss and Plomin's theory has not been supported by any evidence concerning actual genes or combinations of genes that ostensibly are reflected in temperaments (see Haslam et al., 2017). Perhaps the fairest way to evaluate A. H. Buss and Plomin's theory would be to conclude that – as long as one acknowledges that the impact of actual genes, gene x gene interactions, and gene x "environment" interactions likely will be no more than a fraction of the aforementioned 50% heritability estimate (see Munafo, 2009) – the temperament theory of personality development remains viable (Shiner, 2015).

DAVID BUSS AND DAVID SCHMITT'S SEXUAL STRATEGY THEORY

So far, we have commented extensively upon Darwin's (1859) original theory of natural selection – a logical starting point for any discussion of evolutionary influences on the personality characteristics that distinguish humans from members of other species (D. M. Buss, 1997). However, in *The Descent of Man, and Selection in Relation to Sex*, Darwin (1871) delved more deeply into *sexual selection* among humans – a topic that addresses within-sex and between-sex differences in personality (D. M. Buss & Kenrick, 1998). According to Darwin's theory, to the extent that individuals survive long enough to reproduce, those individuals are likely to have benefited from a millennia-long set of adaptive characteristics that enable them to compete successfully against members of the same sex, en route to mating with members of the opposite sex, while contending with various environmental pressures (see Figueredo et al., 2009). A century later, Darwin's ideas about sexual selection inspired Robert Trivers (1972) to develop his *theory of parental investment*, which holds that men and women seek different, albeit complementary, personality and social characteristics from potential mates (e.g., men are more likely to value fidelity in their partners than are women; whereas women are more likely to value upward mobility in their partners than are men; D. M. Buss & Penke, 2015).

In general, *evolutionary psychology* applies Darwin's (1859, 1871) theory of natural selection to human behaviour (Gangestad, 2012). One of the most influential of the evolutionary psychology approaches to personality has been D. M. Buss and Schmitt (1993) *sexual strategy theory*, which draws upon Darwin's theory (as well as the theory of parental investment by Trivers, 1972) in asserting that differing concerns regarding paternity versus maternity lead men and women to pursue different (yet complementary) strategies for short-term and long-term mating; Hazan & Diamond, 2000). D. M. Buss (son of A. H. Buss, whose temperament theory of personality development we reviewed earlier in the present chapter; i.e., A. H. Buss & Plomin, 1975, 1984) and Schmitt have amassed an impressive amount of evidence (e.g., D. M. Buss's [1989] study across 37 nations and more than 10,000 participants) in support of their theory (see Funder, 2001). However, D. M. Buss and Schmitt's theory has been criticised for invoking outdated stereotypes about "typical" men's and women's personality characteristics (see Funder & Fast, 2010). To their credit, D. M. Buss and Schmitt (2011) have demonstrated their willingness to debate their theory with feminist critics (e.g., Pedersen et al., 2011; Smiler, 2011), although Tate (2013) subsequently pointed out that D. M. Buss and Schmitt had placed the burden of proof upon their critics to disconfirm sexual strategy theory. All things considered, D. M. Buss and Schmitt's (1993) theory shows promise as an evolutionary theory of personality, particularly within the field of relationship science (see Kenrick et al., 2013).

CERVONE'S CONSTRUCT OF PERSONALITY ARCHITECTURE: A CHALLENGE TO EXISTING COGNITIVE, BIOLOGICAL, AND OTHER THEORIES OF PERSONALITY

Earlier in the present chapter, we identified the construct of emotions as a possible conceptual bridge between cognitive and biological perspectives on personality; although we have focused on the implications of such a unifying construct for academic theory, Mahoney (1993) emphasised the implications of emotions-as-conceptual-bridge for clinical practice more than thirty years ago. Mahoney pointed out that, since the advent of cognitive psychotherapies in the 1950s, clinical practitioners increasingly have construed emotions as something to be *experienced* (rather than something to be *controlled*) – a viewpoint that dovetails with Gerald Matthews's (2020b, p. 310) recent contention that individuals' real-world adaptive behaviours are influenced directly by skills and aspects of self-knowledge (including individuals' emotional experiences, motives, and self-efficacy), and indirectly by genes as expressed in neural nets (via individuals' arousal/reinforcement systems and information-processing operations). On a related note, Richard M. Ryan et al. (2019) suggested that Bandura's (1986) social-cognitive construct of self-efficacy may be a *feeling* as much as it is a *belief*; if Ryan and colleagues are correct, then one might argue that the construct of self-efficacy likewise promises to unify cognitive and biological perspectives on personality.

When we covered Bandura's (1986) version of social-cognitive theory earlier in the present chapter (and in Chapter 6 of Gaines, 2020), we commented on ambiguity in Bandura's conceptualisation of self-efficacy as a trait versus a state (see also Corcoran, 1991, for a critique of Bandura's shifting definitions of self-efficacy over the years). Even if one does not agree with such commentary, then one may agree that self-efficacy is associated empirically with relatively stable aspects of personality (e.g., clinical depression) as well as relatively unstable aspects of personality (e.g., state anxiety; e.g., Reisenzein et al., 2020). However, after the first edition of the present book was published (Gaines, 2020), Cervone (2020, personal communication) questioned the assumption that ambiguity in the trait–state distinction necessarily made self-efficacy a problematic construct:

> Although writers do engage in the trait/state argument, there's obviously no point in discussing whether self-efficacy "is" a trait or a state; the construct isn't defined with enough specificity for that to be a good question. The following is implicit in… Bandura's writing…, but self-efficacy is essentially defined in terms of propositional content: I-as-agent can/can't do situated action/achievement. Once you say that, it's self-evident that sometimes that propositional content is stored knowledge due to repeated past experiences (and thus stable and "trait-like") and sometimes it's the product of a quick "gee, well, yea I guess I can" appraisal processes (and thus dependent on situational cues and judgmental biases, and "a state").

DANIEL CERVONE'S KNOWLEDGE-AND-APPRAISAL PERSONALITY ARCHITECTURE [KAPA] MODEL

Bandura's (1986) version of social-cognitive theory influenced Cervone's (1986) PhD research on self-efficacy judgment under uncertainty, in which individuals' perceived self-efficacy was unrelated to their persistence on tasks (see also Cervone & Peake, 1986). Not coincidentally, Bandura had served as Cervone's PhD supervisor (for a review linking Bandura's social-cognitive theory with Cervone's subsequent research, see Cervone & W. D. Scott, 1995). Nevertheless, Cervone 2004b) eventually developed his own *knowledge-and-appraisal personality architecture [KAPA] model*, which draws upon Bandura's construct of self-efficacy yet distinguishes between knowledge structures and appraisal dimensions in the process of investigating multiple levels of individuals' personality structure (Artistico et al., 2011). Cervone's (1997) research on the coherence of individuals' perceived self-efficacy across certain situations – specifically, those situations *when attributes that individuals view themselves as possessing are particularly salient* – bridges the gap between Bandura's version of social-cognitive theory to Cervone's KAPA model (see also Cervone, 2005).

Within Cervone's (2004b) KAPA model, *personality architecture* can be defined as "the overall design and operating characteristics of those psychological systems that comprise a person" (Cervone & B. R. Little, 2019, p. 13). Moreover, according to Cervone's model, individuals possess multiple self-schemas that are linked to appraisals of social situations via individuals' beliefs about the relevance of particular situations to particular self-schemas (see also Cervone, 2005). In turn, within the KAPA model, each person possesses a set of cognitive and affective systems that interact at various levels; the resulting interplay between psychological structures and processes at the intra-individual level gives rise to personality (see also Cervone et al., 2008b). In contrast to the preference for between-person or nomothetic methodological tools that currently characterises modern-day personality psychology as a whole, Cervone's KAPA model highlights the utility of within-person or idiographic methodological instruments in academic and (especially) clinical settings (e.g., Cervone, 2004a). By the same token, the KAPA model does not rule out between-person methodology; the "if-then" propositions that Cervone regarded as vital to understanding personality can be assessed within- *and* between-persons (Perugini et al., 2016).

Drawing upon the conceptual framework of Cervone's (2004b) KAPA model, Heather Orom and Daniel Cervone (2009) found that individuals' response times in the process of appraising self-efficacy tended to be relatively fast when the situations in which the appraisals took place seemed to be most relevant to individuals' *positive* attributes, and relatively slow when the situations in question appeared to be most relevant to individuals' *negative* attributes (see Mischel, 2009). Subsequently, building upon Orom and Cervone's (2009) results as well as Cervone's (2004b) KAPA model, Cervone et al. (2020) reported that – even when overall academic self-efficacy was similar across university-level Science, Technology, Engineering, and Mathematics (STEM) students – considerable within-person *and* between-person effects surfaced as a function of the specific situations in which students were engaged (Kuper et al., 2021). Lastly, using Cervone's (2004b) KAPA model as their conceptual base, Cervone et al. (2007) demonstrated that smokers' self-efficacy regarding abstinence was linked to specific situations and perceived attributes (i.e., appraisals for self-efficacy were higher when reflecting upon previous situations in which self-schemas promoted rather than impeded their abstinence efforts (see also Cervone et al., 2008a).

CERVONE'S THEORY OF PERSONALITY ARCHITECTURE

Clearly, Cervone's (2004b) KAPA model fits within the tradition of social-cognitive theories of personality (e.g., Bandura, 1986; Mischel, 1973; see McCrae, 2020). In particular, to the extent that Cervone's model helps in leading personality psychologists toward developing a comprehensive theory of the person, the KAPA model offers a combination of breadth and depth that recalls Mischel and Shoda's (1995) CAPS model (which we reviewed earlier in this chapter; see Reisenzein et al., 2020). However, to a greater degree than one finds within the CAPS model, the KAPA model delves into personality dynamics in a manner that is compatible with Allport's (1937/1951) psychology of the individual (see Kuper et al., 2021). Ironically, given the de-emphasis upon individual differences within Cervone's model, the trait-theory portion of Allport's psychology of the individual had led some reviewers to credit Allport with paving the way for the five-factor model within McCrae and Costa's (1985) version of factor analytic trait theory (e.g., Digman, 1990). Nonetheless, Cervone's KAPA model embraces Allport's advocacy of idiographic or within-person investigation, with the caveat that Cervone has given greater priority to stability versus change across time than did Allport (Krauss, 2008).

Is Daniel Cervone's (2004b) KAPA model sufficiently broad in scope to constitute a theory on its own terms? Across a series of empirical papers concerning the development of individuals' self-efficacy across leisure-related contexts, James Wise first implied that KAPA signifies a theory (Wise, 2007) and later stated explicitly that KAPA signifies a theory (Wise, 2008). However, Cervone initially suggested that – like Mischel and Shoda's (1995) CAPS model (which we reviewed earlier in the present chapter) – his own KAPA model is best understood as a "meta-theory" (i.e., a theory *about* theories of personality; Cervone, 2004b) and subsequently clarified that – again, like the CAPS model – his own KAPA model was designed as a "meta-theory" that eventually could serve as part of the basis for a truly *explanatory* theory of personality (Cervone, 2005). As we write the present chapter, Cervone (2024, personal communication) has recently completed a book entitled *Personality Architecture* (Cervone, 2027); the book is intended to "reset" theories and corresponding studies throughout the field of personality psychology. Given the scope of Cervone's evolving perspective regarding personality architecture, we are inclined to treat Cervone's current conceptual framework as an explanatory theory-in-the-works.

In *Personality Architecture*, Cervone (2027) contends that the knowledge/appraisal distinction should be supplemented with a *beliefs/standards/goals* distinction. Regarding the latter distinction, Cervone builds upon Boldero and Francis's (2002, p. 232) two-fold proposal that a *standard function* (i.e., a desired state of self at the present time) and a *goal function* (i.e., a desired state of self at some time in the future) underlie processes of *self-regulation* (i.e., "the tendency of the self to change with respect to some reference value") among human beings. However, Boldero and Francis implicitly defined *values* as "conceptions of the desirable" (see also Braithwaite & W. A. Scott, 1991, p. 662); whereas Cervone does not define values but *might* be amenable to a definition of beliefs as the building blocks of values (which would be consistent with the working definition that we embrace throughout the present book). Rounding out Cervone's triad of beliefs, standards, and goals as core cognitions underlying self-regulation, we wonder if Cervone's evaluative construct of standards might be (re)interpreted as attitudes. If so, then perhaps Cervone's trichotomy is analogous to the venerable trio of values, attitudes, and goals as conscious constructs within mainstream personality psychology.

CRITIQUE OF COGNITIVE AND BIOLOGICAL PERSPECTIVES

Earlier in the present chapter, we made a passing reference to Gerald Matthews and Kirby Gilliland's (1999) commentary on the intertwined cognitive and biological threads that run throughout H. J. Eysenck's (1967) version of factor-analytic trait theory (see also Brebner, 2000). As it happens, Eysenck's rationale for the cognitive and biological bases of extraversion – as complemented by Gray's (1981) rationale for the cognitive and biological bases of neuroticism, within the framework of reinforcement sensitivity theory – offers a provocative (albeit controversial) argument concerning the possible hard-wiring of fundamental personality traits (see also Pickering et al., 2013). At any rate, Matthews and Gilliland's (1999) review makes it clear that Eysenck's theory in particular has yielded mixed empirical support; whereas Gray's theory has undergone substantial revisions since the Matthews/Gilliland review in question was published, such as Gray and McNaughton's (2000) increasing focus on the neuropsychology of anxiety (see Wilt & Revelle, 2009). In fact, even Eysenck's hypotheses regarding cortical arousal (perhaps the most conceptually compelling aspects of Eysenck's theory) – have met with limited empirical success (DeYoung & Blain, 2020).

At the end of their review article concerning the relative merits of H. J. Eysenck's version of factor-analytic trait theory versus Gray's (1981) reinforcement sensitivity theory, Matthews and Gilliland (1999) concluded that the restricted range of situations in which aspects of Eysenck's and Gray's biologically orientated personality theories provided sufficient justification for personality psychologists to look toward more overtly cognitive and social-cognitive explanations that might underlie empirical links between individuals' traits and behaviour. However, in his subsequent critique of Matthews and Gilliland's (1999) article, Corr (2001) contended that it might be premature for personality psychologists to de-emphasise biological accounts in favour of cognitive accounts concerning trait-behaviour covariance. In particular, Corr argued that Gray's theory had not been put to the test in a sufficiently broad set of situations (or in a methodologically adequate manner). Lastly, Matthews and Gilliland (2001) replied to Corr (2001) by marshalling additional evidence to show that Gray's reinforcement sensitivity theory explained trait-behaviour links in a narrow range of contexts; Matthews and Gilliland (2001) ended by promoting the integration of cognitive and biological approaches to traits and behaviour within cognitive science.

Within his own *cognitive-adaptive theory of traits*, Matthews (1997) purposefully blurred conceptual boundaries between individuals' self-relevant personality dimensions (including traits) and presumed cognitive abilities, using the catchall phrase "skills" to cover both sets of constructs (see also Matthews, 2020b). Consistent with this theory, Matthews et al. (2003) cited evidence that individuals' performance on information-processing tasks regarding social as well as physical features of the environment varies as a function of individuals' extraverted tendencies (e.g., extraversion is associated positively with the utilisation of short-term memory and divided attention; Wilt & Revelle, 2017). More generally, Matthews and colleagues (e.g., Matthews & Gilliland, 1999, 2001) have used this theory to try and anticipate the extent to which individuals' engagement with particular information-processing activities should covary with between-person similarities versus differences in certain traits (but not other traits; M. D. Robinson & Sedikides, 2009). Although the cognitive-adaptive theory of traits might not represent the final word on merging cognitive and biological perspectives on personality, Matthews viewed the co-existence of his theory with various other perspectives as an asset (e.g., Matthews, 2020a).

PRELUDE TO CHAPTER 7

Notwithstanding the relevance of individuals' conscious experience to contemporary twenty-first-century personality theories such as Matthews's (1997) cognitive-adaptive theory of traits, classic twentieth-century personality theories tended to emphasise individuals' *un*-conscious experience (e.g., the psychodynamic-influenced, analytical psychology of Jung, 1921/1971) or *non*-conscious experience (e.g., the behaviourist-influenced, factor-analytic trait theory of H. J. Eysenck, 1967; for a review, see Wilt & Revelle, 2017). Nonetheless, current advances in personality neuroscience offer substantial promise for personality psychologists to make substantive inroads into cognitive and biological correlates, although we note that the clearest signs of progress have emerged from studies of "neurobiological substrates" of personality (DeYoung & Blain, 2020, p. 273). By comparison, progress within personality neuroscience regarding definitive genetic *or* environmental influences upon traits and other dispositions that might be reflected in individuals' behaviour has not been nearly so pronounced (T. A. Allen & DeYoung, 2017). Of course, we would do well to acknowledge the enormous strides that neuroscience as a whole has made since the early decades of psychology (Berntson & Hothersall, 2019).

The present chapter has been conspicuously "culture-free," despite the prominence of culture as a potential moderator of the impact that "cognitive-affective units" may exert when mediating the effects of situational influences upon individuals' behaviour, from the vantage point of Rodolfo Mendoza-Denton et al.'s (1999) *culturally embedded* or *C-CAPS model* – a conceptual framework that was derived directly from Mischel and Shoda's (1995) CAPS model (and indirectly derived from Mischel's [1973] version of social cognitive theory; see Gaines, 2025). It so happens that George Kelly's (1955) *personal construct theory* – a groundbreaking cognitive theory of personality that was covered in the first edition of *Personality Psychology: The Basics* (Gaines, 2020) – not only alluded to culture repeatedly but also proclaimed that perceivers are in a better position to identify cultural influences on targets' behaviours than are targets themselves (although it does not necessarily follow that psychologists know targets' cultural influences better than do the targets; see Butt, 2008). In Chapter 7, we will showcase Manuel Ramirez and Alfredo Castenada's (1974) *cognitive and cultural flex theory* as a vehicle for travelling "back to the future" in personality psychology with regard to ethnic diversity (including racial, religious, and national aspects).

7

PAST, PRESENT, AND FUTURE IN PERSONALITY PSYCHOLOGY

On "Racial," Cultural, and Ethnic Diversity[1]

Just as "racial" and other ethnic groups (e.g., religious, national) might be associated with unique cultures that can influence the development of individuals' personalities, so too may neighbourhoods and other communities (e.g., extended families, workplaces) be associated with distinctive cultures than can exert influence upon individuals' personality development (Dumont, 2010). Of course, a given community may consist primarily (if not exclusively) of persons from the same ethnic group; and individuals who are members of a particular ethnic group may or may not experience acceptance within a community of which they otherwise might be taken for granted as members (e.g., when individuals marry partners whose ethnic group memberships differ from their own group memberships; Gaines, 2017/ 2018). We do not wish to imply that communities (or, more broadly, ethnic groups) are static or unchanging entities; indeed, individual members may consciously strive to change the hearts and minds of fellow community members, sometimes succeeding in altering formal as well as informal community structures and corresponding practices in the process (as proponents of *cultural democracy* might suggest, especially regarding the roles of educational and other societal institutions in facilitating change; e.g., Ramirez, 1999/2017).

During the 1960s and 1970s, the multidisciplinary field of *community psychology* – which incorporates contributions from psychology, sociology, social work, and public health, among

DOI: 10.4324/9781003601777-10

other disciplines and fields – arose as a concerted intellectual and practical response to vivid (and often violent) examples of state-sanctioned *and* vigilante-inflicted forms of stereotyping, prejudice, and discrimination that the Civil Rights Movement and other sociopolitical movements within the US had lain bare for the world to see (and subsequently inspiring the development of an *international* community psychology; Reich et al., 2007). By the end of the 1970s, major works such as Julian Rappaport's authored book *Community Psychology: Values, Research, and Action* (1977) and Ira Iscoe et al.'s edited book *Community Psychology in Transition: Proceedings of the National Conference on Training in Community Psychology* (1977) had amply documented the relevance of community psychology for academicians and practitioners alike (see Ramirez, 1999/2017). Furthermore, by the late 1980s, the Society for Community Research and Action (SCRA)/Community Psychology was established as Division 27 within the American Psychological Association (Levine et al., 2005).

Especially important to the present chapter is a theory that (1) was developed during the early years of community psychology as a distinct field *and* (2) addresses the personality development of individuals from ethnic minority groups within a particular nation, at a time when few comparable theories existed – specifically, Manuel Ramirez and Alfredo Castaneda's (1974) *cognitive and cultural flex theory* (see also Ramirez, 1991). Perhaps more than any other theory that anticipated ethnic psychology as distinct from cross-cultural psychology (yet remaining aligned with the larger field of cultural psychology), cognitive and cultural flex theory has influenced and been influenced by community psychology (see Ramirez, 1983, 1998). This chapter considers cognitive and cultural flex theory in further detail, taking note of the manner in which Ramirez and Castaneda recast Witkin et al.'s (1954) single construct of *field-independent versus field-dependent perception* – which underpinned Witkin et al.'s (1962) *theory of psychological differentiation* – as the two separate constructs of *field-independent as well as field-sensitive perception* that constitute bicognitive styles. Also, we will examine Ramirez and Castaneda's constructs of *traditionalism and modernism* as bicultural styles (see also Ramirez, 1999/2017).

MANUEL RAMIREZ AND ALFREDO CASTANEDA'S (1974) COGNITIVE AND CULTURAL FLEX THEORY I: (RE)CONCEPTUALISING FIELD-INDEPENDENT/ FIELD-"DEPENDENT" PERCEPTIONS

In *Cultural Democracy, Bicognitive Development, and Education*, Ramirez and Castaneda (1974) cited Witkin et al.'s book *Psychological Differentiation: Studies of Development* (1962) when interpreting certain aspects of visual perception (e.g., dis-embedding simple figures from complex patterns when performing upright perception tasks, as assessed via the Embedded Figures Test) as reflecting individual differences in personality *and* cognition – that is, *cognitive styles* (a term that subsequently would be embraced by Witkin & Goodenough, 1981). Witkin and colleagues built upon their own previous work in *Personality through Perception: An Experimental and Clinical Study* (1954/1972), which focused on comparable aspects of visual perception (e.g., dis-embedding a rotating rod from a broader, rotatable frame when performing upright perception tasks, as assessed via the Rod and Frame Test) as reflecting cognitive styles (see also Bertini et al., 1986). Witkin and colleagues concluded that (1) individuals' separation between the part and the whole (i.e., field independence) demonstrated success, and (2) individuals' fusion of the part with the whole (i.e., field dependence) demonstrated failure, in performance on the perceptual task; whereas Ramirez and Castaneda challenged those conclusions (see also Ramirez, 1991).

One key point of contention that Ramirez and Castaneda (1974) raised in response to Witkin et al.'s (1962) theory of psychological differentiation and corresponding research was that the term "field dependence" reflected a premature and, ultimately, incorrect assumption about individuals' fusion of the part with the whole as a perceptual *deficiency* to the extent that this tendency persisted beyond individuals' infancy (see also Ramirez, 1983). Ramirez and Castaneda noted the negative connotation of "dependence" in particular within psychiatry and clinical psychology, such as the pathological pattern known as *dependent personality disorder* within various editions of the American Psychiatric Association's *Diagnostic and Statistical Manual of Mental Disorder* (DSM; e.g., American Psychiatric

Association, 1994). We do not mean to suggest that "independence" inherently represents a lack of psychopathology from the standpoint of the DSM; in principle, independence can take extremely passive (e.g., narcissistic) or extremely active (e.g., aggressive) forms that may reflect personality disorders (Millon, 1996). Nonetheless, one is struck by the overwhelming use of the term "dependence" rather than "independence" to characterise pathological patterns of personality within the DSM (e.g., American Psychiatric Association, 1999).

Another major point of contention that Ramirez and Castaneda (1974) raised in response to Witkin et al.'s (1962) theory of psychological differentiation and accompanying research was that the either/or distinction between field independence versus field "dependence" represented a false dichotomy that did not acknowledge the prospect of a given individual displaying *both* cognitive styles across two or more situational contexts, picking and choosing a particular style to meet the implicit or explicit expectations of that situation – *if* the individual experiences the situation as supportive (see also Ramirez, 1983). Of course, individuals' displays of cognitive styles need not involve conscious decision-making processes at all times, even among adults; Ramirez and Castaneda (1974) and Witkin et al. (1962) were influenced partly by H. A. Murray's (1938) *personology* (which we mentioned briefly in Chapter 2), a psychodynamic personality theory that proposes individual differences in more than 20 unconscious motives that combine with situational demands or "press" to direct individuals' behaviour (with motives originally measured via the Thematic Apperception Test, or TAT; C. D. Morgan & H. A. Murray, 1935). Nevertheless, "top-down" information-processing may guide visual perception (see Witkin & Goodenough, 1981).

Pulling together insights from Ramirez and Castaneda's (1974) responses to Witkin et al.'s (1962) theory of psychological differentiation, we find that the *cognitive* component of Ramirez and Castaneda's cognitive and cultural flex theory proposes *field independence and field sensitivity* as two orthogonal (i.e., conceptually and empirically separate) dimensions that are reflected in individuals' *cognitive styles* (see also Ramirez, 1983). Cognitive and cultural flex theory does not rule out the possibility that a specific individual may overtly or covertly express a preference for field independence over field sensitivity, or vice versa; and cognitive and cultural flex theory specifically identifies socio-cultural contexts that may tend to "call for" field independence over field sensitivity, or vice versa (see also Ramirez, 1991). By the same token, Mexican-descent Americans and other members of various Latina/o ethnic groups in the US were – and are – more likely to navigate home-culture as well as majority-culture contexts on a daily basis, compared to many (if not most) of their European-descent American counterparts (although many Latina women may face socio-structural barriers to entry into majority-culture workplaces at levels that non-Latina women and men from Anglo *or* Latino groups do not face; see Moslimani & Mukherjee, 2024).

Consistent with Ramirez and Castaneda's (1974) cognitive and cultural flex theory, Ramirez (1991) published a 24-item Bicognitive Orientation to Life Scale (BOLS), with 12 items measuring individuals' field-independent orientation and 12 items measuring individuals' field-sensitive orientation (see also Ramirez, 1999/2017). Unlike the Rod and Frame Test (Witkin et al., 1954) or the Embedded Figures Test (Witkin et al., 1962) – both of which assess individuals' perception of nonhuman objects, reflecting the influence of Max Wertheimer's (1945) version of *Gestalt psychology* – the BOLS does *not* measure individuals' object perception. Instead, the BOLS operationalises field-independent orientation in terms of individuals' tendency to pursue competition in situations where the individuals anticipate that *individual* goal attainment will be prized; and the BOLS operationalises field-sensitive orientation in terms of individuals' tendency to pursue collaboration in situations where the individuals expect that *collective* goal attainment will be prized. The BOLS subscales span the life domains of *interpersonal relationships, leadership style, learning style, attitudes toward authority*, and *interest/adeptness in physical & mathematical sciences versus humanities & social sciences* (see also Contreras, 2004).

In addition to the BOLS (which participants can complete outside *or* within the context of psychotherapy), Ramirez (1991) published the eight-item Client Preferred Cognitive Styles Observation Checklist, which therapists complete on the basis of interactions with their clients (see also Ramirez, 1999/2017).

Four therapy-focused field independence options and four therapy-focused field sensitivity options are included within the therapist-assessed list. Therefore, a particular therapist can (1) ask a given client to complete the BOLS in advance of (or during) the first formal session, (2) take notes of the client's apparently preferred cognitive style (if any) beside the ticked boxes from Client Preferred Cognitive Styles Observation Checklist during the first session, and (3) collate the resulting profile from the client-completed BOLS subscale scores alongside the therapist-completed Client Preferred Cognitive Styles Observation Checklist and accompanying notes to compare these two sources of information about the client's cognitive style(s). Although a specific participant in a large-scale study could gain insight into oneself solely by completing the BOLS (assuming that the participant obtains individualised subscale scores), a particular *client* stands to obtain even richer insight via supplemental information from a therapist.

In *Psychotherapy and Counseling with Minorities: A Cognitive Approach to Individual and Cultural Differences*, Ramirez (1991) took the extra step of publishing a Therapist's Cognitive Styles Observation Checklist (see also Ramirez, 1999/2017). Following the logic from Ramirez and Castaneda's (1974) cognitive and cultural flex theory, Ramirez reasoned that a given therapy session serves as an important interpersonal context within which a specific client may display field-independent and/or field-sensitive cognitive styles when interacting with the therapist. For that matter, a particular therapist may display one or both cognitive styles when interacting with the client during that same session; in the tradition of "social-psychological" personality theorist/practitioners such as Karen Horney (1937), whose feminine psychology we covered in Chapter 2, Ramirez encouraged therapists to reflect upon the ways that they *and* their clients influence each other's thoughts, feelings, and behaviour. In fact, Ramirez commented at length upon his initial matching as well as later *mis-matching* expressions of cognitive styles in response to his own clients' expressions of cognitive styles during therapy; we explore Ramirez's candid reflections upon his shifting cognitive style with one client (i.e., "Harold") in Box 7.1.

BOX 7.1 RAMIREZ'S (1991) REFLECTIONS UPON HIS OWN COGNITIVE STYLE(S) WITH "HAROLD" IN PSYCHOTHERAPY

In a section on "Assessing the Therapist" within the book *Psychotherapy and Counseling with Minorities: A Cognitive Approach to Individual and Cultural Differences*, Ramirez (1991) offered insight into his role as a therapist whose efforts at cognitive "flex" (short for *flexibility*) demonstrate the potential for cognitive matches versus mis-matches with clients. Ramirez (a Mexican-descent American man) had commented extensively upon the case study of "Harold" (a European-descent American man), whose life history revealed a default field-sensitive orientation (like his mother) but whose attempts to please his field-independent father – combined with increasing work demands – led him to prefer field-independent orientation. [As it happens, Harold scored considerably higher on the BOLS field independence subscale, compared to the field sensitivity subscale.] Unfortunately, Harold became so unresponsive to his wife (who struck Ramirez as field-sensitive) and three offspring that the wife had threatened to divorce him unless he began to fulfil his marriage vows. Ramirez and Harold agreed that Harold would try to rediscover his previously field-sensitive orientation by preparing interpersonal communication scripts and engaging in role-playing exercises under Ramirez's guidance across sessions.

Ramirez (1991) noticed that, even when he displayed a field-sensitive orientation in an effort to provide a counterpoint or cognitive mismatch to Harold's preferred field-independent orientation during later sessions (instead of cognitive match during the initial sessions), Harold ended up "pulling" Ramirez toward a *matching* field-independent orientation within minutes. Upon reflection, Ramirez mused that the ease with which he slipped into a pattern of field-independent behaviour toward Harold (e.g., formal, business-like, willing to serve as a consultant) might reflect Ramirez's own unexplored preference for field independence. Subsequently, Ramirez discussed this turn of events with a trusted colleague and devised a strategic plan for facilitating cognitive flex on the part of Harold and himself, alerting Harold to this problematic situation and separately pursuing "empty chair" role-playing whereby Ramirez devised scripts in which he successively enacted the roles of client *and* therapist (and recording himself in order to observe his own performance and strive to change his default responses to Harold's field-independent behaviour). Along the way, Ramirez completed the Client Preferred Cognitive Styles Observation Checklist *and* the Therapist's Cognitive Styles Observation Checklist on himself(!).

During the later therapy sessions, Ramirez (1991) and Harold agreed to work on ways that Harold could get back in touch with his field-sensitive orientation; having acknowledged experiencing burnout with regard to his field-independence-promoting career as a technical professional (which was far removed from his pre-career interests in the arts), Harold ended up forming a support group for technical professionals who were grappling with comparable burnout issues within Harold's workplace. Additionally, Ramirez helped Harold create alternative scripts to guide interactions with workplace officers (i.e., the persons whose approval Harold would need to establish the support group and serve as a peer counsellor) whose preferred cognitive styles were field independence *or* field sensitivity. In the process of anticipating optimal ways to tailor his peer-counselling pitch to officers with varying cognitive styles, Harold acquired a bicognitive orientation for himself. Over time, Harold's self-acceptance blossomed; and Harold became more of a "family man" with his wife and offspring than he had ever experienced during his years of interacting with his own father from childhood onward. Indeed, Harold's relationship with his father improved as a result of the therapy sessions with Ramirez; Harold had learned to "flex" throughout his relationships.

RAMIREZ AND CASTANEDA'S (1974) COGNITIVE AND CULTURAL FLEX THEORY II: (RE) CONCEPTUALISING TRADITIONAL AND MODERN IDEOLOGIES

Thus far, we have discussed cultural aspects of Ramirez and Castaneda's (1974) cognitive and cultural flex theory exclusively in terms of different ethnic communities' possibly differential promotion of field-independent as distinct from field-sensitive forms of cognition-influenced perceptions. However, cognitive and cultural flex theory also posits that different ethnic communities promote *traditional* as distinct from *modern* forms of *political and/or economic ideologies* (see also Ramirez, 1983). For instance, from the perspective of Ramirez and Castaneda, Mexican Catholic ideology exemplifies traditionalism within Mexican-descent American communities by championing national and religious ideals that may have originated in the Eastern Hemisphere but have evolved in a manner that has enabled them to retain their appeal for large segments of the Mexican American population (among other ethnic groups in the Americas) across several centuries (see also Ramirez, 1998). Conversely, according to Ramirez and Castaneda, European secular ideology epitomises modernism within European-descent American communities by embracing *universalist* ideals that ostentibly transcend nations and religions (see Marchland, 1991).

In *Cultural Democracy, Bicognitive Development, and Education,* Ramirez and Castaneda (1974) cited Nathan Glazer and Daniel Patrick Moynihan's previous book *Beyond the Melting Pot: The Negroes, Puerto Ricans, Jews, Italians, and Irish of New York City* (1963) en route to contending that the "melting pot" ideology that was so intertwined with universalism in the United States was disconnected from the lived experiences of many persons from a variety of "racial," religious, and national minority groups. Not coincidentally, in *The Negro Family: The Case for National Action* – often dubbed "The Moynihan Report," due to Moynihan's leading role (albeit uncredited at the time) in writing the book – the US Department of Labor's Office of Policy Planning and Research (1965) focused upon the plight of African-descent Americans as so severely disadvantaged via a century of enslavement and a subsequent century of segregation that the federal government could not credibly claim that universalism was working for most members of that particular ethnic group. Unfortunately, as James M. Jones noted in the first edition of *Prejudice and Racism* (1972), the Department's simultaneous criticism of "unstable" African American family structure *and* failure to make specific policy recommendations led to widespread backlash.

Also, in *Cultural Democracy, Bicognitive Development, and Education,* Ramirez and Castaneda (1974) cited Robert Nisbet's previous book *Community and Power* (1962) as a prelude to arguing that universalism has not been nearly as engrained within the histories of European-descent communities as some social commentators would suggest. [*NOTE: Community and Power* (1962) was the retitled second edition of *The Quest for Community: A Study in the Ethics of Order and Freedom* (1953).] As it turns out, as Brad Lowell Stone observed in the book *Robert Nisbet: Communitarian Traditionalist* (2000), Nisbet's own trajectory as a social commentator took him away from his conservative-yet "New Left"-friendly roots and toward a thoroughly *conservative pluralism* that depicted liberty and equality as locked in direct conflict within US society. Perhaps the most clear-cut instance of such a pivot regarding Nisbet's ideology is the book *Conservatism: Dream and Reality* (1986), which was keenly attuned to the so-called Reagan Revolution of the 1980s and expressed disdain toward liberal as well as progressive forms of pluralism across the US and Europe. In fact, Nisbet's *Conservatism* casts equality as antagonistic toward liberty – and liberty (rather than equality) as ultimately worth defending within US society.

In all fairness, the aforementioned books by Moynihan (e.g., Glazer & Moynihan, 1963; US Department of Labor Office of Policy Planning and Research, 1965) and Nisbet (1953, 1962, 1986) never invoked pejorative terms such as "culture of poverty" that appeared in the subtitles of certain Latina/o-themed anthropological books by Oscar Lewis during the 1950s and 1960s, such as *Five Families: Mexican Case Studies in the Culture of Poverty* (1959) and *La Vida: A Puerto Rican Family in the Culture of Poverty – San Juan and New York* (1966). Nonetheless, Ramirez and Castaneda (1974) charted a decidedly different course for themselves by offering a cognitive and cultural flex theory that embraced a progressive form of pluralism for the post-Civil Rights Era in the US:

> [C]ultural democracy… states that an individual can be bicultural and still be loyal to American ideals…. Furthermore, educational environments or policies that do not recognize the individual's right, as guaranteed by the Civil Rights Act of 1964, to remain identified with the culture and language of his [or her] cultural group are culturally undemocratic (p. 23).

In Ramirez and Castaneda's view, *biculturalism* is operationalised in terms of individuals' development of *traditionalism and modernism* as orthogonal *cultural styles* to fit situational demands.

Consistent with Ramirez and Castaneda's (1974) cognitive and cultural flex theory, Ramirez (1991) published a 40-item, original version of the Traditionalism–Modernism Inventory (TMI), with 20 items measuring traditional cultural style and 20 items measuring modernist cultural style (this original version was credited to Ramirez & Doell, 1982). Subsequently, Ramirez (1999/2017) published a 52-item, revised version of the TMI, with 26 items measuring traditional cultural style and 26 items measuring modernist cultural style (this revised version was credited to Ramirez, Doell, & Rodriguez [n.d.]). Ramirez (1998) explained that the original TMI measures individuals' *attitudes toward gender roles*, *ritual and tradition*, *religion*, *age status*, *family orientation*, *respect for authority*, and *time orientation*; whereas the revised TMI supplements those attitudinal domains with *attitudes toward homosexuality*, *abortion*, and *the death penalty*. Although Ramirez (1998) cited Castaneda's (1984) description of traditionalism and modernism as values and goals, the politically orientated content of the attitudinal domains and corresponding items within original and revised versions of the TMI leads us to adopt Ramirez's (1983) earlier description of traditionalism and modernism as *ideologies* (see also Rappaport, 1977).

In addition to the TMI (which participants can complete outside *or* within psychotherapy), Ramirez (1991) published the 10-item Client Preferred *Cultural* Styles Observation Checklist, which therapists complete on the basis of interactions with their clients (see also Ramirez, 1999/2017). Five therapy-focused traditionalist options and five therapy-focused modernist options are included within the therapist-assessed list. As was the case for the BOLS and the Client Preferred Cognitive Styles Observation Checklist (both of which we covered in the preceding section), a particular therapist can (1) ask a given client to complete the TMI in advance of (or during) the first formal session, (2) take notes of the client's apparently preferred cognitive style (if any) beside the ticked boxes from Client Preferred Cultural Styles Observation Checklist during the first session, and (3) collate the resulting profile from the client-completed TMI subscale scores alongside the therapist-completed Client Preferred Cultural Styles Observation Checklist and accompanying notes to compare the two sources of information about the client's cultural style(s). Thus, a specific participant in a large-scale study can gain insight into oneself just by completing the TMI; yet a given *client* may obtain even richer insight via supplemental information from a therapist.

Unlike the Therapist's Cognitive Styles Observation Checklist, Ramirez did not include a Therapist's *Cultural* Styles Observation Checklist within his Appendices of therapy-based instruments in *Psychotherapy and Counseling with Minorities: A Cognitive Approach to Individual and Cultural Differences* (1991) or *Multicultural Psychotherapy: An Approach to Individual and Cultural Differences* (1999/2017). However, Ramirez *did* allude to a Therapist's Cultural Styles Observation Checklist in both books. Moreover, Ramirez listed nine sample questions for an open-ended Self Life History that therapists might wish to answer for themselves; all nine questions invite respondents to reflect upon their attitudes toward one or more cultural as well as cognitive forms of diversity. Lastly, Ramirez indicated that therapists might find it useful to administer the TMI and the BOLS (among other closed-question surveys) to assess their own social-psychological resources for learning and teaching cultural as well as cognitive flex. Ramirez commented upon his initial matching and later *mis*-matching expressions of cultural styles in response to clients' expressions of cultural styles; we explore Ramirez's candour in reflecting upon his shifting cultural style with another client (i.e., "Imelda") in Box 7.2.[2]

BOX 7.2 RAMIREZ'S (1991) REFLECTIONS UPON HIS OWN CULTURAL STYLE(S) WITH "IMELDA" IN PSYCHOTHERAPY

In the aforementioned section on "Assessing the Therapist" within the book *Psychotherapy and Counseling with Minorities: A Cognitive Approach to Individual and Cultural Differences*, Ramirez (1991) provided insight into his role as a therapist whose efforts at cultural "flex" demonstrate the potential for cultural as well as cognitive matches versus mis-matches with clients. Ramirez had commented at length upon the case study of "Imelda" (a Mexican-descent American girl in her mid-teens), whose life history revealed a default traditionalist ideology but also was an athlete *and* was the offspring of divorced parents (two atypical details that may have contributed to her relatively modernist attitudes toward gender roles, as indicated on her responses to the TMI subscales). The most jarring aspect of Imelda's life history was that she had attempted suicide after her boyfriend's parents pressured him to end their years-long relationship; as a matter of priority, Ramirez recommended that Imelda undergo evaluation for antidepressant medication – especially considering such suboptimal dynamics as Imelda's conflicts with her stepmother following her father's remarriage (living with her father yet remaining connected to her mother), difficulties with most of her grandparents, and clashes with her teachers over authority.

Alongside his recommendation of drug therapy for Imelda, Ramirez (1991) entered into a contract with Imelda to undertake psychotherapy that would address Imelda's social and psychological issues from the standpoint of cognitive and cultural flex theory (Ramirez & Castaneda, 1974). Ramirez and Imelda agreed that Imelda should develop interpersonal goals with the potential for decreasing her loneliness and feelings of being misunderstood within various social and personal relationships in the wake of her breakup with her boyfriend. Also, Ramirez and Imelda agreed that Imelda would try to expand upon her modernistic leanings in terms of gender roles by preparing interpersonal communication scripts (specifically identifying the only Latina coach at the school as a source of balanced advice concerning traditionalism and modernism) and engaging in role-playing exercises under Ramirez's guidance across sessions. Finally, Ramirez and Imelda agreed that Imelda would seek a specific White female teammate (who was competitive as an athlete but was friendly to Imelda, off the basketball and volleyball courts) as a peer role model concerning modernism in gender role attitudes. Given that Imelda tended to be traditional in areas other than gender roles, Ramirez concluded that Imelda was expressing her genuine self.

When Ramirez tried to introduce cultural mismatch into their later therapy sessions (i.e., discussing modernist ideology across political issues), Imelda responded by "pulling" Ramirez back toward her overarching traditionalist cultural style; such a response led Ramirez to engage in the same self-evaluation in terms of cultural styles with Imelda that we noted in Box 7.1 when considering Ramirez's self-evaluation of cognitive styles with Harold. Ironically, by virtue of her evolving therapeutic relationship with Ramirez, Imelda as the client gradually became less deferential and more assertive (i.e., lower in socially undesirable forms of "feminine" behaviour and higher in socially desirable forms of "masculine" behaviour; see Ramirez, 1983) toward Ramirez as the therapist – a development that was entirely consistent with Ramirez's efforts toward helping Imelda cultivate her modernist cultural style after all. By the end of therapy, not only had Imelda taken the lead in proposing an alliance between coaches and counsellors to assist young women in dealing with traditionalist expectations from many of their friends and family members regarding gender roles; but Imelda's previously established relationship with the only Latina coach at the school emboldened Imelda to approach that particular coach to serve as a liaison.

DISTINGUISHING BETWEEN "FAMILY VALUES" AND "FAMILY ATTITUDES" WITHIN RAMIREZ AND CASTANEDA'S (1974) THEORY

In *Cultural Democracy, Bicognitive Development, and Education*, Ramirez and Castaneda (1974) contended that a *Mexican American value system* has continued to thrive among Mexican-descent persons in the US *and* Mexico across centuries and is composed of four *value clusters*: (1) *Identification with family, community, and ethnic group*; (2) *personalisation of interpersonal relationships*; (3) *status and role definition in family and community*; and (4) *Mexican Catholic ideology*. Ramirez and Castaneda (1974, p. 44) published five items from a "Family Values" subscale (credited to Ramirez & Price-Williams, 1971) that measured individuals' level of identification with family, community, and ethnic group; the percentage of Mexican-descent Americans who agreed with the family-affirming items generally was higher than the percentage of European-descent Americans who agreed with those items. Additionally, Ramirez and Castaneda (1974, p. 47) published four items from another "Family Values" subscale (Ramirez & Price-Williams, 1971) that measured individuals' status and role definition in family and community; the percentage of Mexican-descent Americans who agreed with the family-affirming items invariably was higher than the percentage of European-descent Americans who agreed with those items.

The measures of "family values" from Ramirez and Castaneda's book *Cultural Democracy, Bicognitive Development, and Education* (1974) do not appear in Ramirez's subsequent books *Psychotherapy and Counseling with Minorities: A Cognitive Approach to Individual and Cultural Differences* (1991) or *Multicultural Psychotherapy: An Approach to Individual and Cultural Differences* (1999/2017). Also, Ramirez and Castaneda's (1974) measures of "family values" are not mentioned within Ramirez's (1991, 1999/2017) summaries of case studies with various clients from Ramirez's psychotherapy sessions. Nevertheless, Ramirez (1991) *did* include an initial, 37-item Family Attitudes Scale (FAS) – whereas Ramirez (1999/2017) included a revised, 30-item FAS (credited to Ramirez & Carrasco, 1996) – that was designed to measure individuals' "degree of identification with traditional Mexican American values" (Ramirez, 1999/2017, p. 180). The FAS includes six domains: (1) *Loyalty to the family*, (2) *strictness in childrearing*, (3) *respect for adults*, (4) *separation of gender roles*, (5) *male superiority*, and (6) *time orientation*. The content domains in the FAS overlap with the domains in the previously mentioned TMI; yet both surveys are administered to clients.

The initial and revised versions of the FAS (Ramirez, 1999/2017) do not figure prominently in most of the case studies that Ramirez (1991, 1999/2017) summarised. One exception is the case of Wanda (a White/European-descent woman) who was married to Javier (a Latino man); the couple had two young offspring. Although Wanda initially sought psychotherapy on her own, Ramirez encouraged her to invite Javier from the second session onward, thus transforming the context from individual to couple counselling. At the time that Wanda attended her first (solo) session with Ramirez, it became obvious that Wanda's primary social-psychological difficulties lay in pursuing an increasingly demanding yet rewarding career as a company manager, while maintaining a stable family life that nonetheless left Javier and their children increasingly dissatisfied by her level of engagement at home. On the basis of Wanda's and Javier's respective FAS scores (via the initial version of the survey), once Javier joined Wanda in therapy, Ramirez provided evidence of ongoing cultural mismatch (e.g., Wanda was permissive, whereas Javier was strict, where child-rearing attitudes were concerned). Wanda and Javier responded by agreeing that their offspring could decide whether to watch TV or do homework first during each weeknight.

We do not seek to reduce conflict between Wanda and Javier in the above scenario (Ramirez, 1991, 1999/2017) of cultural mismatch involving family attitudes. Rather, we intend to emphasise Wanda and Javier's couple-level demonstration that they could *de-escalate* marital conflict (following Ramirez's intervention) in a manner that not only was satisfactory to each of them but also offered promise for Wanda's as well as Javier's quality of relationships with their offspring, all while observing respect for each other's pre-marriage cultural backgrounds (for more information on Mestizo perspectives concerning marriage and the family in the late twentieth century, see Ramirez, 1983, 1998). These constructive results for Wanda and Javier with regard to individual-level child-rearing attitudes and couple-level child-rearing behaviours may be understood within the context of a broader literature on interethnic marriage (disproportionately focusing on Black–White interracial marriage) in the US – a literature that offers few (if any) clear-cut examples of parents with differing "racial" and/or cultural heritage working together to solve interpersonal problems to the benefit of each other, let alone the benefit of their offspring (for critiques of the literature on interethnic marriage across the late twentieth and early twenty-first centuries, see Gaines, 1997, 2017/2018).

Returning to the question of what the FAS (Ramirez, 1991, 1999/2017) measures, perhaps a designation such as "traditionalist versus modernist family-themed ideology" is most accurate; *conservatism* is linked to traditionalist family-themed ideology, whereas *liberalism* (if not *progressivism*) is linked to modernist family-themed ideology (see Nisbet, 1970). Consequently, if the FAS measures a specific form of traditionalist ideology, then it may be interpreted as a survey of *family attitudes* (i.e., evaluations of behavioural expectations accompanying the constellation of time-tested relational roles that individuals occupy by virtue of their age, gender, and generation within nuclear and extended families) as indicated by the title that Ramirez (1991, 1999/2017) originally gave to his survey (see Nisbet, 1988). Two important implications of such an interpretation are that – like other attitudes that individuals may hold at a given point in time – (1) particular individuals' family attitudes are susceptible to change; and (2) even in the absence of change, particular individuals may or may not act upon their pre-existing family attitudes, depending on the social-psychological and socio-structural circumstances with which they must contend at the time (see Nisbet, 1975).

If the FAS (Ramirez, 1991, 1999/2017) does in fact measure family attitudes, then how have followers of Ramirez and Castaneda's (1974) cognitive and cultural flex theory measured family values among Mexican-descent persons? The answer to that question may be found largely in the ways that various followers have responded to Ramirez's book *Psychology of the Americas: Mestizo Perspectives on Personality and Mental Health* (1983), which had drawn substantially upon Ramirez and Castaneda's aforementioned book *Cultural Democracy, Bicognitive Development, and Education* (1974) but expanded the scope of inquiry from Mexican-descent Americans' social and psychological experiences to Latinas/os' social and psychological experiences throughout North America, Central America, South America, and the Caribbean Islands (keeping in mind that Mexican-descent Americans consistently have comprised more than 60% of Latinas/os within the US across the past several decades; see Pina & G. Martinez, 2025). For example, relationship scientists such as Gaines et al. (1997a) cited Ramirez's (1983) perspective on *Mestizo world view* as inspiration for operationalising *familism* as individuals' orientation toward the welfare of their immediate and extended families in their respective surveys (Gaines, 1997).

Before we shift our attention more fully toward Ramirez's post-1970s-era writings that bear upon cognitive and cultural flex theory (e.g., Ramirez, 1983, 1998), we wish to tie up a few loose ends concerning the conceptualisation and measurement of individuals' cultural styles in Ramirez and Castaneda's (1974) initial formulation of the theory. First, even if familism were operationalised as an organised set of beliefs reflecting individuals' orientation toward the welfare of their families (e.g., Gaines et al., 1997a), Verkuyten (2005) has noted that the cultural value of familism is conceptually and empirically distinct from *ethnic identity* (which is individuals' sense of "who they are" as a function of their racial, religious, and/or other ethnic group memberships; e.g., Phinney & Ong, 2007). Second, Gaines (1997) has pointed out that – even if the distinction between familism as a cultural value and familism as a set of cultural attitudes is not stated as overtly (see Freeberg & Stein, 1996) – familism nonetheless is conceptually and empirically distinct from Mexican Catholicism. Third, Goodwin (2009) concluded that ideologies and corresponding attitudes in nations around the world are in flux like never before; even the dichotomy of traditionalist versus modernist ideologies has been subjected to debate.

EVOLUTION OF COGNITIVE AND CULTURAL FLEX THEORY: BEYOND ITS ROOTS IN COMMUNITY PSYCHOLOGY

Notwithstanding the concerns that some critics have voiced with regard to the dichotomisation of traditionalism versus modernism, Ramirez (1983) credited Nisbet – whose book *Tradition and Revolt: Historical and Sociological Essays* (1968) helped to popularise the traditionalist/modernist dichotomy, within and beyond sociology – with contemplating the possibility that *a given individual* may struggle to manage internal conflict over competing demands from two or more communities between which the individual migrates on a daily basis (literally and figuratively; see also Castaneda, 1984). Furthermore, Ramirez argued that an individual's internal battles over conflict management may plant the seeds of *conflict resolution*, in the form of mobilising tangible as well as intangible resources that enable the individual to function effectively in each of the communities (consistent with a *multicultural person-environment fit paradigm*; see also Ramirez, 1991). Lastly, if co-existence between traditionalist and modernist cultural styles is possible within the same person, then Ramirez and Castaneda's (1974) cognitive and cultural flex theory would contend that co-existence between traditionalist and modernist ideologies is possible within communities, within nations, and throughout the world (Ramirez, 1984).

In *Psychology of the Americas: Mestizo Perspectives on Personality and Mental Health*, Ramirez (1983) praised community psychology – especially as practised by Rappaport (1977) – for affirming the dignity and capabilities of persons across a myriad of "racial," religious, national, and other ethnic groups. On the one hand,

Ramirez (1983) acknowledged the compatibility between guiding principles underpinning the field of community psychology and core assumptions underlying his own cognitive and cultural flex theory (Ramirez & Castaneda, 1974; see also Ramirez, 1991). On the other hand, Ramirez's (1983) *Mestizo theory of personality psychology and psychiatry* – which posits that centuries of intergroup contact between persons of European (particularly Spanish) descent and persons of Indigenous descent within the US and throughout the Americas have produced a pan-ethnic group with unique heritage(s) as evident in their fusion of multiple languages, customs, and ways of being-in-the-world – represents a substantive evolution beyond cognitive and cultural flex theory (see also Ramirez, 1998). Indeed, Ramirez's Mestizo theory inspired Gaines (1997) to propose that familism serves as a foundation for *interpersonal resource exchange* among Latina/o couples (if not other couples; see Gaines, 2016/2018).

Ramirez's (1983) Mestizo theory suggests that, if an accurate contrast is to be drawn between European-descent persons and Latinas/os in the US and elsewhere regarding cultural values, then the contrast likely will involve differences between (1) an embrace of individualism as a singular value among European-descent persons, versus (2) an embrace of *individualism in addition to familism* as dual values among Latinas/os (perhaps facilitated by high levels of bilingualism among Latinas/os in the US; see Mora & Lopez, 2023). Such a predicted contrast *might* be supported by Freeberg and Stein's (1996) finding that (1) European-descent and Mexican-descent Americans scored equally high in individualism; whereas (2) Mexican-descent Americans scored significantly higher in familism than did European-descent persons (see Oyserman et al., 2002a). However, we do not wish to overgeneralise group similarities in individualism *or* group differences in familism; as Phinney (1996) noted, "acculturation" to mainstream US society among Latinas/os tends to nullify the impact of ethnic group membership on familism when compared to European-descent Americans (and US-born Latinas/os are less likely than immigrant Latinas/os to use terms such as "Latina/o" to describe themselves; Lopez et al., 2024).

Ramirez's (1983) development of Mestizo theory coincides with the late 1970s/early 1980s-era rise of psychometric advances such as *confirmatory factor analysis* (in which strong theory frequently drives researchers' specification of expected associations between broadly conceived constructs and the narrowly tailored items that have been designed to measure those constructs; e.g., Joreskog & Sorbom, 1979). For instance, the 10-item measure of familism that was created by Gaines et al. (1997a) as a direct application of Mestizo theory demonstrated satisfactory construct validity across several US samples via confirmatory factor analyses, including a Mexican-descent sample for which the scale was translated from English to Spanish (see Lunt, 2010). Some researchers (e.g., Campos et al., 2008) have used Gaines and colleagues' full scale with Latina/o-only samples; whereas other researchers (e.g., Villarreal et al., 2005) have used portions of Gaines et al.'s (1997a) familism scale alongside portions of additional, similarly valid scales (e.g., part of a 7-item familism scale by Gil et al., 2000) with Latina/o-only samples. By the same token, still other researchers (e.g., Campos et al., 2019) have opted to use familism scales that were developed specifically for Latina/o samples (e.g., the 14-item scale by Sabogal et al., 1987).

We are unaware of any case studies based on Ramirez's (1983) Mestizo theory that have utilised Gaines et al.'s (1997a) familism scale. However, the aforementioned study by Campos et al. (2008) *did* use Gaines and colleagues' scale in examining covariance between familism and perceived social support among medium-to-large samples of Latina as well as European-descent pregnant women. Although the resulting correlation was significant and positive for both groups, the magnitude or strength of the correlation was significantly higher for Latinas compared to European-descent women (as one would anticipate from the standpoint of Ramirez's theory). Furthermore, even though Campos et al. did not mention Mestizo theory in particular, key principles from the field of community psychology that influenced and has been influenced by Mestizo theory (e.g., appreciation for familism as a core component of respondents' world view; real-world implications of research outcomes, such as the knock-on effects of perceived social support on the birth weight of infants whose mothers initially participated in the study while pregnant; attention toward public health issues, such as mothers' anxiety during their pregnancies) are reflected in Campos et al.'s study.

We hasten to add that, although scales that measure individualism (i.e., individuals' orientation toward the welfare of themselves) are much more numerous than are scales that measure familism, Oyserman et al.'s (2002a) meta-analysis revealed that individualism scales often perform poorly in terms of internal consistency (i.e., frequently plagued by substantially higher-than-desired measurement error, resulting in Cronbach's alphas below .70). Oyserman et al.'s (2002a) meta-analysis included Gaines et al.'s (1997a) previously mentioned individualism scale (for which Cronbach's alpha < .60 on average), as well as Freeberg and Stein's (1996) aforementioned individualism scale (for which Cronbach's alpha < .50), among dozens of other scales. Like many of their counterparts, those particular surveys yielded suboptimal internal consistency coefficients; Coon and Kemmelmeier (2001) observed that measurement error issues with individualism scales generalise across respondents' ethnic group memberships. Fortunately, as Oyserman et al. (2000b) noted, the question for individualism scales is not *whether* individualism can be measured (i.e., construct validity is not a problem). Instead, as Gaines et al. (1997a) acknowledged, the question is *how well* individualism is measured (i.e., an internal consistency issue).

In an indication of how far confirmatory factor analysis has come since the late 1970s/early 1980s, Kline (2023) pointed out that contemporary researchers possess the statistical tools for identifying and controlling for unexpected sources of measurement error within and/or across scale items in general. Gaines et al. (1997a) noted during the late 1990s that it was already possible, and sometimes necessary, for "ethnic" psychologists (investigating "racial" and other ethnic group differences/similarities within a given nation) to control for differences in correlated measurement error among items when evaluating the goodness-of-fit for factor models involving cultural value scale items in particular – not just regarding individualism, but also regarding familism (and *collectivism*). Gaines and Ramkissoon (2008) added during the early 2000s that it was possible, even necessary in some instances, for "cross-cultural" psychologists (investigating "national" ethnic group differences/similarities) to control for differences in entire scales (not just specific items) measuring cultural values – again, not just for individualism, but also for familism and other values (i.e., collectivism, romanticism, spiritualism).

PRELUDE TO CHAPTER 8

As we learned near the beginning of the present chapter, Ramirez and Castaneda's (1974) cognitive and cultural flex theory of personality took constructs from Witkin's et al.'s (1962) theory of psychological differentiation (i.e., field-independent and field-sensitive cognitive styles) in cultural-psychological directions that even Witkin had not foreseen (though these advances subsequently were recognised by Witkin & Goodenough, 1981). Subsequently, as we learned nearer the end of the present chapter, Ramirez's (1983) Mestizo theory of personality psychology and psychiatry took Ramirez and Castaneda's own cognitive and cultural flex theory into new directions by maintaining an emphasis on Chicana/o or Mexican-descent American psychology while incorporating conceptual and empirical insights from a variety of Latina/o ethnic groups throughout the continents of North America, Central America, South America; as well as island nations throughout the Caribbean Sea (see also Ramirez, 1991). In retrospect, Ramirez's evolving theoretical perspective not only foreshadowed but also helped to set the stage for the emergence of the 1990s as the "decade of ethnicity" in psychology, as Shweder and M. A. Sullivan (1993, p. 517) would put it (see Gaines, 2025).

Following the publication of *Psychology of the Americas* (1983), Ramirez contended in *Psychotherapy and Counseling with Minorities* (1991) that a "psychology of differentness, of respect for individual and cultural differences" (p. 10) had been coalescing since the pre-World War II era. Ramirez singled out the influences of three trailblazers who advocated a *psychology of differentness* from a variety of lived experiences and sociocultural standpoints: (1) Karen Horney (1937), whose feminine psychology (1922–37/1966) we covered in Chapter 2; (2) Frantz Fanon (1952/1967), whose version of existential psychology (1961/1963) we covered in Chapter 4; and (3) George Sanchez (1932), whose critique of racial and cultural biases in mainstream accounts of intelligence testing (1934) might be equally relevant to the content of another book in Routledge's *The Basics* series – namely, *Cognitive Psychology: The Basics* (S. Taylor & Workman, 2022). In any event, the evolution beyond Ramirez and Castaneda's (1974) cognitive and cultural flex theory of personality continued beyond Ramirez's (1983) Mestizo theory; as we discover in Chapter 8, Ramirez's (1998) *multicultural/multiracial theory of personality* provides an especially broad framework for us to integrate as well as expand upon the subject matter of mainstream personality psychology.

NOTES

1 Stanley O. Gaines, Jr., Manuel Ramirez III, and Norma Rodriguez co-authored the present Chapter 7.

2 Some of the content in Box 7.2 refers to attempted suicide. Although the client in question benefitted greatly from therapy and was no longer suicidal by the time that therapy session came to a close, individual readers may prefer to skip that particular breakout box. Even if you decide to read Box 7.2, you might find it helpful to talk with a significant other and/or qualified mental health professional before you read that breakout box.

CONCLUSION

8

CONCLUDING THOUGHTS ON PERSONALITY PSYCHOLOGY

At various points in the present book, we have referred to G. W. Allport's (1937/1951, 1961/1963) psychology of the individual as a foundational theory for personality psychology. We have emphasised Allport's conceptualisation of traits as individuals' answer to the question "What are you like/How would you describe yourself?" (see especially Chapter 5 of the present book). However, we could have commented at greater length upon G. W. Allport's conceptualisation of values as individuals' answer to the question "What do you believe in?" *and* Allport's accompanying survey, which is known as A Study of Values (Allport et al., 1960; Vernon & Allport, 1931); Allport's distinction among *theoretical*, *economic*, *aesthetic*, *social*, *political*, and *religious* values has continued to intrigue scholars in personality and social psychology throughout the past century (for a twenty-first-century update to the survey, see the fourth edition of the Study of Values survey by Kopelman et al., 2003). The Study of Values survey is unusual in that it was designed for use with individual participants but also has been adapted for administration to large samples (see Oles & Hermans, 2010). Especially important for our purposes is Allport's operationalisation of values as sets of attitudes, following Spranger (1928; see also Braithwaite & W. A. Scott, 1991).

For the most part, we have been silent thus far regarding Allport's perspective on attitudes as individuals' answers to the question, "How do you think and feel about that 'entity' (e.g., person, place, abstract concept)?" G. W. Allport (1954/1979)

DOI: 10.4324/9781003601777-12

is well-known for his perspective on *intergroup attitudes*, which include a combination of *stereotyping* (cognitive/thought component) and *prejudice* (affective/feeling component) as potential influences on *intergroup behaviour* in the form of *discrimination* (S. T. Fiske, 1998). Allport's "lens model" contends that, in order to understand individuals' formation of *authoritarian attitudes* as precursors to discrimination, one ideally should take into account *historical*, *sociocultural*, and *situational* effects on individuals' personality development (thus proceeding from macro-level to micro-level influences; see also G. W. Allport, 1950a). Allport's acknowledgement of societal structures as playing a role in shaping individuals' personality structure – including the communication of stereotypes that individuals may internalise, even as they learn which socially defined groups are "legitimate" targets of prejudicial scorn versus sentiment – was ahead of the curve (e.g., anticipating the modern-day construct of *systemic racism*; Richeson et al., 2025).

G. W. Allport's (1954/1979) identification of sociocultural influences on individuals' personality development concerning intergroup attitudes provides a conceptual opening for us to introduce Manuel Ramirez III's (1998) *multicultural/multiracial theory of personality* as noteworthy in its own right *and* as a means toward understanding authoritarian tendencies as expressed by "Jenny," the namesake of *Letters from Jenny* (Allport, 1965). In the present chapter, not only will we consider the applicability of Ramirez's theory to Jenny's ethnocentric attitudes at greater length; but we will utilise a similar conceptual approach as we apply Ramirez's theory to the "bicultural immersion status" (Wiggins, 2003/2005, p. 249) of "Madeline G," the namesake of *Personality Assessment Paradigms and Methods: A Collaborative Reassessment of Madeline G* (edited by Hopwood & Waugh, 2020). By the end of this chapter, we shall offer a path forward for idiographic and nomothetic research methods to coexist within personality psychology, offering Jenny and Madeline G as examples of the individualised insight that researchers can gain via the two methods. Specifically, we contend that Ramirez's multicultural/multiracial theory can be aligned with Cervone's (2027) aforementioned theory of personality architecture, using the unifying construct of values.

RAMIREZ'S (1998) MULTICULTURAL/MULTIRACIAL THEORY OF PERSONALITY: ON THE ADAPTIVE POTENTIAL OF MULTICULTURALISM AS A PROPERTY OF PERSONS

According to Ramirez's (1998) multicultural/multiracial theory, in an increasingly interconnected and ethnically diverse world, individuals' capacity for crafting a personal worldview that fuses together two or more complementary sets of cultural values, attitudes, and beliefs will enable the individuals to navigate a variety of interpersonal and intergroup contexts in an adaptive manner (Arredondo, 2008). Multicultural/multiracial theory expands upon Ramirez's (1983) *psychology of the Americas*, which had proposed that individuals throughout North American, Central American, South American, and Caribbean nations whose cultural and biological heritage reflects a combination of European (particularly Spanish), Indigenous, and possibly African influences will tend to define themselves on the basis of the prevailing values, attitudes, or beliefs that are associated implicitly or explicitly with each of the socially defined groups in question (see also Ramirez, 2004). In Ramirez's multicultural/multiracial theory, individuals who are figuratively or literally *Mestiza/o* (i.e., descended from members of European, Indigenous, and perhaps other ethnic groups) not only *need* to possess multiple cultural competencies but generally *want* to develop those competencies (Arredondo et al., 2006).

In *Psychology of the Americas: Mestizo Perspectives on Personality and Mental Health*, Ramirez (1983) introduced a 69-item Biculturalism/Multiculturalism Experience Inventory to measure individual differences in demographic/linguistic background, personal history, and multicultural participation; quantitative results were interpreted primarily in terms of subscores on Historical Development Patterns (HDP) and Contemporary Multicultural Identities (CMI) among Latinas/os (see also Ramirez, 1991). Afterward, in *Multicultural/Multiracial Psychology: Mestizo Perspectives on Personality and Mental Health*, Ramirez (1998) unveiled two versions of a revised Multiculturalism Experience Inventory (which we shall abbreviate as MEI from this point onward) – one 48-item version for persons of colour (including, but not limited to, Latinas/

os); and one 45-item version for White/European-descent persons (with the CMI subscale items differing in content and number between the persons-of-colour and White versions of the survey; see also Ramirez, 1999/2017). Three additional items regarding respondents' degree of comfort with, felt acceptance by, and degree to which they are identified as members of various ethnic groups, were included within both versions of the survey but are not formally part of the MEI.

Generally speaking, scores on the HDP subscale, CMI subscale, and total multiculturalism (MC) scale of the persons-of-colour and White versions of the MEI have been reported within case studies of clients with whom Ramirez (1998) has interacted within his role as a psychotherapist (see also Ramirez, 1999/2017). Therefore, within published research, the MEI tends to be discussed as a quantitative tool (in combination with a given client's life history as a qualitative tool) in idiographic studies of $n = 1$ participant at a time, consistent with the methodologies that were promoted within G. W. Allport's (1937/1951) psychology of the individual (see also G. W. Allport, 1961/1963). Although Ramirez summarised the results of two clients' case studies in *Multicultural/Multiracial Psychology: Mestizo Perspectives on Personality and Mental Health* (1998) and several clients' case studies in *Multicultural Psychotherapy: An Approach to Individual and Cultural Differences* (1999/2017), the story of one multicultural/multiracial client named "Raul" is unique in that it spans both of those books (owing to Raul's separate stints within psychotherapy with Ramirez across several years). In Box 8.1, we delve into Raul's story in greater detail, including Raul's profile on the persons-of-colour version of the MEI.

BOX 8.1 THE STORY OF "RAUL," PARTS 1 AND 2

As described by Ramirez (1998), "Raul" was an employed American man (cisgender, heterosexual) of Latino, Indigenous, and African descent. Raul was the eldest of five children to parents who also were multiracial (and Raul's mother had relatives along the border between the United States and Mexico, in South Texas). Raul was raised in the southwestern US; Raul's parents were married throughout his childhood and adolescence, although (1) his father was unfaithful to his mother and was absent without explanation for days at a time; and (2) his mother worked *two* jobs to support the family (as the first-born offspring, Raul was obligated to serve as a *de facto* parent to his younger siblings). Following high school, Raul was drafted to serve in the Vietnam War; within Southeast Asia, Raul experienced acceptance for the first time from persons of various multiracial heritages. Raul had never been married, but he entered (and exited) multiple romantic relationships as an adult. Upon leaving the service, Raul returned ambivalently to his hometown in Central Texas. Thus, Raul scored as *more* multicultural on HDP during his childhood in Central Texas, compared to his adolescence in South Texas; yet he scored as *less* multicultural on CMI during his then-current time in Central Texas, compared to his years in the service.

Also, as noted by Ramirez (1998), Raul agreed to engage in guided self-assessment within his counselling sessions with Ramirez. Given that Raul was a client, Ramirez was able to use additional counselling-related qualitative information in order to supplement Raul's quantitative MEI subscale and total scale scores, in the process of directing Raul toward guided self-assessment. A primary goal of therapy was for Ramirez to help Raul obtain increased awareness of self in relation to persons from ethnic groups other than Raul's own group (and to gain greater awareness of persons from other ethnic groups in relation to the self). Moreover, Ramirez sought to bolster Raul's self-esteem by acknowledging Raul's intra-personal and interpersonal strengths. Raul benefitted from multicultural therapy as a means toward reconciling his ambivalent thoughts and feelings regarding his own multicultural/ multiracial heritage and his ultimately unsuccessful romantic relationships (especially relationships with some White/ European-descent women, whom he suspected were attracted to his multiracial appearance but not to him as an individual). Raul ultimately made substantial progress toward becoming a "multicultural/multiracial educator, peer counselor, and ambassador" via his initial round of multicultural therapy.

As it turns out, Raul would return to Ramirez (1999/2017) two years later. Raul re-entered therapy following the death of one of his younger brothers; Raul blamed himself for his brother's succumbing to lung cancer, rationalising that his harsh behaviour as the oldest sibling over the years had driven the younger sibling to smoke in the first instance (and Raul himself was a smoker, which could have led Raul to criticise his past performance as a role model/*de facto* parent). Even though Raul had struggled with bouts of anxiety and depression during his earlier round of therapy, Raul's return to therapy two years later was distinguished by feelings of personal guilt that could not be explained sufficiently as understandable consequences of the bereavement process. On the one hand, Raul had maintained positive relationships with his sister and her family (but not with other members of his immediate and extended family) in the aftermath of his brother's death. On the other hand, Raul was not looking after himself in terms of maintaining physical health to the extent that he previously accomplished, at the time of his re-entry into therapy. Fortunately, Raul responded positively to the goals that he and Ramirez agreed during the second round (e.g., Raul becoming a mentor to the son of the deceased brother – Raul's nephew).

MULTICULTURAL/MULTIRACIAL THEORY AND "JENNY" (ALLPORT, 1965), *CONTRA* "JILL" (RAMIREZ, 1998): HISTORICAL DEVELOPMENT PATTERN → AUTHORITARIANISM(?)

In *Multicultural/Multiracial Psychology: Mestizo Perspectives on Personality and Mental Health*, Ramirez (1998) also summarised the case study of "Jill," a retired American woman (cisgender, heterosexual) of European descent. Jill was the only child of parents who born in the US, and Jill's grandparents were White European immigrants. Jill was raised in the northeastern US; Jill's parents were married throughout her formative years, although (1) her father was a travelling salesman and was away from home for long intervals; and (2) her stay-at-home mother was a strict disciplinarian (up to Jill's early adulthood, following the death of Jill's father *and* Jill's entry into university). After graduating from university, Jill entered the Peace Corps and travelled around the world, marrying (and divorcing) an American man of Japanese descent and raising her own offspring in the southwestern US. Although Jill's pre-retirement experience as an adult was highly multicultural (including renouncement of her Catholic religion and adopting her then-husband's Buddhist faith), Jill did not maintain many cross-ethnic social contacts after retirement. Thus, Jill scored high on multicultural HDP (no change from pre-retirement to post-retirement) but added that her post-retirement CMI was *lower* than her pre-retirement CMI.

Like Raul (whom we discussed in the preceding section), Jill provided qualitative Life History Information that facilitated Ramirez's (1998) efforts toward working with her to achieve further development of her multicultural/multiracial orientation, alongside data from the MEI. Furthermore, like Raul, Jill benefitted from multicultural therapy – in Jill's case, as a means toward resolving negative thoughts and feelings toward her mother, ex-husband, *and her own children and grandchildren* (owing to her descendants' biracial heritage), keeping in mind that her relatives had distanced themselves from her once she married and had children across racial lines. Lastly, as was the case for Raul, Ramirez (1998) described Jill as ultimately making substantial progress toward becoming a "multicultural/multiracial educator, peer counselor, and ambassador" via multicultural therapy. Jill's path toward increased self-understanding differed from that of Raul; Jill's forte was literature (rather than art) and had been suffering from "writer's block" until her sessions with Ramirez helped to un-block Jill's strides toward completing her autobiography. Nonetheless, exploring spirituality proved to be as self-enlightening for Jill as it had been for Raul; Jill enrolled in a creative writing course and subsequently formed a Buddhist-Catholic study group.

Considering Jill's largely negative family experiences (particularly with regard to her authoritarian mother) throughout childhood, adolescence, and early adulthood as recounted by Ramirez (1998), one could be forgiven for assuming that Jill would have ended up displaying authoritarian tendencies toward her own offspring. However, Jill's guided self-assessment revealed a pattern of *non-engagement* (rather than authoritarianism) with her offspring, which made her feel guilty once she found it necessary to depend upon them for financial support upon retirement; indeed, Ramirez did not diagnose Jill as authoritarian. Conversely, when we learned about "Jenny" via *Letters from Jenny* (Allport, 1965) in Chapter 1 of the present book, we did not discuss evidence of Jenny's authoritarianism – partly because Allport did not know Jenny's life history and consequently was reluctant to attach such a negative label to Jenny, let alone attribute her personality to an Elektra complex or other childhood-based precursor. Ironically, Allport discounted Jenny's own tendency to insert ethnic slurs against outgroups such as Catholic, Jewish, and Irish persons into her letters – even though Allport's synopsis of the "prejudiced personality" in *The Nature of Prejudice* (1954/1979) would have justified characterising Jenny as authoritarian.

In *Letters from Jenny*, Allport (1965) summarised results of a study that he conducted with 36 participants who had read Jenny's letters and subsequently chose adjectives from a list that comprised hundreds of terms; "prejudiced" was one of the terms that participants consistently attributed to Jenny. Allport interpreted the adjective "prejudiced" as indicative of a central *trait* that he labelled as "quarrelsome-suspicious"; such an overarching label bears some resemblance to Wiggins's (1979) lower-order interpersonal trait of "cold-quarrelsome" (which, in turn, comprises the negative pole of *nurturance* as a higher-order interpersonal trait within Wiggins's [1991] interpersonal circumplex theory). However, Wiggins (2003/2005) never obtained any evidence for "prejudiced" as part of an interpersonal trait, despite the fact that Wiggins's Interpersonal Adjective Scales (IAS) drew upon Allport and Odbert's (1936) then-exhaustive list of several thousand trait terms. Without belabouring the point, we wonder if Allport's counterintuitive decision to file his data regarding Jenny's authoritarian or prejudiced *attitudes* under an interpersonal trait (sub) scale that is neither conceptually nor empirically supported has inadvertently led personality psychologists to de-emphasise one of the more compelling aspects of Jenny's personality.

Before leaving the subject of Jenny's authoritarian or prejudiced personality as implicit (but seldom explicit) within Allport's *Letters from Jenny* (1965), we note that Allport's earlier book *The Nature of Prejudice* (1954/1979) also alluded to the *tolerant* or *non-prejudiced personality*; this latter constellation of attitudes within the psyches of some individuals has received comparatively little attention within personality psychology *or* social psychology. If Ramirez's (1998) multicultural/multiracial theory is correct, then we would expect the adoption of a multicultural worldview to steer individuals away from stereotyping, prejudice, and discrimination – in short, to develop the hallmarks of a tolerant personality. Unfortunately, mainstream perspectives in personality and social psychology have not incorporated Ramirez's theory into theories or research on intergroup relations. To Allport's (1965) knowledge, Jenny never underwent psychotherapy for her so-called "cardinal trait" of neuroticism, not to mention her ill-scrutinised intolerant attitudes toward members of stigmatised ethnic groups within American society at the time. Nonetheless, during an era in which ethnic relations remain tenuous within the US and around the world, multicultural/multiracial theory offers considerable insight into the tolerant personality.

MULTICULTURAL/MULTIRACIAL THEORY AND "MADELINE G" (HOPWOOD & WAUGH, 2020): HISTORICAL DEVELOPMENT PATTERN → BICULTURAL IMMERSION(?)

Allport published *Letters from Jenny* (1965) during the height of the US Civil Rights Era; in hindsight, modern-day readers might find it unsurprising that Allport did not comment more extensively upon Jenny's attitudes as prejudiced versus unprejudiced, or intolerant versus tolerant. In contrast, today's readers might well be surprised if Wiggins and his team did not comment at length upon research participant "Madeline G's" comparatively unprejudiced/tolerant versus prejudiced/intolerant attitudes in the second, collaborative half of *Paradigms of Personality Assessment* (2003/2005), which was published 3–5 years before the dawn of a supposedly "post-racial" era in the US (following premature conclusions from some observers regarding the ramifications of Barack Obama's election as President in 2008 and 2012). As it happens, on the basis of results from a battery of qualitative and quantitative questionnaires that accompanied a Life History Interview, Wiggins and colleagues made several references to Madeline G – who, like Jenny, was not a client in psychotherapy – as tolerant in her attitudes toward other persons. [Wiggins and his team speculated that, if Madeline G *had* been a client, then she might have been diagnosed with narcissistic personality disorder on the basis of her tendency to exaggerate her successes.]

In *Paradigms of Personality Assessment*, Wiggins and his research team (2003/2005) did not specifically refer to Ramirez's book *Multicultural/Multiracial Psychology: Mestizo Perspectives on Personality and Mental Health* (1998) when elaborating upon Madeline G's personality characteristics. Nevertheless, Wiggins and collaborators *did* cite the phrase "bicultural immersion" from an article by J. Allen on "Personality Assessment With American Indians and Alaska Natives: Instrument Considerations and Service Delivery Style" (1998, p. 28); the article in question was published in the same year as Ramirez's 1998 book and cited LaFromboise et al.'s earlier article on "Psychological Impact of Biculturalism: Evidence and Theory" (1993) with regard to the construct of bicultural competence. Connecting the last of the dots from Wiggins and colleagues' brief commentary on Madeline G's "bicultural immersion" status (i.e., integrating White/European American and her familial Indigenous American worldviews) to Ramirez's evolving theory, LaFramboise and colleagues cited a chapter by Ramirez (1984) on "Assessing and Understanding Biculturalism-Multiculturalism among Mexican American Adults" from the book *Chicano Psychology* (edited by Mendoza & Martinez, 1984).

Following Wiggins's death, editors Christopher Hopwood and Mark Waugh published results from a 17-year follow-up study of Madeline G in the book *Personality Assessment Paradigms and Methods: A Collaborative Reassessment of Madeline G* (2020). In many respects, Madeline G's personality profile remained consistent over the years, even as some of her life circumstances changed (e.g., still scoring high on agentic and [to a lesser extent] communal aspects of personality, albeit no longer scoring at extreme levels; still living in the southwestern US, although she moved from a less conservative to a more conservative state, which did not mesh well with her liberal political views; still a force of nature, albeit suffering from bouts of depression as she has progressed from young adulthood to middle-age adulthood). One of the most noteworthy changes for our purposes has been Madeline G's less-active role as a civil rights advocate for Indigenous Americans, although she continued to serve as a lawyer and trainer of legal professionals who wish to specialise in issues that specifically affect persons in Indigenous American communities. All in all, Madeline G's bicultural immersion status continued to serve her well, though her long-term neglect of close relationships was taking a social and psychological toll on her psyche.

FINAL THOUGHTS

Our reviews of multiple case studies remind us that we had hoped to link Ramirez's (1998) multicultural/multiracial theory with Cervone's (2027) theory of personality architecture within the present chapter. As we bring this chapter (and the book as a whole) to a close, we anticipate that – in the wake of ongoing critiques about the utility of *trait* as the predominant construct within personality psychology at the present time – theorists' and researchers' interests will shift increasingly toward *value* in the not-too-distant future. Although we hesitate to predict that value will replace trait as the main construct within this field, the value construct strikes us as well-aligned with the current transition from social psychology to cognitive psychology as a primary site of intellectual activity for personality psychologists. Moreover, the construct of value figures prominently in Ramirez's and Cervone's respective theories; the prospect of mid-level attitudes serving as mediators of the impact of generalised values on specialised beliefs is sufficiently promising for both theories that we can envision well-defined points of intersection emerging between diversity science (in the venerable tradition of Ramirez) and personality science (in the "new classic" tradition of Cervone). In any event, we are bullish regarding the potential for this field.

REFERENCES

Acton, G. S., & Revelle, W. (2002). Interpersonal personality measures show circumplex structure based on new psychometric criteria. *Journal of Personality Assessment*, *79*, 456–481.

Adams, W. W. (2010). Nature's participatory psyche: A study of consciousness in the shared Earth community. *The Humanistic Psychologist*, *38*, 15–39.

Adkins, A. V. (2013). Black/feminist futures: Reading Beauvoir in *Black Skin, White Masks*. *The South African Quarterly*, *112*, 697–723.

Adler, A. (1925). *The practice and theory of individual psychology*. Routledge.

Adler, A. (1932). The meaning of life. *Individual Psychology and Social Problems*, *5*, 9–23.

Adler, A. (1935). What is neurosis? *International Journal of Individual Psychology*, *1*, 9–17.

Adler, A. (1957). *Understanding human nature*. Greenberg. (Original work published 1927)

Ainsworth, M. D. S. (1963). The development of infant–mother interaction among the Ganda. In B. M. Foss (Ed.). *Determinants of infant behavior* (pp. 67–104). Wiley.

Ainsworth, M. D. S. (1967). *Infancy in Uganda: Infant care and the growth of love*. Johns Hopkins University Press.

Ainsworth, M. D. S., Blehar, M. C., Waters, E., & Wall, S. (1978). *Patterns of attachment: A psychological study of the Strange Situation*. Erlbaum.

Ainsworth, M. D. S., & Bowlby, J. (1991). An ethological approach to personality development. *American Psychologist*, *46*, 333–341.

Allen, J. (1998). Personality assessment with American Indians and Alaska Natives: Instrument considerations and service delivery style. *Journal of Personality Assessment, 70*(1), 17–42. https://doi.org/10.1207/s15327752jpa7001_2

Allen, T. A., & DeYoung, C. G. (2017). Personality neuroscience and the Five Factor Model. In T. A. Widiger (Ed.), *The Oxford handbook of the Five Factor Model* (pp. 319–349). Oxford University Press.

Allport, F. H. & Allport, G. W. (1921). Personality traits: Their classification and measurement. *Journal of Abnormal and Social Psychology, 16*, 6–40.

Allport, G. W. (1927). Concepts of trait and personality. *Psychological Bulletin, 24*, 284–293.

Allport, G. W. (1928). A test for ascendance-submission. *Journal of Abnormal and Social Psychology, 23*, 118–136.

Allport, G. W. (1950a). Prejudice: A problem in psychological and social causation. *Journal of Social Issues, 6*, 4–23.

Allport, G. W. (1950b). *The individual and his religion: A psychological interpretation*. Macmillan.

Allport, G. W. (1951). *Personality: A psychological interpretation*. Holt. (Original work published 1937)

Allport, G. W. (1955). *Becoming: Basic considerations for a psychology of personality*. Yale University Press.

Allport, G. W. (1963). *Pattern and growth in personality*. (Original work published 1961)

Allport, G. W. (ed. & interpret.) (1965). *Letters from Jenny*. Harcourt, Brace and World.

Allport, G. W. (1979). *The nature of prejudice*. Addison-Wesley. (Original work published 1954)

Allport, G. W. (1985). The historical background of social psychology. In G. Lindzey & E. Aronson (Eds.), *Handbook of social psychology* (3rd ed., Vol. 1, pp. 1–107). Random House. (Original work published 1968)

Allport, G. W., & Odbert, H. S. (1936). Trait-names: A psycho-lexical study. *Psychological Monographs, 47* (Whole No. 211).

Allport, G. W., Vernon, P. E., & Lindzey, G. (1960). *Study of values: Manual and test booklet* (3rd ed.). Houghton Mifflin.

Amelang, M., & Borkenau, P. (1982). Uber die faktorielle Struktur und externe validitat einiger fragebogen-skalen zur erfassung von dimensionen der extraversion und emotionalen stabilitat. *Zeitschrift für Differentielle und Diagnostische Psychologie, 3*, 119–146.

American Psychiatric Association (1980). *Diagnostic and statistical manual of mental disorders* (3rd ed.). American Psychiatric Press.

American Psychiatric Association (1999). *Diagnostic and statistical manual of mental disorders* (4th ed.). American Psychiatric Press.

American Psychiatric Association (1994). *DSM-IV sourcebook*. American Psychiatric Press.

American Psychiatric Association (2017). *Diagnostic and statistical manual of mental disorders* (5th ed.). American Psychiatric Press.

Ansbacher, H. L. (1978). The development of Adler's concept of social interest: A critical study. *Journal of Individual Psychology, 34*, 118–152.

Ansbacher, H. L. (1988). Dreikurs's four goals of children's disturbing behavior and Adler's social interest-activity typology. *Individual Psychology: The Journal of Adlerian Theory, Research & Practice, 44*, 282–289.

Arlow, J. A. (2002). Transference as defense. *Journal of the American Psychoanalytic Association, 50*, 1139–1150.

Arredondo, P. (2008). Using professional leadership to promote multicultural understanding and social justice. *Journal of Pacific Rim Psychology, 2*(1), 13–17. https://doi.org/10.1375/prp.2.1.13

Arredondo, P., Aviles, R. M. D., Zalaquett, C. P., Grazioso, M. D. P., Bordes, V., Hita, L., & Lopez, B. J. (2006). The psychohistorical approach in family counseling with Mestizo/Latino immigrants: A continuum and synergy of worldviews. *The Family Journal, 14*(1), 13–27. https://doi.org/10.1177/1066480705283089

Artistico, D., Berry, J. M., Black, J., Cervone, D., Lee, C., & Orom, H. (2011). Psychological functioning in adulthood: A self-efficacy analysis. In C. Hoare (Ed.), *The Oxford handbook of reciprocal adult development and learning* (2nd ed., pp. 215–247). Oxford University Press.

Ashton, M. C. (1998). Personality and job performance: The importance of narrow traits. *Journal of Organizational Behavior, 19*, 289–303.

Ashton, M. C., Jackson, D. N., Helmes, E., & Paunonen, S. V. (1998a). Joint factor analysis of the Personality Research Form and the Jackson Personality Inventory: Comparisons with the Big Five. *Journal of Research in Personality, 32*, 243–250.

Ashton, M. C. & Lee, K. (2001). A theoretical basis for the major dimensions of personality. *European Journal of Personality, 15*, 327–353.

Ashton, M. C., Lee, K., & Son, C. (2000). Honesty as the sixth factor of personality: Correlations with Machiavellianism, primary psychopathy, and social adroitness. *European Journal of Personality, 14*, 359–368.

Ashton, M. C., Lee, K., & Visser, B. A. (2019). Where's the H? Relations between BFI-2 and HEXACO-60 scales. *Personality and Individual Differences, 137*, 71–75. https://doi.org/10.1016/j.paid.2018.08.013

Ashton, M. C., Paunonen, S. V., Helmes, E., & Jackson, D. N. (1998b). Kin altruism, reciprocal altruism, and the Big Five personality factors. *Evolution and Human Behaviour, 19*, 243–255.

Atalay, M. (2007). Psychology of crisis: An overall account of the psychology of Erikson. *Ekev Academic Review, 11*, 15–34.

Augustine, A. A., & Larsen, R. J. (2015). Personality, affect, and affect regulation. In M. Mikulincer & P. R. Shaver (Eds.), *APA handbook of personality and social psychology* (Vol. 4: Personality processes and individual differences, pp. 147–165). American Psychological Association.

Azim, H. F. A., & Piper, W. E. (1991). The Quality of Object Relations Scale. *Bulletin of the Menninger Clinic, 55*, 323–343.

Baldwin, M. W. (1992). Relational schemas and the processing of social information. *Psychological Bulletin, 112*, 461–484.

Balleine, B. W., & Ostlund, S. B. (2007). Still at the choice-point: Action selection and initiation in instrumental conditioning. *Annals of the New York Academy of Sciences, 1104*, 147–171.

Bandura A. (1978). The self-system in reciprocal determinism. *American Psychologist, 33*, 344–358.

Bandura, A. (1986). *Social foundations of thought and action: A social cognitive theory.* Cambridge University Press.

Bandura, A., Ross, D., & Ross, S. A. (1961). Transmission of aggression through the imitation of aggressive models. *Journal of Abnormal and Social Psychology, 63*, 575–582.

Bandura, A., & Walters, R. (1963). *Social learning and personality development.* Holt, Rinehart and Winston.

Banks, C. (1948). Primary personality factors in women: A re-analysis. *British Journal of Statistical Psychology, 1*, 204–218. https://doi.org/10.1111/j.2044-8317.1948.tb00237.x

Barker, M. (2010). Self-care and relationship conflict. *Sexual and Relationship Therapy, 25*, 37–47.

Bartholomew, K. (1990). Avoidance of intimacy: An attachment perspective. *Journal of Social and Personal Relationships, 7*, 147–178.

Bartholomew, K. (1994). The assessment of individual differences in adult attachment. *Psychological Inquiry, 5*, 23–27.

Bartholomew, K., & Horowitz, L. M. (1991). Attachment styles among young adults: A test of a four-category model. *Journal of Personality and Social Psychology, 61*, 226–244.

Baumeister, R. F. (1997). Identity, self-concept, and self-esteem: The self lost and found. In R. Hogan, J. Johnson, & S. Briggs (Eds.), *Handbook of personality psychology* (pp. 681–710). Academic Press.

Baumeister, R. F. (1998). The self. In D. T. Gilbert, S. T. Fiske, & G. Lindzey (Eds.), *The handbook of social psychology* (4th ed., Vol. 1, pp. 680–740). McGraw-Hill.

Baumeister, R. F., Dale, K., & Sommer, K. L. (1998). Freudian defense mechanisms and empirical findings in modern social psychology: Reaction formation, projection, displacement, undoing, isolation, sublimation, and denial. *Journal of Personality, 66*, 1081–1124.

Beaton, E. A., Schmidt, L. A., Ashbaugh, A. R., Santesso, D. L., Antony, M. M., McCabe, R. E., Seaglowitz, D. J., & Schulkin, J. (2006). Low salivary cortisol levels among socially anxious young adults: Preliminary evidence from a selected and a non-selected sample. *Personality and Individual Differences, 41*, 1217–1228.

Beck, H. P., Levinson, S., & Irons, G. (2009). Finding Little Albert: A journey to John B. Watson's infant laboratory. *American Psychologist, 64*, 605–614.

Bem, D. J. (1965). An experimental analysis of self-persuasion. *Journal of Experimental Social Psychology, 1*, 199–218.

Bem, D. J. (1967). Self-perception: An alternative interpretation of cognitive dissonance phenomena. *Psychological Review, 74*, 183–200.

Bem, D. J. (1972). Self-perception theory. In L. Berkowitz (Ed.), *Advances in Experimental Social Psychology* (Vol. 6, pp. 1–62). Academic Press.

Bem, S. L. (1974). The measurement of psychological androgyny. *Journal of Consulting and Clinical Psychology, 42*, 155–62.

Bem, S. L. (1981). Gender schema theory: A cognitive account of sex typing. *Psychological Review, 88*, 354–364.

Bem, S. L. (1985). Androgyny and gender schema theory: A conceptual and empirical integration. In T. B. Sonderegger (Ed.), *Nebraska Symposium on Motivation 1984: Psychology and gender* (pp. 76–103). University of Nebraska Press.

Bem, S. L. (1994). *The lenses of gender: Transforming the debate on sexual inequality.* Yale University Press.

Benet-Martínez, V., & John, O. P. (1998). *Los Cinco Grandes* across cultures and ethnic groups: Multitrait-multimethod analyses of the Big Five in Spanish and English. *Journal of Personality and Social Psychology, 75*(3), 729–750. https://doi.org/10.1037/0022-3514.75.3.729

Benjafield, J. G. (2008). George Kelly: Cognitive psychologist, humanistic psychologist, or something else entirely? *History of Psychology, 11*, 239–262.

Benjafield, J. G. (2019). Major paradigms and approaches in psychology. In R. J. Sternberg & W. E. Pickren (Eds.), *The Cambridge handbook of the intellectual history of psychology* (pp. 4–28). Cambridge University Press.

Benjamin, L. B. (2011). Structural analysis of social behavior (SASB). In L. M. Horowitz & S. Strack (Eds.), *Handbook of interpersonal psychology: Theory, research, assessment, and therapeutic implications* (pp. 325–342). John Wiley & Sons.

Bernasconi, R. (2000). Almost always more than philosophy proper. *Research in Phenomenology, 30*, 1–11.

Berntson, G. G., & Hothersall, D. (2019). Neuroscience in psychology. In R. J. Sternberg & W. E. Pickren (Eds.), *The Cambridge handbook of the intellectual history of psychology* (pp. 63–87). Cambridge University Press.

Berry, J. W. (1990). Psychology of acculturation. In J. J. Berman (Ed.), *Nebraska Symposium on Motivation, 1989: Cross–cultural perspectives* (pp. 201–234). University of Nebraska Press.

Berry, J. W. (1997). Immigration, acculturation, and adaptation. *Applied Psychology: An International Review, 46*(1), 5–34. https://doi.org/10.1080/026999497378467

Berscheid, E. (1994). Interpersonal relationships. *Annual Review of Psychology, 45*, 79–129.

Berscheid, E. (1999). The greening of relationship science. *American Psychologist, 54*, 260–266.

Bertini, M., Pizzamiglio, L., Wapner, S., & Wapner, S. (Eds.). (1986). *Field dependence in psychological theory, research and application: Two symposia in memory of Herman A. Witkin*. Routledge. https://doi.org/10.4324/9781315825564

Binswanger, L. (1963). *Being-in-the-world: Selected papers of Ludwig Binswanger.* Basic Books.

Bitter, J. R., Robertson, P. E., Healey, A. C., & Cole, L. K. J. (2009). Reclaiming a profeminist orientation in Adlerian therapy. *Journal of Individual Psychology, 65*, 13–33.

Blair, I. V., Dasgupta, N., & Glaser, J. (2015). Implicit attitudes. In M. Mikulincer & P. R. Shaver (Eds.), *APA handbook of personality and social psychology* (Vol. 1: Attitudes and social cognition, pp. 665–691). American Psychological Association.

Bland, A. M., & DeRobertis, E. M. (2019). Humanistic perspective. In V. Zeigler-Hill & T. Shackelford (eds.), *Encyclopedia of personality and individual differences*. Springer. https://doi.org/10.1007/978-3-319-28099-8_1484-2

Blascovich, J., & Tomaka, J. (1991). Measures of self-esteem. In J. Robinson, P. Shaver, & L. Wrightsman (Eds.), *Measures of personality and social psychological attitudes* (pp. 161–194). Academic Press.

Blaser, R. E., & Bellizzi, C. (2014). The comparative study of learning from 1994–2013. *International Journal of Comparative Psychology, 27*, 31–49.

Boag, S. (2006). Freudian repression, the common view, and pathological science. *Review of General Psychology, 10*, 74–86.

Boldero, J., & Francis, J. (2002). Goals, standards, and the self: Reference values serving different functions. *Personality and Social Psychology Review, 6*, 232–241.

Borgatta, E. F. (1964). The structure of personality characteristics. *Behavioral Science, 9*(1), 8–17.

Boss, M. (1963). *Psychoanalysis and Daseinsanalysis*. Basic Books.

Bouton, M. E., & Boakes, R. A. (2019). Learning. In R. J. Sternberg & W. E. Pickren (Eds.), *The Cambridge handbook of the intellectual history of psychology* (pp. 135–164). Cambridge University Press.

Bowlby, J. (1953). *Child care and the growth of love*. Penguin.
Bowlby, J. (1997). *Attachment and loss* (Vol. 1: Attachment). Pimlico. (Original work published 1969)
Bowlby, J. (1998). *Attachment and loss* (Vol. 2: Separation: Anxiety and anger). Pimlico. (Original work published 1973)
Bowlby, J. (1998). *Attachment and loss* (Vol. 3: Loss: Sadness and depression). Pimlico. (Original work published 1980)
Bradford, G. K. (2015). Romantic love as a path: Tensions between erotic desire and security needs. In K. J. Schneider, J. F. Pierson, & J. F. T. Bugental (Eds.), *The handbook of humanistic psychology: Theory, research, and practice* (2nd ed., pp. 653–680). Sage.
Braithwaite, V. A., & Scott, W. A. (1991). Values. In J. P. Robinson, P. R. Shaver, & L. S. Wrightsman (Eds.), *Measures of personality and social psychological attitudes* (pp. 661–753). Academic Press.
Brebner, J. A. (2000). The personality theories of H. J. Eysenck and J. A. Gray: A comparative review. [Review of article by G. Matthews and K. Gilliland (1999) From *Personality and Individual Differences, 26*, 583–626.] *Personality and Individual Differences, 28*, 1191–1192.
Brennan, J. F. (2003). *History and systems of psychology* (6th ed.). Prentice Hall.
Brennan, K. A., Clark, C. L., & Shaver, P. R. (1998). Self-report measurement of adult romantic attachment: An integrative overview. In J. A. Simpson & W. S. Rholes (Eds.), *Attachment theory and close relationships* (pp. 46–76). Guilford Press.
Bretherton, I. (1992). The origins of attachment theory: John Bowlby and Mary Ainsworth. *Developmental Psychology, 28*, 759–775.
Breuer, J., & Freud, S. (1995). Studies on hysteria. In J. Strachey (Ed.), *The standard edition of the complete psychological works of Sigmund Freud* (Vol. 2, xxxii, pp. 1–335). Hogarth Press. (Original work published 1895)
Brewer, M. B., & Brown, R. J. (1998). Intergroup relations. In D. T. Gilbert, S. T. Fiske, & G. Lindzey (Eds.), *The handbook of social psychology* (4th ed., pp. 554–594). McGraw-Hill.
Brewin, C. R. (1996). Theoretical foundations of cognitive-behavior therapy for anxiety and depression. *Annual Review of Psychology, 47*, 33–57.
Brown, R. (1965). *Social psychology*. Free Press.
Brown, R. (1986). *Social psychology* (2nd ed.). Free Press.
Buchanan, R. D., & Haslam, N. (2019). Psychotherapy. In R. J. Sternberg & W. E. Pickren (Eds.), *The Cambridge handbook of the intellectual history of psychology* (pp. 468–494). Cambridge University Press.
Bugental, D. B., & Johnston, C. (2000). Parental and child cognitions in the context of the family. *Annual Review of Psychology, 51*, 315–344.
Buhler, C. (1968). The general structure of the human life cycle. In C. Buhler & F. Massarik (Eds.), *The course of human life: A study of goals in the humanistic perspective* (pp. 12–26). Springer.

Buhler, C. & Allen, M. (1972). *Introduction to humanistic psychology.* Brooks/Cole Publishing Co.

Burghardt, G. M. (2009). Darwin's legacy to comparative psychology and ethology. *American Psychologist, 64,* 102–110.

Burney, V., Arnold-Saritepe, A., & McCann, C. M. (2023). Rethinking the place of qualitative methods in behavior analysis. *Perspectives on Behavior Science, 46,* 185–200.

Burt, C. L. (1966). The genetic determination of differences in intelligence: A study of monozygotic twins reared together and apart. *British Journal of Psychology, 57,* 137–153.

Buss, A. H. (1989). Personality as traits. *American Psychologist, 44,* 1348–1378.

Buss, A. H., & Plomin, R. (1975). *A temperament theory of personality development.* Wiley.

Buss, A. H., & Plomin, R. (1984). *Temperament: Early developing personality traits.* Erlbaum.

Buss, A. H., Plomin, R., & Willerman, L. (1973). The inheritance of personality traits. *Journal of Personality, 41,* 513–524.

Buss, D. M. (1989). Sex differences in human mate preferences: Evolutionary hypotheses tested in 37 cultures. *Behavioral and Brain Sciences, 12,* 1–14.

Buss, D. M. (1997). Evolutionary foundations of personality. In R. Hogan, J. Johnson, & S. Briggs (Eds.), *Handbook of personality psychology* (pp. 317–344). Academic Press.

Buss, D. M., & Kenrick, D. T. (1998). Evolutionary social psychology. In D. T. Gilbert, S. T. Fiske, & G. Lindzey (Eds.), *The handbook of social psychology* (4th ed., Vol. 2, pp. 982–1026). McGraw-Hill.

Buss, D. M., & Penke, L. (2015). Evolutionary personality psychology. In M. Mikulincer & P. R. Shaver (Eds.), *APA handbook of personality and social psychology* (Vol. 4: Personality Processes and Individual Differences, pp. 3–29). American Psychological Association.

Buss, D. M., & Schmitt, D. P. (1993). Sexual strategies theory: An evolutionary perspective on human mating. *Psychological Review, 100,* 204–232.

Buss, D. M., & Schmitt, D. P. (2011). Evolutionary psychology and feminism. *Sex Roles, 64,* 768–787.

Butt, T. (2004). *Understanding people.* Palgrave Macmillan.

Butt, T. (2008). *George Kelly: The psychology of personal constructs.* Palgrave Macmillan.

Calkins, M. W. (1917). The case of self against soul. *Psychological Review, 24,* 278–300.

Campos, B., Roesch, S. C., Gonzalez, P., Hooker, E. D., Castañeda, S. F., Giachello, A. L., Perreira, K. M., & Gallo, L. C. (2019). Measurement properties of Sabogal's Familism Scale: Findings from the Hispanic Community Health Study/Study of Latinos (HCHS/SOL) sociocultural ancillary study. *Journal of Latinx Psychology, 7*(4), 257–272. https://doi.org/10.1037/lat0000126

Campos, B., Schetter, C. D., Abdou, C. M., Hobel, C. J., Glynn, L. M., & Sandman, C. A. (2008). Familialism, social support, and stress: Positive implications for pregnant Latinas. *Cultural Diversity & Ethnic Minority Psychology, 14*(2), 155–162. https://doi.org/10.1037/1099-9809.14.2.155

Capps, D. (2012). Erikson's schedule of human strengths and the childhood origins of the resourceful self. *Pastoral Psychology, 61*, 269–283.

Capuano, A. M., & Killu, K. (2021). Understanding and addressing pseudoscientific practices in the treatment of neurodevelopmental disorders: Considerations for applied behavior analysis practitioners. *Behavioral Interventions, 36*, 242–260.

Carlin, N. (2010). The paranoia of everyday life: Some personal, psychological, and pastoral thoughts. *Pastoral Psychology, 59*, 679–695.

Carroll, E. N., Zuckerman, M., & Vogel, W. H. (1982). A test of the optimal level of arousal theory of sensation seeking. *Journal of Personality and Social Psychology, 42*, 572–575.

Carton, J. S., & Nowicki, S. (1994). Antecedents of individual differences in locus of control of reinforcement: A critical review. *Genetic, Social, and General Psychology Monographs, 120*, 31–81.

Carver, C. S. (2015). Behavioral approach, behavioural avoidance, and behavioural inhibition. In M. Mikulincer & P. R. Shaver (Eds.), *APA Handbook of Personality and Social Psychology* (Vol. 4: Personality Processes and Individual Differences, pp. 307–327). American Psychological Association.

Castagna, P. J., Davis, T. E., III, & Lilly, M. E. (2017). The Behavioral Avoidance Task with anxious youth: A review of procedures, properties, and criticisms. *Clinical Child & Family Psychology Review, 20*, 162–184.

Castaneda, A. (1984). Traditionalism, modernism, and ethnicity. In J. L. Martinez & R. H. Mendoza (Eds.), *Chicano psychology* (2nd ed., pp. 35–40). Academic Press.

Cattell, R. B. (1946). *Development and measurement of personality.* World Book Co.

Cattell, R. B. (1950). *Personality: A systematic, theoretical, and factual study.* McGraw-Hill.

Cattell, R. B. (1965). Factor analysis: An introduction to essentials I: The purpose and underlying models. *Biometrics, 21*, 190–215.

Cattell, R. B. (1970). *Personality and social psychology: Collected papers of Raymond B. Cattell.* Knapp.

Cattell, R. B. (1973). *Personality and mood by questionnaire.* Jossey-Bass.

Cervone, D. (1986). Self-efficacy judgment under uncertainty: Availability biases in perceived self-efficacy and behavior. *Dissertation Abstracts International*, 46(12-B, Pt 1), pp. 4442–4443.

Cervone, D. (1997). Social-cognitive mechanisms and personality coherence: Self-knowledge, situational beliefs, and cross-situational coherence in perceived self-efficacy. *Psychological Science, 8*, 43–50.

Cervone, D. (2004a). Personality assessment: Tapping the social-cognitive architecture of personality. *Behavior Therapy, 35*, 113–129.

Cervone, D. (2004b). The architecture of personality. *Psychological Review, 111*, 183–204.

Cervone, D. (2005). Personality architecture: Within-person structures and processes. *Annual Review of Psychology, 56*, 423–452.

Cervone, D. (2027). *Personality architecture: Making sense of people who think*. Cambridge University Press.

Cervone, D., Caldwell, T. L., Fiori, M., Orom, H., Shadel, W. G., Kassel, J. D., & Artistico, D. (2008a). What underlies appraisals? Experimentally testing a knowledge-and- appraisal model of personality architecture among smokers contemplating high-risk situations. *Journal of Personality, 76*, 929–968.

Cervone, D., Caldwell, T. L., & Orom, H. (2008b). Beyond person and situation effects: Intraindividual personality architecture and its implications for the study of personality and social behavior. In F. Rhodewalt (Ed.), *Personality and social behavior* (pp. 9–48). Psychology Press.

Cervone, D., & Little, B. R. (2019). Personality architecture and dynamics: The new agenda and what's new about it. *Personality and Individual Differences, 136*, 12–23.

Cervone, D., Mercurio, L., & Lilley, C. (2020). The individual STEM student in context: Idiographic methods for understanding self-knowledge and intraindividual patterns of self-efficacy appraisal. *Journal of Educational Psychology, 112*, 1597–1613.

Cervone, D., Orom, H., Artistico, D., Shadel, W. G., & Kassel, J. D. (2007). Using a knowledge-and-appraisal model of personality architecture to understand consistency and variability in smokers' self-efficacy appraisals in high-risk situations. *Psychology of Addictive Behaviors, 21*, 44–54.

Cervone, D., & Peake, P. K. (1986). Anchoring, efficacy, and action: The influence of judgmental heuristics on self-efficacy judgments and behavior. *Journal of Personality and Social Psychology, 50*, 492–501.

Cervone, D., & Scott, W. D. (1995). Self-efficacy theory of behavioral change: Foundations, conceptual issues, and therapeutic implications. In W. T. O'Donohue & L. Krasner (Eds.), *Theories of behavior therapy: Exploring behavior change* (pp. 349–383). American Psychological Association.

Chase, C. I. (1998). A chat room – educational psychologists but no curriculum methodologists? *Educational Psychology Review, 10*, 239–248.

Chodorow, N. J. (1978). *The reproduction of mothering: Psychoanalysis and the sociology of gender*. University of California Press.

Chodorow, N. J. (2004). The American independent tradition: Loewald, Erikson, and the (possible) rise of intersubjective ego psychology. *Psychoanalytic Dialogues, 14*, 207–232.

Chomsky N. (1959). Review of Skinner's *Verbal Behavior. Language, 35*, 26–58.

Church, A. T. (2000). Culture and personality: Toward an integrated cultural trait psychology. *Journal of Personality, 68*, 651–703.

Church, A. T., Katigbak, M. S., & Reyes, J. A. S. (1998). Further exploration of Filipino personality structure using the lexical approach: Do the Big-Five or Big-Seven dimensions emerge? *European Journal of Personality, 12*, 249–269.

Church, A. T., & Lonner, W. J. (1998). The cross-cultural perspective in the study of personality: Rationale and current research. *Journal of Cross-Cultural Psychology, 29*, 32–62.

Church, A. T., Reyes, J. A. S., Katigbak, M. S., & Grimm, S. D. (1997). Filipino personality structure and the Big Five model: A lexical approach. *Journal of Personality, 65*, 477–528.

Churchill, S. D., & Wertz, F. J. (2015). An introduction to phenomenological research in psychology: Historical, conceptual, and methodological foundations. In K. J. Schneider, J. F. Pierson, & J. F. T. Bugental (Eds.), *The handbook of humanistic psychology: Theory, research, and practice* (2nd ed., pp. 275–293). Sage.

Clark, D. O. (2005). From philosopher to psychologist: The early career of Edwin Ray Guthrie, Jr. *History of Psychology, 8*, 235–254.

Clarke, S. (2000). Psychoanalysis, psychoexistentialism and racism. *Psychoanalytic Studies, 2*, 343–355.

Clavijo, A. (2013). The psyche as behavior. *Revista Columbiana de Psicologia, 22*, 377–387.

Cloninger, C. R. (1987). A systematic method for clinical description and classification of personality variants. *Archives of General Psychiatry, 44*, 573–588.

Cloninger, C. R., Svrakic, D. M., & Przybeck, T. R. (1993). A psychobiological model of temperament and character. *Archives of General Psychiatry, 50*, 975–990.

Cloninger, S. C. (2020). Conceptual and historical perspectives. In P. J. Corr & G. Matthews (Eds.), *The Cambridge handbook of personality psychology* (pp. 13–30). Cambridge University Press.

Cohen, J., Cohen, P., West, S. G., & Aiken, L. S. (2003). *Applied multiple regression/ correlation analysis for the behavioral sciences* (3rd ed.). Erlbaum.

Cokley, K. (2007). Critical issues in the measurement of ethnic and racial identity: A referendum on the state of the field. *Journal of Counseling Psychology, 54*, 224–234.

Constantinople, A. (1969). An Eriksonian measure of personality development in college students. *Developmental Psychology, 1*, 357–372.

Constantinople, A. (1973). Masculinity–Femininity: An exception to a famous dictum? *Psychological Bulletin, 80*, 389–407.

Contreras, C. L. M. (2004). Predicting computer self-confidence from demographic and personality variables and computer use. *Quarterly Review of Distance Education, 5*(3), 173–181.

Cooley, C. H. (1902). *Human nature and the social order.* Scribner's.

Coolidge, F. L., Moor, C., Yamazaki, G. F., Stewart, S. E., & Segal, D. L. (2001). On the relationship between Karen Horney's tripartite neurotic type theory and personality disorder features. *Personality and Individual Differences, 30*, 1387–1400.

Coon, H. M., & Kemmelmeier, M. (2001). Cultural orientations in the United States: (Re)examining differences among ethnic groups. *Journal of Cross-Cultural Psychology, 32*(3), 348–364. https://doi.org/10.1177/0022022101032003006

Cooper, C. R., & Denner, J. (1998). Theories linking culture and psychology: Universal and community-specific processes. *Annual Review of Psychology, 49*, 559–584.

Corcoran, K. J. (1991). Efficacy, "skills," reinforcement, and choice behavior. *American Psychologist, 46*, 155–157.

Corr, P. J. (2001). Testing problems in J. A. Gray's personality theory: A commentary on Matthews and Gilliland (1999). *Personality and Individual Differences, 30*(2), 333–352. https://doi.org/10.1016/S0191-8869(00)00028-3

Corr, P. J. (2009). The reinforcement sensitivity theory of personality. In P. J. Corr & G. Matthews (Eds), *The Cambridge handbook of personality psychology* (pp. 347–376). Cambridge University Press.

Corr, P. J., & Matthews, G., eds. (2020). *The Cambridge handbook of personality psychology* (2nd ed.). Cambridge University Press.

Cortina, J. M. (1993). What is coefficient alpha? An examination of theory and applications. *Journal of Applied Psychology, 78*(1), 98–104. https://doi.org/10.1037/00219010.78.1.98

Cortina, M. (2015). The greatness and limitations of Erich Fromm's humanism. *Contemporary Psychoanalysis, 51*, 388–422.

Costa, P. T., Jr., & McCrae, R. R. (1985). *The NEO personality inventory manual.* Psychological Assessment Resources.

Costa, P. T., Jr., & McCrae, R. R. (1989). *The NEO PI manual supplement.* Psychological Assessment Resources.

Costa, P T., Jr., & McCrae, R. (1992). *Revised NEO Personality Inventory (NEO-PI-R) and NEO Five Factor Model (NEO-FFI) professional manual.* Psychological Assessment Center.

Craig, E. (2008). The human and the hidden: Existential wonderings about depth, soul, and the unconscious. *The Humanistic Psychologist, 36*, 227–282.

Curlette, W. L., Kern, R. M., & Wheeler, M. (1996). Uses and interpretations of scores on the BASIS-A Inventory. *Individual Psychology, 52*, 95–103.

Danzer, G. (2012). Integrating ego psychology and strengths–based social work. *Journal of Theory Construction & Testing, 16*, 9–15.

Darwin, C. R. (1859). *On the origin of species by means of natural selection, or the preservation of favoured races in the struggle for life*. John Murray.

Darwin, C. R. (1871). *The descent of man, and selection in relation to sex*. John Murray.

Davis, M., Barad, M., Otto, M., & Southwick, S. (2006). Combining pharmacotherapy with cognitive behavioral therapy: Traditional and new approaches. *Journal of Traumatic Stress, 19*, 571–581.

Davis, T. (2007). The relevance of the Freudian concept of "transference" to existential psychotherapy. *Existential Analysis, 18*, 348–357.

Davison, K., & MacGregor, M. W. (1998). A critical appraisal of self-report defense mechanism measures. *Journal of Personality, 66*, 965–992.

Deary, I. J. (2009). The trait approach to personality. In P. J. Corr & G. Matthews (Eds.), *The Cambridge handbook of personality psychology* (pp. 89–109). Cambridge University Press.

Deaux, K., & Lafrance, M. (1998). Gender. In D. T. Gilbert, S. T. Fiske, & G. Lindzey (Eds.), *The handbook of social psychology* (4th ed., Vol. 1, pp. 788–827). McGraw-Hill.

Debbane, E. (2011). Envy and its relation to destructiveness. *Canadian Journal of Psychoanalysis, 19*, 108–124.

de Beauvoir, S. (1947). *The ethics of ambiguity*. Philosophical Library.

de Beauvoir, S. (2009). *The second sex* (Vols 1 & 2). Knopf. (Original work published 1949)

DeCarvalho, R. J. (1990). The growth hypothesis and self–actualization: An existential alternative. *The Humanistic Psychologist, 18*, 252–258.

Deci, E. L., & Ryan, R. M. (2000). The "what" and "why" of goal pursuits: Human needs and the self-determination of behavior. *Psychological Inquiry, 11*, 227–268.

Delval, I., Fernandez-Bolanos, M., & Izar, P. (2024). Towards an integrated concept of personality in human and nonhuman animals. *Integrative Psychological & Behavioral Science, 58*, 271–302.

Demanarig, D. L., Cokley, K., Beasley, S. T., Hita, L., Hashem, H., Mamidanna, P., Mujica, C., & Mercado, A. (2024). Mending fragile alliances to fight racism: A developing framework for cross-racial/ethnic solidarity. *American Psychologist, 79*, 553–568.

Denis, D. J., & Young, B. (2019). Methodology in psychology. In R. J. Sternberg & W. E. Pickren (Eds.), *The Cambridge handbook of the intellectual history of psychology* (pp. 29–62). Cambridge University Press.

Depue, R. A. (1995). Neurobiological factors in personality and depression. *European Journal of Personality, 9*, 413–439.

Depue, R. A., & Collins, P. F. (1999). Neurobiology of the structure of personality: Dopamine, facilitation of incentive motivation, and extraversion. *Behavioral and Brain Sciences, 22*, 491–569.

DeRobertis, E. M. (2006). Charlotte Buhler's existential-humanistic contributions to child and adolescent psychology. *Journal of Humanistic Psychology, 46*, 48–76.

DeRobertis, E. M. (2015). Toward a humanistic-multicultural model of development. In K. J. Schneider, J. F. Pierson, & J. F. T. Bugental (Eds.), *The handbook of humanistic psychology: Theory, research, and practice* (2nd ed., pp. 227–242). Sage.

Devonis, D. (2019). Emotion. In R. J. Sternberg & W. E. Pickren (Eds.), *The Cambridge handbook of the intellectual history of psychology* (pp. 371–390). Cambridge University Press.

Dewey, J. (1909). *Moral principles in education.* Houghton Mifflin.

Dewsbury, D. A. (2000). Comparative cognition in the 1930s. *Psychonomic Bulletin & Review, 7*, 267–283.

DeYoung, C. G. (2015). Openness/intellect: A dimension of personality reflecting cognitive exploration. In M. Mikulincer & P. R. Shaver (Eds.), *APA Handbook of Personality and Social Psychology* (Vol. 4: Personality Processes and Individual Differences, pp. 369–399). American Psychological Association.

DeYoung, C. G., & Blain, S. D. (2020). Personality neuroscience. In P. J. Corr & G. Matthews (Eds.), *The Cambridge handbook of personality psychology* (2nd ed., pp. 273–291). Cambridge University Press.

DeYoung, C. G. & Gray, J. R. (2009). Personality neuroscience: Explaining individual differences in affect, behavior, and cognition. In P. J. Corr & G. Matthews (Eds.), *The Cambridge handbook of personality psychology* (pp. 323–346). Cambridge University Press.

Diener, E. (1984). Subjective well-being. *Psychological Bulletin, 95*, 542–575.

Diener, E., Emmons, R. A., Larsen, R. J., & Griffin, S. (1985). The Satisfaction with Life Scale. *Journal of Personality Assessment, 49*, 71–75.

Diener, E., Oishi, S., & Lucas, R. E. (2003). Personality, culture, and subjective well-being: Emotional and cognitive evaluations of life. *Annual Review of Psychology, 54*, 403–425.

Diener, E., Sapyta, J. J., & Suh, E. (1998). Subjective well-being is essential to well-being. *Psychological Inquiry, 9*, 33–37.

Diener, E., Wirtz, D., Tov, W., Kim-Prieto, C., Choi, D.-W., Oishi, S., & Biswas-Diener, R. (2010). New well-being measures: Short scales to assess flourishing and positive and negative feelings. *Social Indicators Research, 97*, 143–156.

Digman, J. M. (1990). Personality structure: Emergence of the Five-Factor Model. *Annual Review of Psychology, 41*, 417–440.

Dixon, J., & Levine, M. (2012). Introduction. In J. Dixon & M. Levine (Eds.), *Beyond prejudice: Extending the social psychology of conflict, inequality and social change* (pp. 1–22). Cambridge University Press.

Djikic, M., & Oatley, K. (2004). Love and personal relationships: Navigating on the border between the ideal and the real. *Journal for the Theory of Social Behaviour, 34*(2), 199–209.

Dolezal, L. (2012). Reconsidering the Look in Sartre's *Being and Nothingness. Sartre Studies International, 18*, 9–28.

Dollard, J., Doob, L. W., Miller, N. E., Mowrer, O. H., & Robert Sears, R. R. (1939). *Frustration and aggression*. Yale University Press.

Dollard, J., & Miller, N. E. (1950). *Personality and psychotherapy: An analysis in terms of learning, thinking, and culture*. McGraw-Hill.

Donahoe, J. W. (1999). Edward L Thorndike: The selectionist connectionist. *Journal of the Experimental Analysis of Behavior, 72*, 451–454.

Douglass, S., & Umana-Taylor, A. J. (2015). A brief form of the Ethnic Identity Scale: Development and empirical validation. *Identity, 15*, 48–65.

Draguns, J. G., & Tanaka-Matsumi, J. (2020). Personality in cross-cultural perspective. In P. J. Corr & G. Matthews (Eds.), *The Cambridge handbook of personality psychology* (2nd ed., pp. 400–412). Cambridge University Press.

Dumont, F. (2010). *History of personality psychology: Theory, science, and research from Hellenism to the twenty-first century*. Cambridge University Press.

Duschinsky, R. (2020). *Cornerstones of attachment research*. Oxford University Press.

Eccles, J. S., & Wigfield, A. (2002). Motivational beliefs, values, and goals. *Annual Review of Psychology, 53*, 109–132.

Eibl-Eibesfeldt, I. (1977). Evolution of destructive aggression. *Aggressive Behavior, 3*, 127–144.

Elkind, D. (1999). Educational research and the science of education. *Educational Psychology Review, 11*, 271–287.

Endler, N. S. (2000). The interface between personality and cognition. *European Journal of Personality, 14*, 377–389.

Enns, C. Z. (1989). Toward teaching inclusive personality theories. *Teaching of Psychology, 16*, 111–117.

Erikson, E. H. (1950). *Childhood and society*. Norton.

Erikson, E. H. (1980). *Identity and the life cycle*. Norton. (Original work published 1959)

Erikson, E. H. (1994). *Identity: Youth and crisis*. Norton. (Original work published 1968)

Erikson, E. H. (1995). *Childhood and society*. Vintage. (Original work published 1963)

Escobar, R., & Roca, A. (2012). Edwin Guthrie's theory of association by temporal contiguity. *Revista Mexicana de Psicologia, 29*, 5–15.

Etcheverry, P. E., Le, B., Wu, T.-F., & Wei, M. (2013). Attachment and the investment model: Predictors of relationship commitment, maintenance, and persistence. *Personal Relationships, 20*, 546–567.

Ewen, R. B. (1998). *An introduction to theories of personality* (5th ed.). Erlbaum.

Eysenck, H. J. (1947). *Dimensions of personality*. Methuen.

Eysenck, H. J. (1967). *The biological basis of personality*. Charles C. Thomas.

Eysenck, H. J., & Eysenck, S. B. G. (1968). *Manual for the Eysenck Personality Inventory*. Educational and Industrial Testing.

Eysenck, H. J. & Eysenck, S. B. G. (1975). *Manual of the Eysenck Personality Questionnaire*. EdITS/Educational and Industrial Testing Service.

Fabrigar, L. R., Visser, P. S., & Browne, M. W. (1997). Conceptual and methodological issues in testing the circumplex structure of data in personality and social psychology. *Personality and Social Psychology Review, 1*, 184–203.

Fairbairn, W. R. D. (1952). *Psychoanalytic studies of personality*. Routledge.

Fairchild, H. H., Yee, A. H., Wyatt, G., & Weizmann, F. (1995). Readdressing psychology's problems with race. *American Psychologist, 50*, 46–47.

Fancher, R. & Rutherford, A. (2017). *Pioneers of psychology* (5th ed.). Norton.

Fanon, F. (1963). *The wretched of the earth*. Grove Weidenfeld. (Original work published 1961)

Fanon, F. (1967). *Black skin, White masks*. Grove Press. (Original version published 1952)

Feest, U. (2005). Operationism in psychology: What the debate is about, what the debate should be about. *Journal of the History of the Behavioral Sciences, 41*, 131–149.

Feij, J. A., Orlebeke, J. F., Gazendam, A., & van Zuilen, R. W. (1985). Sensation seeking: Measurement and psychophysiological correlates. In *The biological bases of personality and behaviour, volume 1: Theories, measurement techniques and development*, edited by J. Strelau, F. H. Farley, & A. Gale. New York: Hemisphere Publishing.

Ferguson, E. (2013). Personality is of central concern to understand health: Towards a theoretical model for health psychology, *Health Psychology Review, 7*, S32–S70.

Ferreira, T. A. d. S., Simoes, A. S., Santos, F. M. S., Matos, J. P. A., & Moura, M. C. B. L. (2021). Methods of conceptual research in clinical behavior analysis. *The Psychological Record, 71*, 257–264.

Festinger, L. (1957). *A theory of cognitive dissonance*. Stanford University Press.

Field, A. P., & Nightingale, Z. C. (2009). Test of time: What if Little Albert had escaped? *Clinical Child Psychology and Psychiatry, 14*, 311–319.

Figueredo, A. J., Gladden, P., Vasquez, G., Wolf, P. A. A., & Jones, D. N. (2009). Evolutionary theories of personality. In P. J. Corr & G. Matthews (Eds.), *The Cambridge handbook of personality psychology* (pp. 265–274). Cambridge University Press.

Fincham, F. D., & Beach, S. R. (1999). Marital conflict: Implications for working with couples. *Annual Review of Psychology, 50*, 47–77.

Finkel, E. J., Simpson, J. A., & Eastwick, P. W. (2017). The psychology of close relationships: Fourteen core principles. *Annual Review of Psychology, 68*, 383–411.

Fisher, S. (1949). An overview of trends in research dealing with personality rigidity. *Journal of Personality, 17*, 342–351.

Fiske, D. W. (1949). Consistency of the factorial structures of personality ratings from different sources. *Journal of Abnormal and Social Psychology, 44*, 329–344.

Fiske, S. T. (1998). Prejudice, stereotyping, and discrimination. In D. T. Gilbert, S. T. Fiske, & G. Lindzey (Eds.), *The handbook of social psychology* (4th ed., pp. 357–411). McGraw–Hill.

Fiske, S. T., & Taylor, S. E. (1991). *Social cognition* (2nd ed.). McGraw–Hill.

Foa, U. G., & Foa, E. B. (1974). *Societal structures of the mind*. Charles C. Thomas.

Forest, J., & Sicz, G. (1981). A review of the Personal Orientation Dimensions. *Journal of Personality Assessment, 45*, 433–435.

Frable, D. E. S. (1997). Gender, racial, sexual, and class identities. *Annual Review of Psychology, 48*, 139–163.

Freeberg, A. L., & Stein, C. H. (1996). Felt obligations towards parents in Mexican-American and Anglo-American young adults. *Journal of Social and Personal Relationships, 13*(3), 457–471. https://doi.org/10.1177/02654 07596133009

Freud, A. (1958). Adolescence. *Psychoanalytic Study of the Child, 13*, 255–278.

Freud, A. (1966). *The ego and the mechanisms of defense*. International Universities Press. (Original work published 1936)

Freud, A. (1975). *Introduction to the technique of child analysis*. Ayer Company Publishers. (Original work published 1927)

Freud, S. (1925). Character and anal eroticism. n S. Freud, *Collected papers* (Vol. 2). Hogarth. (Original work published 1908)

Freud, S. (1927). *The ego and the id*. Hogarth. (Original work published 1923)

Freud, S. (1953). On narcissism: An introduction. In J. Strachey (Ed. & Trans.), *The standard edition of the complete psychological works of Sigmund Freud* (Vol. 14, pp. 69–102). Hogarth Press. (Original work published 1914)

Freud, S. (1961). *Beyond the pleasure principle*. Norton. (Original work published 1920)

Freud, S. (1962). *Three essays on the theory of sexuality* (James Strachey, trans.). Basic Books. (Original work published 1905)
Freud, S. (1965). *The interpretation of dreams*. Avon. (Original work published 1900)
Freud, S. (1990). *New introductory lectures on psychoanalysis*. Norton. (Original work published 1933)
Fridlund, A. J., Beck, H. P., Goldie, W. D., & Irons, G. (2012). Little Albert: A neurologically impaired child. *History of Psychology, 15*, 302–327.
Friedan, B. (1963). *The feminine mystique*. Norton.
Friedman, H. (2008). Humanistic and positive psychology: The methodological and epistemological divide. *Humanistic Psychologist, 36*, 113–126.
Frings, D. (2018). *Social psychology: The basics*. Routledge.
Fromm, E. (1941). *Escape from freedom*. Farrar & Rinehart.
Fromm, E. (1955). *The sane society*. Rinehart & Co.
Fromm, E. (1956). *The art of loving*. George Allen & Unwin.
Funder, D. C. (1991). Global traits: A neo-Allportian approach to personality. *Psychological Science, 2*, 31–39.
Funder, D. C. (2001). Personality. *Annual Review of Psychology, 52*, 197–221.
Funder, D. C., & Fast, L. A. (2010). Personality in social psychology. In S. T. Fiske, D. T. Gilbert, & G. Lindzey (Eds.), *The handbook of social psychology* (5th ed., Vol. 1, pp. 668–697). John Wiley & Sons, Inc.
Gaines, S. O., Jr. (with Buriel, R., Liu, J. H., & Rios, D. I.) (1997). *Culture, ethnicity, and personal relationship processes*. Routledge.
Gaines, S. O., Jr. (2007a). Personality and personal relationship processes: An introduction to the special issue. *Journal of Social and Personal Relationships, 24*, 475–478.
Gaines, S. O., Jr. (2007b). Personality and personal relationship processes: Concluding thoughts. *Journal of Social and Personal Relationships, 24*, 613–617.
Gaines, S. O., Jr. (2012). Stereotyping, prejudice and discrimination revisited: From William James to W. E. B. Du Bois. In J. Dixon, & M. Levine (Eds.), *Beyond prejudice: Extending the social psychology of conflict, inequality and social change* (pp. 105–119). Cambridge University Press.
Gaines, S. O., Jr. (2018). *Identity and interethnic marriage in the United States*. Routledge. (Original work published 2017)
Gaines, S. O., Jr. (2018). *Personality and close relationship processes*. Cambridge University Press. (Original work published 2016)
Gaines, S. O., Jr. (2020). *Personality psychology: The basics* (1st ed.). Routledge.
Gaines, S. O., Jr. (2023). *The self in relationships: Social-personality theory, research, and new directions*. Oxford University Press.
Gaines, S. O., Jr. (2025). *A critical approach to conceptual and historical issues in psychology: Soul, self, and science*. Routledge.

Gaines, S. O., Jr., Marelich, W. D., Bledsoe, K. L., Steers, W. N., Henderson, M. C.,

Granrose, C. S., Barajas, L., Hicks, D., Lyde, M., Takahashi, Y., Yum, N., Rios, D. I., Garcia, B. F., Farris, K., & Page, M. S. (1997a). Links between race/ethnicity and cultural values as mediated by racial/ethnic identity and moderated by gender. *Journal of Personality and Social Psychology, 72*, 1460–1476.

Gaines, S. O., Jr., Marelich, W. D., Bunce, D., Robertson, T., & Wright, B. C. (2013). MEIM expansion: Racial, religious, and national aspects of sense of ethnic identity within the United Kingdom. *Identity, 13*, 289–317.

Gaines, S. O., Jr., Panter, A. T., Lyde, M. D., Steers, W. N., Rusbult, C. E., Cox, C. L., & Wexler, M. O. (1997b). Evaluating the circumplexity of interpersonal traits and the manifestation of interpersonal traits in interpersonal trust. *Journal of Personality and Social Psychology, 73*, 610–623.

Gaines, S. O., Jr., & Ramkissoon, M. (2008). US/Caribbean relationships: Perspectives from Caribbean psychology and mainstream social psychology. In T. A. Karis, & K. D. Killian (Eds.), *Intercultural couples: Exploring diversity in intimate relationships* (pp. 227–250). Routledge.

Gaines, S. O., Jr. & Reed, E. S. (1994). Two social psychologies of prejudice: Gordon W. Allport, W. E. B. Du Bois, and the legacy of Booker T. Washington. *Journal of Black Psychology, 20*, 8–28.

Gaines, S. O., Jr. & Reed, E. S. (1995). Prejudice: From Allport to Du Bois. *American Psychologist, 50*, 96–103.

Galton, F. (1869). *Hereditary genius*. Macmillan.

Gangestad, S. W. (2012). Evolutionary perspectives. In K. Deaux & M. Snyder (Eds.), *The Oxford handbook of personality and social psychology* (pp. 151–181). Oxford University Press.

Garcia-Valdecases, M. (2005). Psychology and mind in Aquinas. *History of Psychiatry, 16*, 291–310.

Gaughan, E.T., Miller, J. D., & Lynam, D. R. (2012). Examining the utility of general models of personality in the study of psychopathy: A comparison of the HEXACO–PI–R and NEO PI–R. *Journal of Personality Disorders, 26*, 513–523.

Geen, R. G. (1997). Psychophysiological approaches to personality. In R. Hogan, J. A. Johnson, & S. R. Briggs (eds.), *Handbook of personality psychology* (pp. 387–414). Academic Press.

Gieser, M. T. (1993). The first behavior therapist as I knew her. *Journal of Behavior Therapy and Experimental Psychiatry, 24*, 321–324.

Gil, A. G., Wagner, E. F., & Vega, W. A. (2000). Acculturation, familism and alcohol use among Latino adolescent males: Longitudinal relations. *Journal of Community Psychology, 28*(4), 443–458. https://doi.org/10.1002/1520-6629(200007)28:4<443::AID-JCOP6>3.0.CO;2-A

Gildersleeve, M. (2015). Beauvoir and demystifying paradoxical characteristics of Narcissistic Personality Disorder. *Indian Journal of Psychological Medicine, 37*, 251–253.

Gilliam, C. (2017). The existential unconscious: Sartre and the dialectic of freedom. *Existential Analysis, 28*, 351–360.

Glazer, N., & Moynihan, D. P. (1963). *Beyond the melting pot: The Negroes, Puerto Ricans, Jews, Italians and Irish of New York City.* Massachusetts Institute of Technology Press.

Goddard, M. J. (2012). On certain similarities between mainstream psychology and the writings of B. F. Skinner. *Psychological Record, 62*, 563–576.

Goffman, E. (1959). *The presentation of self in everyday life.* Doubleday.

Goffman, E. (1963). *Stigma: Notes on the management of spoiled identity.* Prentice–Hall.

Goldberg, L. (1981). Language and individual differences: The search for universals in personality lexicons. In L. Wheeler (Ed.), *Review of Personality and Social Psychology* (pp. 141–165). Sage.

Goldberg, L. R. (1999). A broad-bandwidth, public domain, personality inventory measuring the lower-level facets of several five-factor models. In I. Mervielde, I. Deary, F. DeFruyt, & F. Ostendorf (Eds.), *Personality Psychology in Europe* (Vol. 7, pp. 7–28). Tilburg University Press.

Goldsmith, H. H., Buss, A. H., Plomin, R., Rothbart, M. K., Thomas, A., Chess, S., Hinde, R. A., & McCall, R. B. (1987). What is temperament? Four approaches. *Child Development, 58*, 505–529.

Goldstein, K. (1939). *The organism: A holistic approach to biology derived from pathological data in man.* American Book Company.

Goldstein, K. (1940). *Human nature in the light of psychopathology.* Harvard University Press.

Good, J., & Still, A. (1986). Tolman and the tradition of direct perception. *British Journal of Psychology, 77*(4), 533–539. https://doi.org/10.1111/j.2044–8295.1986.tb02218.x

Goodwin, R. (2009). *Changing relations: Achieving intimacy in a time of social transition.* Cambridge University Press.

Gore, P. M., & Rotter, J. B. (1963). A personality correlate of social action. *Journal of Personality, 31*(1), 58–64. https://doi.org/10.1111/j.1467–6494.1963.tb01840.x

Gorycki, K. A., Ruppel, P. R., & Zane, T. (2020). Is long-term ABA therapy abusive: A response to Sandoval-Norton and Shkedy. *Cogent Psychology, 7*(1), 1823615.

Gray, J. A. (1970). The psychophysical basis of Introversion–Extraversion. *Behavior Research and Therapy, 8*, 249–266.

Gray, J. A. (1972). The psychophysiological nature of introversion–extraversion: A modification of Eysenck's theory. In V. D. Nebylitsyn &

J. A. Gray (Eds.), *The biological bases of individual behaviour* (pp. 182–205). Academic Press.

Gray, J. A. (1981). A critique of Eysenck's theory of personality. In H. J. Eysenck (Ed.), *A model for personality* (pp. 246–277). Springer–Verlag.

Gray, J. A., & McNaughton, N. (2000). *The neuropsychology of anxiety: An enquiry into functions of the septo-hippocampal system*. Oxford University Press.

Greening, T. (1992). Existential challenges and responses. *The Humanistic Psychologist, 20*, 111–115.

Gross, C. (2010). Alfred Russell Wallace and the evolution of the human mind. *Neuroscientist, 16*, 496–507.

Grotstein, J. (2008). The overarching role of unconscious phantasy. *Psychoanalytic Inquiry, 28*, 190–205.

Grusec, J. E. (1992). Social learning theory and developmental psychology: The legacies of Robert Sears and Albert Bandura. *Developmental Psychology, 28*, 776–786.

Guest, H. S. (2014). Maslow's hierarchy of needs – the sixth level. *The Psychologist, 27*, 982–983.

Guilford, J. P. (1975). Factors and factors of personality. *Psychological Bulletin, 82*, 802–814.

Guilford, J. P., & Guilford, R. B. (1934). An analysis of the factors in a typical test of introversion–extroversion. *Journal of Abnormal and Social Psychology, 28*, 377–399.

Guilford, J. P., & Zimmerman, W. S. (1949). *The Guilford-Zimmerman Temperament Survey: Manual*. Sheridan Supply.

Guntrip, H. (1969). *Schizoid phenomena, object-relations, and the self*. International Universities Press.

Gurtman, M. B., & Pincus, A. L. (2000). Interpersonal Adjective Scales: Confirmation of circumplex structure from multiple perspectives. *Personality and Social Psychology Bulletin, 26*, 374–384.

Guthrie, E. R. (1930). Conditioning as a principle of learning. *Psychological Review, 37*, 412–428.

Guthrie, E. R. (1934). Discussion: Pavlov's theory of conditioning. *Psychological Review, 41*, 199–206.

Guthrie, E. R. (1935). *The psychology of learning*. Harper.

Guthrie, E. R. (1942). Conditioning: A theory of learning in terms of stimulus, response, and association. *Teachers College Record, 43*, 17–60.

Guthrie, E. R., & Powers, F. F. (1950). *Educational psychology*. Ronald Press.

Hall, C. S., & Lindzey, G. (1957). *Theories of personality*. Wiley & Sons.

Hall, C. S., & Lindzey, G. (1970). *Theories of personality* (2nd ed.). Wiley & Sons.

Hall, C. S., & Lindzey, G. (1978). *Theories of personality* (3rd ed.). Wiley & Sons.

Hall, C. S., Lindzey, G., & Campbell, J. B. (1998). *Theories of personality* (4th ed.). Wiley & Sons.
Hall, C. S., Lindzey, G., Loehlin, J. C., & Manosevitz, M. (1985). *An introduction to theories of personality.* Wiley & Sons.
Hall, T. W. (2007). Psychoanalysis, attachment, and spirituality Part 1: The emergence of two relational traditions. *Journal of Psychology and Theology, 35*, 14–28.
Haslam, N., Smillie, L., & Song, J. (2017). *An introduction to personality, individual differences and intelligence.* 2nd ed. Los Angeles: SAGE Publications.
Hazan, C., & Diamond, L. M. (2000). The place of attachment in human mating. *Journal of General Psychology, 4*, 186–204.
Hazan, C., & Shaver, P. R. (1987). Romantic love conceptualized as an attachment process. *Journal of Personality and Social Psychology, 52*, 511–524.
Hazan, C., & Shaver, P.R. (1994a). Attachment as an organizational framework for research on close relationships. *Psychological Inquiry, 5*, 1–22.
Hazan, C., & Shaver, P. R. (1994b). Deeper into attachment theory: Reply to commentaries. *Psychological Inquiry, 5*, 68–79.
Hebb, D. O. (1960). The American revolution. *American Psychologist, 15*, 735–745.
Heider, F. (1958). *The psychology of interpersonal relations.* John Wiley & Sons.
Heilmayr, D., & Friedman, H. S. (2020). Models of physical health and personality. In P. J. Corr & G. Matthews (Eds.), *The Cambridge handbook of personality psychology* (2nd ed., pp. 193–207). Cambridge University Press.
Hekman, S. J. (1999). *The future of differences: Truth and method in feminist theory.* Polity Press.
Hekman, S. J. (2015). Simone de Beauvoir and the beginnings of the feminine subject. *Feminist Theory, 16*, 137–151.
Helgeson, V. S. (2015). Gender and personality. In M. Mikulincer & P. R. Shaver (Eds.), *APA handbook of personality and social psychology* (Vol. 4: Personality processes and individual differences, pp. 515–534.) American Psychological Association.
Helmreich, R. L., & Spence, J. T. (1978). The Work and Family Orientation Questionnaire: An objective instrument to assess components of achievement motivation and attitudes toward family and career. *JSAS Catalog of Selected Documents in Psychology, 8*, 35.
Helmreich, R. L, Spence, J. T., & Wilhelm, J. A. (1981). A psychometric analysis of the Personal Attributes Questionnaire. *Sex Roles, 7*, 1097–1108.
Helms, J. E. (2007). Some better practices for measuring racial and ethnic identity constructs. *Journal of Counseling Psychology, 54*, 235–246.
Hendrick, C., & Hendrick, S. S. (1986). A theory and method of love. *Journal of Personality and Social Psychology, 50*, 392–402.

Hendrick, C., Hendrick, S. S., & Dicke, A. (1998). The Love Attitudes Scale: Short form. *Journal of Social and Personal Relationships*, *15*, 147–159.

Hendrick, C., Hendrick, S., Foote, F. H., & Slapion–Foote, M. J (1984). Do men and women love differently? *Journal of Social and Personal Relationships*, *1*, 177–195.

Hepworth, J. X, & West, S. G. (1988). Lynchings and the economy: A time–series reanalysis of Hovland and Sears (1940). *Journal of Personality and Social Psychology*, *55*, 239–247.

Higgins E. T. (1987). Self–discrepancy: A theory relating self and affect. *Psychological Review*, 94, 319–340.

Hirsch, P. (2005). Apostle of freedom: Alfred Adler and his British disciples. *History of Education*, *34*, 473–481.

Hoffman, D. (2003). Sandor Ferenczi and the origins of humanistic psychology. *Journal of Humanistic Psychology*, *43*, 59–86.

Hoffman, L., Stewart, S., Warren, D. M., & Meek, L. (2015). Toward a sustainable myth of self: An existential response to the postmodern condition. In K. J. Schneider, J. F. Pierson, & J. F. T. Bugental (Eds.), *The handbook of humanistic psychology: Theory, research, and practice* (2nd ed., pp. 105–133). Sage.

Holmes, J. G. (2000). Social relationships: The nature and function of relational schemas. *European Journal of Social Psychology*, *30*, 447–495.

Holmes, J. G. (2002). Interpersonal expectations as the building blocks of social cognition: An interdependence theory perspective. *Personal Relationships*, *9*, 1–26.

Hopwood, C. J., & Waugh, M. H., eds. (2020). *Personality assessment paradigms and methods: A collaborative reassessment of Madeline* G. Routledge.

Horney, K. (1937). *The neurotic personality of our time*. Norton.

Horney, K. (1967). *Feminine psychology*. Norton. (Original work published 1922–37)

Hough, L. M., Oswald, F. L., & Ock, J. (2015). Beyond the Big Five: New directions for personality research and practice in organizations. *Annual Review of Organizational Psychology and Organizational Behavior*, *2*, 183–209.

Hovland, C., & Sears, R. R. (1940). Minor studies in aggression: Correlation of lynchings with economic indices. *Journal of Psychology*, *9*, 301–310.

Howard, J. A. (2000). Social psychology of identities. *Annual Review of Sociology*, *26*, 367–393.

Hull, C. (1943). *Principles of behavior*. Appleton-Century-Crofts.

Hull, C. L., Hovland, C. I., Ross, R. T., Hall, M., Perkins, D. T., & Fitch, F. B. (1940). *Mathematico-deductive theory of rote learning*. Yale University Press.

Ickes, W., Snyder, M., & Garcia, S. (1997). Personality influences on the choice of situations. In R. Hogan; J. Johnson; & S. Briggs. (Eds.), *Handbook of personality psychology* (pp. 165–195). Academic Press.

Innis, N. K. (1992). Tolman and Tryon: Early research on the inheritance of the ability to learn. *American Psychologist, 47*, 190–197.
Iscoe, I., Bloom, B. L., & Spielberger, C. D. (Eds.). (1977). *Community psychology in transition: Proceedings of the National Conference on Training in Community Psychology*. Hemisphere.
Jacobsen, B. (2007). What is happiness? The concept of happiness in existential psychology and therapy. *Existential Analysis, 18*, 39–50.
Jahoda, M. (1958). *Current concepts of positive mental health*. Basic Books.
James, W. (1902). *The varieties of religious experience*. Collins.
James, W. (2010). *The principles of psychology* (Vols. 1 & 2). Martino Publishing. (Original work published 1890)
Jamison, D. F. (2010). Fanon revisited: Exploring the relationship between African-centered psychology and Fanonian psychology. *The Journal of Pan African Studies, 3*, 179–193.
Joffe, P. E., & Naditch, M.P. (1977). Paper and pencil measures of coping and defense processes. In N. Haan (Ed.), *Coping and defending: Processes of self-environmental organization* (pp. 280–294). Academic Press.
John, O. P., Donahue, E. M., & Kentle, R. L. (1991). *The Big Five Inventory—Versions 4a and 5a*. University of California.
Jones, A. (2001). Absurdity and being-in-itself. The third phase of phenomenology: Jean-Paul Sartre and existential psychoanalysis. *Journal of Psychiatric and Mental Health Nursing, 8*, 367–372.
Jones, E. E. (1998). Major developments in five decades of social psychology. In D. T. Gilbert, S. T. Fiske, & G. Lindzey (Eds.), *The handbook of social psychology* (4th ed., Vol. 1, pp. 3–57). McGraw-Hill. (Original work published 1985)
Jones, J. M. (1972). *Prejudice and racism*. Addison-Wesley.
Jones, J. M. (1997). *Prejudice and racism* (2nd ed.). McGraw-Hill.
Jones, M. C. (1924a). A laboratory study of fear: The case of Peter. *The Pedagogical Seminary, 31*, 308–315.
Jones, M. C. (1924b). The elimination of children's fears. *Journal of Experimental Psychology, 7*, 382–392.
Joreskog, K. G., & Sorbom, D. (1979). *Advances in factor analysis and structural equation models*. Abt Books.
Jung, C. G. (1916). *Psychology of the unconscious: A study of the transformations and symbolisms of the libido, a contribution to the history of the evolution of thought*. Kegan Paul Trench Trubner. (Original work published 1912)
Jung, C. G. (1971). *Psychological types*. Routledge. (Original work published 1921)
Juni, S. (2009). Conceptualization of hostile psychopathy and sadism: Drive theory and object relations perspectives. *International Forum of Psychoanalysis, 18*, 11–22.

Karniol, R., & Ross, M. (1996). The motivational impact of temporal focus: Thinking about the future and the past. *Annual Review of Psychology, 47*, 593–620.

Kelley, H. H. (1979). *Personal relationships: Their structures and processes.* Erlbaum.

Kelley, H. H., Holmes, J. G., Kerr, N. L., Reis, H. T., Rusbult, C. E., & Van Lange, P. A. M. (2003). *An atlas of interpersonal situations.* Cambridge University Press. https://doi.org/10.1017/CBO9780511499845.

Kelley, H. H., & Thibaut, J. (1978). *Interpersonal relations: A theory of interdependence.* Wiley.

Kelly, G. A. (1955). *The psychology of personal constructs* (Vols 1 & 2). Norton.

Kenrick, D. T., Neuberg, S. L., & White, A. E. (2013). Relationships from an evolutionary life history perspective. In J. A. Simpson & L. Campbell (Eds.), *The Oxford handbook of close relationships* (pp. 13–38). Oxford University Press.

Kensit, D. A. (2000). Rogerian theory: A critique of the effectiveness of pure client-centred therapy. *Counselling Psychology Quarterly, 13*, 345–351.

Kernberg, P. F. (1994). Mechanisms of defense: Development and research perspectives. *Bulletin of the Menninger Clinic, 58*, 55–87.

Kihlstrom, J. F. (2004). Unity within psychology, and unity between science and practice. *Journal of Clinical Psychology, 60*, 1243–1247

Kihlstrom, J. F., & Harackiewicz, J. M. (1990). An evolutionary milestone in the psychology of personality. *Psychological Inquiry, 1*, 86–100.

Kim, J. O., & Mueller, C. W. (1978). *Factor analysis: Statistical methods and practical issues.* Sage.

Kirsch, I., Lynn, S. J., Vigorito, M., & Miller, R. R. (2004). The role of cognition in classical and operant conditioning. *Journal of Clinical Psychology, 60*, 369–392.

Kiser, S. (2007). Sacred dialectic: The centrality of paradox in the worldview of Rollo May. *The Humanistic Psychologist, 35*, 191–201.

Klein, M. (1927). Symposium on child analysis. *International Journal of Psychoanalysis, 8*, 339–391.

Kline, R. B. (2023). *Principles and practice of structural equation modeling* (5th ed.). Guilford.

Koffka, K. (1935). *Principles of Gestalt psychology.* Harcourt & Brace.

Koltko-Rivera, M. E. (2006). Rediscovering the later version of Maslow's hierarchy of needs: Self-transcendence and opportunities for theory, research, and unification. *Review of General Psychology, 10*, 302–317.

Kopelman, R. E., Rovenpor, J. L., & Guan, M. (2003). The Study of Values: Construction of the fourth edition. *Journal of Vocational Behavior, 62*(2), 203–220. https://doi.org/10.1016/S0001-8791(02)00047-7

Kornfeld, A. D. (1989). Mary Cover Jones and the Peter case: Social learning versus conditioning. *Journal of Anxiety Disorders, 3*, 187–195.

Kostromina, S. N., & Grishina, N. (2023). Psychology of changeability: Basic principles of description of processual nature of personality. *Integrative Psychological & Behavioral Science, 57*, 569–589.

Krauss, S.W. (2008). A tripartite model of idiographic research: Progressing past the concept of idiographic research as a singular entity. *Social Behavior and Personality, 36*, 1123–1140.

Kuper, N., Modersitzki, N., Phan, L. V., & Rauthmann, J. F. (2021). The dynamics, processes, mechanisms, and functioning of personality: An overview of the field. *British Journal of Psychology, 112*, 1–51.

Kwan, V. S. Y., & Herrmann, S. D. (2015). The interplay between culture and personality. In M. Mikulincer & P. R. Shaver (Eds.), *APA handbook of personality and social psychology* (Vol. 4: Personality processes and individual differences, pp. 553–574). American Psychological Association.

LaFromboise, T., Coleman, H. L. K., & Gerton, J. (1993). Psychological impact of biculturalism: Evidence and theory. *Psychological Bulletin, 114*(3), 395–412. https://doi.org/10.1037/0033-2909.114.3.395

Laing, R. D. (1960). *The divided self: An existential study in sanity and madness*. Penguin.

Layard, R., & De Neve, J.-E. (2023). *Wellbeing: Science and policy*. Cambridge University Press.

Leaf, J. B., Cihon, J. H., Ferguson, J. L., & Weinkauf, S. M. (2017). An introduction to Applied Behavior Analysis. In J. L. Matson (ed.), *Handbook of childhood psychopathology and developmental disabilities treatment* (pp. 25–42). Springer International.

Leaf, J. B., Cihon, J. H., Leaf, R., McEachin, J., Liu, N,. Russell, N., Unumb, L., Shapiro, S., & Khosrowshahi, D. (2022). Concerns about ABA-based intervention: An evaluation and recommendations. *Journal of Autism and Developmental Disorders, 52*, 2838–2853.

Leary, D. E. (2004). On the conceptual and linguistic activity of psychologists: The study of behaviour from the 1890s to the 1990s and beyond. *Behavior and Philosophy, 32*, 13–35.

Leary, T. (1957). *Interpersonal diagnosis of personality*. Ronald.

Lee, J. A. (1973). *Colours of love: An exploration of the ways of loving*. New Press.

Lee, J. A. (1976). Forbidden colors of love: Patterns of gay love and gay liberation. *Journal of Homosexuality, 1*, 401–418.

Lee, K., & Ashton, M. C. (2004). Psychometric properties of the HEXACO Personality Inventory. *Multivariate Behavioral Research, 39*, 329–358.

Lee, K., & Ashton, M. C. (2006). Further assessment of the HEXACO Personality Inventory: Two new facet scales and an observer report form. *Psychological Assessment, 18*, 182–191.

Lefcourt, H. M. (1991). Locus of control. In J. P. Robinson, P. R. Shaver, & L. S. Wrightsman (Eds.), *Measures of personality and social psychological attitudes* (pp. 413–499). Academic Press.

Lenney, E. (1991). Sex roles. In J. P. Robinson, & P. R. Shaver (Eds.), *Measures of personality and social psychological attitudes* (pp. 573–660). Academic Press.

LeUnes, A. (1983). Little Albert from the viewpoint of abnormal psychology textbook authors. *Teaching of Psychology, 10*, 230–231.

Levenson, H. (1973a). Multidimensional locus of control in psychiatric patients. *Journal of Consulting and Clinical Psychology, 41*, 397–404.

Levenson, H. (1973b). Reliability and validity of the I, P, and C scales: A multidimensional view of locus of control. In *Proceedings from the American Psychological Association Convention.*

Levenson, H. (1974). Activism and powerful others: Distinctions within the concept of internal–external control. *Journal of Personality Assessment, 38*, 377–383.

Levenson, H. (1981). Differentiating among internality, powerful others, and chance. In H. Lefcourt (Ed.), *Research with the Locus of Control Construct* (Vol. 1, pp. 15–63). Academic Press.

Levine, M., Perkins, D. D., & Perkins, D. V. (2005). *Principles of community psychology: Perspectives and applications* (3rd ed.). Oxford University Press.

Lewin, K. (1936). *Principles of topological psychology* (F. Heider & G. M. Heider, Trans.). McGraw-Hill. https://doi.org/10.1037/10019-000.

Lewis, O. (1959). *Five families: Mexican case studies in the culture of poverty.* Basic Books.

Lewis, O. (1966). *La Vida: A Puerto Rican family in the culture of poverty – San Juan and New York.* Alfred A. Knopf, Inc. and Random House, Inc.

Liu, Y., Fu, Q., & Fu, X. (2009). The interaction between cognition and emotion. *Chinese Science Bulletin, 54*, 4102–4116.

Lopez, M. H., Krogstad, J. M., & Passel, J. S. (2024). *Who is Hispanic?* Retrieved January 25, 2026, from https://www.pewresearch.org/short–reads/2024/09/12/who–is–hispanic/

Lorr, M., & McNair, D. M. (1963). An interpersonal behavior circle. *Journal of Abnormal and Social Psychology, 67*(1), 68–75. https://doi.org/10.1037/h0049326

Lorr, M., & McNair, D. M. (1965). Expansion of the interpersonal behavior circle. *Journal of Personality and Social Psychology, 2*, 823–830.

Lovaas, I. O. (1981). *Teaching developmentally disabled children: The me book.* University Park Press.

Lovaas, I. O. (1987). Behavioral treatment and normal educational and intellectual functioning in young autistic children. *Journal of Consulting and Clinical Psychology, 55*, 3–9.

Lubbe, T. (2008). A Kleinian theory of sexuality. *British Journal of Psychotherapy, 24*, 299–316.

Lucas, R. E., & Diener, E. (2015). Personality and subjective well–being: Current issues and controversies. In M. Mikulincer & P. R. Shaver

(Eds.), *APA handbook of personality and social psychology* (Vol. 4, pp. 577–599). American Psychological Association.

Lunt, R. (2010). *Mexicans; and United States Whites' commitment to familism and its relation with psychosocial adjustment: A cross national comparison.* Unpublished doctoral dissertation, University of Central Florida.

MacDonald, G. & Leary, M. R. (2012). Individual differences in self–esteem: A review and theoretical integration. In M. R. Leary & J. P. Tangney (Eds.), *Handbook of self and identity* (2nd ed., pp. 354–377). Guilford.

MacDonald, S. G. (2001). The real and the researchable: A brief review of the contribution of John Bowlby (1907–1990). *Perspectives in Psychiatric Care, 37*, 60–64.

Mackintosh, N. J. (1981). Tolman and modern conditioning theory. *British Journal of Psychology, 77*, 517–523.

Madowitz, J., & Boutelle, K. N. (2014). Ethical implications of using the term "non–White" in psychological research. *Ethics & Behavior, 24*, 306–310.

Magnusson. D., & Endler, N. S. (1977). *Personality at the crossroads*. Erlbaum.

Mahoney, M. J. (1993). Introduction to special section: Theoretical developments in the cognitive psychotherapies. *Journal of Consulting and Clinical Psychology, 61*, 187–193.

Maldonado-Torres, N. (2017). Frantz Fanon and the decolonial turn in psychology: From modern/colonial methods to the decolonial attitude. *South African Journal of Psychology, 47*, 432–441.

Malone, J. C. (2014). Did John B. Watson really "found" behaviorism? *The Behavior Analyst, 37*, 1–12.

Malone, J. C. (2016). E. R. Guthrie: A behaviorism for everyone. In D. Zilio & K. Carrara (Eds.). *Behaviorisms. Historical and conceptual issues* (Vol. 1, pp. 199–222). Nucleo Paradigma Press.

Malott, R. W. (2018). A science–based practitioner model. *Education and Treatment of Children, 41*, 371–384.

Mandin, P. (2007). The contribution of system and object–relation theories to an understanding of the therapeutic relationship in social work practice. *Journal of Social Work Practice, 21*, 149–162.

Mandler, G. (2002). Origins of the cognitive (r)evolution. *Journal of the History of the Behavioral Sciences, 38*, 339–353.

Marchland, B., ed. (1991). *Higher education and the practice of democratic politics: A political education reader.* Kettering Foundation.

Marcia, J. E. (1966). Development and validation of ego–identity status. *Journal of Personality and Social Psychology, 3*, 551–558.

Marcia, J. E. (1967). Ego identity status: Relationship to change in self–esteem, "general maladjustment", and authoritarianism. *Journal of Personality, 35*, 119–133.

Marcus-Newhall, A., Pedersen, W. C., Carlson, M., & Miller, N. (2000). Displaced aggression is alive and well: A meta-analytic review. *Journal of Personality and Social Psychology, 78*, 670–689.

Margolis, M. L. (1984). *Mothers and such: Views of American women and why they changed*. University of California Press.

Markey, P. M., & Markey, C. N. (2009). A brief assessment of the interpersonal circumplex: The IPIP–IPC. *Assessment, 16*, 352–361.

Markus, H. R. (2008). Pride, prejudice, and ambivalence: Toward a unified theory of race and ethnicity. *American Psychologist, 63*, 651–670.

Markus, H., & Zajonc, R. B. (1985). The cognitive perspective in social psychology. In G. Lindzey & E. Aronson (Eds.), *Handbook of social psychology* (3rd ed., pp. 137–229). Random House.

Maslow, A. H. (1954). *Motivation and personality*. Harper & Row.

Maslow, A. H. (1962). *Toward a psychology of being*. Van Nostrand.

Maslow, A. H. (1968). *Toward a psychology of being* (2nd ed). Van Nostrand Reinhold.

Maslow, A. H. (1969). The farther reaches of human nature. *Journal of Transpersonal Psychology, 1*(1), 1–9.

Massey, R. F. (1988). Adler's missing quadrant: Berne's solution. *Individual Psychology, 44*, 447–452.

Matson, J. (2009). Aggression and tantrums in children with autism: A review of behavioral treatments and maintaining variables. *Journal of Mental Health Research in Intellectual Disabilities, 2*, 169–187.

Matthews, G. (1997). Extraversion, emotion and performance: A cognitive-adaptive model. *Advances in Psychology, 124*, 399–442.

Matthews, G. (2013). Integrating biological and cognitive perspectives on personality and health: Commentary on Ferguson (2011). *Health Psychology Review, 7*, S75–S78.

Matthews, G. (2016). Traits, cognitive processes and adaptation: An elegy for Hans Eysenck's personality theory. *Personality and Individual Differences, 103*, 61–67.

Matthews, G. (2020a). Against consensus: Embracing the disunity of personality theory. *Personality and Individual Differences, 152*, Article 109535.

Matthews, G. (2020b). Cognitive processes and models. In P. J. Corr & G. Matthews (Eds.), *The Cambridge handbook of personality psychology* (pp. 295–315). Cambridge University Press.

Matthews, G., Deary, I. J., & Whiteman, M. C. (2003). *Personality traits* (2nd ed.). Cambridge University Press.

Matthews, G., & Gilliland, K. (1999). The personality theories of H. J. Eysenck and J. A. Gray: A comparative review. *Personality and Individual Differences, 26*, 583–626.

Matthews, G., & Gilliland, K. (2001). Personality, biology and cognitive science: A reply to Corr (2001). *Personality and Individual Differences, 30*(2), 353–362. https://doi.org/10.1016/S0191–8869(00)00029–5

May, R. (1953). *Man's search for himself.* Norton.

May, R. (1969). *Love and will.* Norton.

May, R. (1999). *Freedom and destiny.* Norton. (Original work published 1981)

McAdams, D. P. (1997). A conceptual history of personality psychology. In R. Hogan, J. Johnson, & S. R. Briggs (Eds.), *Handbook of Personality* (pp. 3–39). Academic Press.

McAdams, D. P., & Manczak, E. (2015). Personality and the life story. In M. Mikulincer & P. R. Shaver (Eds.), *APA handbook of personality and social psychology* (Vol. 4: Personality processes and individual differences, pp. 425–446). American Psychological Association.

McClelland, D. C. (1987). *Human motivation.* Cambridge University Press. (Original work published 1985)

McCrae, R. (2009). The Five–Factor Model of personality traits: Consensus and controversy. In P. J. Corr & G. Matthews (Eds.), *The Cambridge handbook of personality psychology* (pp. 148–161). Cambridge University Press.

McCrae, R. R. (2020). The five-factor model of personality: Consensus and controversy. In P. J. Corr & G. Matthews (Eds.), *The Cambridge handbook of personality psychology* (2nd ed., pp. 129–141). Cambridge University Press.

McCrae, R. R., & Costa, P. C., Jr. (1985). Using Norman's "adequacy taxonomy": Intelligence and personality dimensions in natural language and in questionnaires. *Journal of Personality and Social Psychology, 49*, 710–721.

McCrae, R. R., & Costa, P. T., Jr. (1986). Clinical assessment can benefit from recent advances in personality psychology. *American Psychologist, 41*, 1001–1003.

McCrae, R. R., & Costa, P. T., Jr. (1989). More reasons to adopt the Five–Factor Model. *American Psychologist, 44*, 451–452.

McCrae, R. R., & Costa, P. T., Jr. (1997). Personality trait structure as a human universal. *American Psychologist, 52*(5), 509–516. https://doi.org/10.1037/0003-066X.52.5.509

McCrae, R. R., & Costa, P. T., Jr. (2006). *Personality in adulthood: A five–factor theory perspective* (2nd ed.). Guilford Press. (Original work published 2003)

McDonald, M., & Wearing, S. (2013). A reconceptualisation of the self in humanistic psychology: Heidegger, Foucault and the sociocultural turn. *Journal of Phenomenological Psychology, 44*, 37–59.

McNulty, J. K. (2013). Personality and relationships. In J. A. Simpson & L. Campbell (Eds.), *The Oxford handbook of close relationships* (pp. 535–552). Oxford University Press.

Medina, M. (2008). Everyday courage: Living courageously without being a hero. *Existential Analysis, 19*, 280–299.

Mendoza, R. H., & Martinez, J. L., eds. (1984). *Chicano psychology* (2nd ed.). Academic Press.

Mendoza-Denton, R., Shoda, Y., Ayduk, O., & Mischel, W. (1999). Applying cognitive-affective processing system (CAPS) theory to cultural differences in social behavior. In W. L. Lonner, D. L. Dinnel, D. K. Forgays, & S. A. Hayes (Eds.), *Merging past, present, and future in cross-cultural psychology* (pp. 205–217). Swets & Zeitlinger.

Mikulincer, M., & Shaver, P. R. (2016). *Attachment in adulthood: Structure, dynamics, and change* (2nd ed.). Guilford.

Miller, A. L., Stern, C., & Neville, H. (2019). Forging diversity-science-informed guidelines for research on race and racism in psychological science. *Journal of Social Issues, 75*, 1240–1261.

Miller, N. E., & Dollard, J. (1941). *Social learning and imitation.* Yale University Press.

Millon, T. (1996). *Disorders of personality: DSM-IV and beyond.* Wiley.

Mischel, W. (1968). *Personality and assessment.* Wiley.

Mischel, W. (1973). Toward a cognitive social learning reconceptualization of personality. *Psychological Review, 80*, 252–283.

Mischel, W. (2004). Toward an integrative science of the person. *Annual Review of Psychology, 55*, 1–22

Mischel, W. (2009). From *Personality and Assessment* (1968) to personality science, 2009. *Journal of Research in Personality, 43*, 282–290.

Mischel, W., & Shoda, Y. (1995). A cognitive–affective system theory of personality: Reconceptualizing situations, dispositions, dynamics, and invariance in personality structure. *Psychological Review, 102*, 246–268.

Mitchell, R. L. C., & Kumari, V. (2016). Hans Eysenck's interface between the brain and personality: Modern evidence on the cognitive neuroscience of personality. *Personality and Individual Differences, 103*, 74–81.

Molouki, S., & Pronin, E. (2015). Self and other. In M. Mikullincer & P. R. Shaver (Eds.), *APA handbook of personality and social psychology* (Vol.1: Attitudes and social cognition, pp. 387–414). American Psychological Association.

Montag, C., & Panksepp, J. (2017). Primary emotional systems and personality: An evolutionary perspective. *Frontiers in Psychology, 8*, Article 464.

Montuori, A., & Purser, R. (2015). Humanistic psychology in the workplace. In K. J. Schneider, J. F. Pierson, & J. F. T. Bugental (Eds.), *The handbook of humanistic psychology: Theory, research, and practice* (2nd ed., pp. 723–734). Sage.

Moore, J. (2013). Sketch: Three views of behaviorism. *Psychological Record, 63*, 681–692.

Mora, L., & Lopez, M. H. (2023). *Latinos' views of and experiences with the Spanish language.* Retrieved January 25, 2026, from https://www.pewresearch.org/wp–content/uploads/sites/20/2023/09/RE_2023.09.20_Latinos–Speaking–Spanish_Report.pdf

Morf, C. C. & Mischel, W. (2012). The self as a psycho-social dynamic processing system: Toward a converging science of self-hood. In M. R. Leary & J. P. Tangney (Eds.), *Handbook of self and identity* (2nd ed., pp. 21–49). Guilford.

Morgan, C. D., & Murray, H. A. (1935). A method for investigating fantasies. *Archives of Neurological Psychiatry, 34*, 289–306.

Morris, E. K., Smith, N. G., & Altus, D. E. (2005). B. F. Skinner's contributions to applied behavior analysis. *The Behavior Analyst, 28*, 99–131.

Moslimani, M., & Mukherjee, S. (2024). *Half of Latinas say Hispanic women's situation has improved in the past decade and expect more gains.* Retrieved January 25, 2026, from https://www.pewresearch.org/wp–content/uploads/sites/20/2024/05/RE_2024.05.15_Latinas–Gains_REPORT.pdf

Moss, D. (2015). The roots and genealogy of humanistic psychology. In K. J. Schneider, J. F. Pierson, & J. F. T. Bugental (Eds.), *The handbook of humanistic psychology: Theory, research, and practice* (2nd ed., pp. 3–18). Sage.

Munafo, M. R. (2009). Behavioural genetics: From variance to DNA. In P. J. Corr & G. Matthews (Eds), *The Cambridge handbook of personality psychology* (pp. 287–304). Cambridge University Press.

Murray, H. A. (1938). *Explorations in personality.* Oxford University Press.

Mussen, P., & Eichorn, D. (1988). Mary Cover Jones (1896–1987). *American Psychologist, 43*, 818.

Myers, D. G., & Diener, E. (1995). Who is happy? *Psychological Science, 6*, 10–19.

Myers, D. G., & Diener, E. (2018). The scientific pursuit of happiness. *Perspectives on Psychological Science, 13*, 218–225.

Myers, I. B. (1962). *The Myers-Briggs Type Indicator: Manual.* Consulting Psychologists Press.

Neary, R. S., & Zuckerman, M. (1976). Sensation seeking, trait and state anxiety, and the electrodermal orienting reflex. *Psychophysiology, 13*, 205–211.

Nisbet, R. A. (1953). *The quest for community: A study in the ethics of order and freedom.* Oxford University Press.

Nisbet, R. A. (1962). *Community and power.* Oxford University Press.

Nisbet, R. A. (1968). *Tradition and revolt: Historical and sociological essays.* Random House.

Nisbet, R. A. (1970). *The social bond: An introduction to the study of society.* Alfred A. Knopf.

Nisbet, R. A. (1975). *Twilight of authority.* Oxford University Press.

Nisbet, R. A. (1986). *Conservatism: Dream and reality.* University of Minnesota Press.

Nisbet, R. A. (1988). *The present age: Progress and anarchy in modern America.* World Press.

Noppeney, U. (2001). Kurt Goldstein – a philosophical scientist. *Journal of the History of the Neurosciences, 10*, 67–78.

Nunnally, J. C., & Bernstein, I. H. (1994). *Psychometric theory* (3rd ed.). McGraw-Hill.

O'Connell, A. N. (1980). Karen Horney: Theorist in psychoanalysis and feminine psychology. *Psychology of Women Quarterly, 5*, 81–93.

O'Dell, J. W. (1978). *Letters from Jenny* revisited: The computer content analysis redone. *Journal of Clinical Psychology, 34*, 161–164.

Okon–Singer, H., Hendler, T., Pessoa, L., & Shackman, A. J. (2015). The neurobiology of emotion–cognition interactions: Fundamental questions and strategies for future research. *Frontiers in Human Neuroscience, 9*, Article 58.

Oles, P. K., & Hermans, H. (2010). Allport-Vernon Study of Values. In I. B. Weiner & W. E. Craighead (Eds.), *The Corsini Encyclopedia of Psychology* (pp. 67–68). John Wiley & Sons, Inc. https://doi.org/10.1002/9780470479216.corpsy0038

Omar, S. M. (2009). Fanon in Algeria: A case of horizontal (post)-colonial encounter? *Journal of Transatlantic Studies, 7*, 264–278.

Ormond, J. E. (2008). *Beyond Thorndike, Pavlov, and Skinner: Other early behaviorist theorists.* [Supplementary reading in the companion website accompanying *Human Learning*, 5th ed.] Merrill/Prentice Hall.

Orom, H., & Cervone, D. (2009). Personality dynamics, meaning, and idiosyncrasy: Identifying cross-situational coherence by assessing personality architecture. *Journal of Research in Personality, 43*, 228–240.

Oyserman, D., Coon, H. M., & Kemmelmeier, M. (2002a). Rethinking individualism and collectivism: Evaluation of theoretical assumptions and meta-analyses. *Psychological Bulletin, 128*(1), 3–72. https://doi.org/10.1037/0033-2909.128.1.3

Oyserman, D., Kemmelmeier, M., & Coon, H. M. (2002b). Cultural psychology, a new look: Reply to Bond (2002), Fiske (2002), Kitayama (2002), and Miller (2002). *Psychological Bulletin, 128*(1), 110–117. https://doi.org/10.1037/0033-2909.128.1.110

Ozer, D. J., & Reise, S. P. (1994). Personality assessment. *Annual Review of Psychology, 45*, 357–388.

Paunonen, S. V., & Hong, R. Y. (2015). On the properties of personality traits. In M. Mikulincer & P. R. Shaver (Eds.), *APA handbook of personality and social psychology* (Vol. 4: Personality processes and individual differences, pp. 233–259). American Psychological Association.

Pavlov, I. P. (1927). *Conditioned reflexes: An investigation of the physiological activity of the cerebral cortex.* Routledge and Kegan Paul.

Pavlov, I. P. (1928). *Lectures on conditioned reflexes: Twenty–five years of objective study of the higher nervous system*. International Publishers. (Original work published 1926)

Pavlov, I. P. (1932). The reply of a physiologist to psychologists. *Psychological Review, 39*, 91–127.

Pearce, R. (2011). On being a person: Sartre's contribution to psychotherapy. *Existential Analysis, 22*, 83–95.

Pedersen, W. D., Putcha–Bhagavatula, A., & Miller, L. C. (2011). Are men and women really that different? Some of sexual strategy theory's (SST) key assumptions about sex-distinct mating mechanisms. *Sex Roles, 64*, 629–643.

Peluso, P. R., Peluso, J., P., White, J., & Kern, R. M. (2004). A comparison of attachment theory and individual psychology: A review of the literature. *Journal of Counseling & Development, 82*, 139–145.

Perugini, M., Costantini, G., Hughes, S., & de Houwer, J. (2016). A functional perspective on personality. *International Journal of Psychology, 51*, 33–39.

Perugini, M., Richetin, J., & Costantini, G. (2020). Personality and the unconscious. In P. J. Corr & G. Matthews (Eds.), *The Cambridge handbook of personality psychology* (2nd ed., pp. 69–80). Cambridge University Press. https://doi.org/10.1017/9781108264822.008

Peterson, C., & Seligman, M. E. P. (2004). *Character strengths and virtues: A handbook and classification*. Oxford University Press.

Petty, R. E., & Brinol, P. (2015). Processes of social influence through attitude change. In M. Mikullincer & P. R. Shaver (Eds.), *APA handbook of personality and social psychology* (Vol.1: Attitudes and social cognition, pp. 509–545). American Psychological Association.

Phinney, J. S. (1990). Ethnic identity in adolescents and adults: A review of research. *Psychological Bulletin, 108*, 499–514.

Phinney, J. S. (1992). The Multigroup Ethnic Identity Measure: A new scale for use with adolescents and young adults from diverse groups. *Journal of Adolescent Research, 7*, 156–176.

Phinney, J. S. (1996). When we talk about American ethnic groups, what do we mean? *American Psychologist, 51*(9), 918–927. https://doi.org/10.1037/0003-066X.51.9.918

Phinney, J. S., Horenczyk, G., Liebkind, K., & Vedder, P. (2001). Ethnic identity, immigration, and well-being: An interactional perspective. *Journal of Social Issues, 57*(3), 493–510. https://doi.org/10.1111/0022-4537.00225

Phinney, J. S., & Ong, A. D. (2007). Conceptualization and measurement of ethnic identity: Current status and future directions. *Journal of Counseling Psychology, 54*, 271–281.

Pickering, A. D., Cooper, A. J., Smillie, L. D., & Corr, P. J. (2013). On the shoulders of giants. *The Psychologist, 26*(1), 22–25.

Pietikainen, P. (2019). Abnormal psychology. In R. J. Sternberg & W. E. Pickren (Eds.), *The Cambridge handbook of the intellectual history of psychology* (pp. 441–467). Cambridge University Press.

Pina, G., & Martinez, G. (2025). *Key facts about U.S. Latinos.* Retrieved January 25, 2026, from https://www.pewresearch.org/short–reads/2025/10/22/key–facts–about–us–latinos/#the–share–of–u–s–hispanics–who–speak–english–proficiently–is–growing

Piper, W. E., Debbane, E. G., Bienvenu, J. P., & Garant, J. (1984). A comparative study of four forms of psychotherapy. *Journal of Consulting and Clinical Psychology, 52*, 268–279.

Pitchford, D. B. (2009). The existentialism of Rollo May: An influence on trauma treatment. *Journal of Humanistic Psychology, 49*, 441–461.

Poll, J. B., & Smith, T. B. (2003). The spiritual self: Toward a conceptualization of spiritual identity development. *Journal of Psychology and Theology, 31*, 129–142.

Popkewitz, T. S. (2011). Curriculum history, schooling and the history of the present. *History of Education, 40*, 1–19.

Posner, M. I. (2019). Attention: Awareness and control. In R. J. Sternberg & W. E. Pickren (Eds.), *The Cambridge handbook of the intellectual history of psychology* (pp. 111–134). Cambridge University Press.

Prado de Oliviera, L. E. (2001). The nature of the transference between Anna Freud and Melanie Klein: Learning from the controversies. *International Forum of Psychoanalysis, 10*, 247–258.

Puhakka, K. (2000). Beyond reflection: Loss and transformation of self. *The Humanistic Psychologist, 28*, 334–342.

Qizilbash, M. (1998). The concept of well-being. *Economics and Philosophy, 14*(1), 51–73. Doi:10.1017/S0266267100004934.

Raad, B. D., & Barelds, D. P. H. (2020). Models of personality structure. In P. J. Corr & G. Matthews (Eds.), *The Cambridge handbook of personality psychology* (pp. 115–128). Cambridge University Press.

Ramirez, M., III (1983). *Psychology of the Americas: Mestizo perspectives on personality and mental health*. Pergamon Press.

Ramirez, M., III (1984). Assessing and understanding biculturalism–multiculturalism in Mexican-American adults. In J. L. Martinez & R. H. Mendoza (Eds.), *Chicano psychology* (2nd ed., pp. 77–94). Springer–Verlag.

Ramirez, M., III. (1991). *Psychotherapy and counseling with minorities: A cognitive approach to individual and cultural differences*. Pergamon Press.

Ramirez, M., III (1998). *Multicultural/multiracial psychology: Mestizo perspectives on personality and mental health*. Jason Aronson Inc.

Ramirez, M., III (2004). Mestiza/o and Chicana/o psychology: Theory, research, and application. In R. J. Velasquez, L. M. Arellano, & B. W. McNeill (Eds.), *The handbook of Chicana/o psychology and mental health* (pp. 3–21). Erlbaum.

Ramirez, M., III. (2017). *Multicultural psychotherapy: An approach to individual and cultural differences.* Allyn and Bacon. (Original work published 1999)

Ramirez, M., III, & Carrasco, N. (1996). *Revision of the Family Attitude Scale.* Unpublished manuscript, University of Texas at Austin.

Ramirez M., III, & Castaneda, A. (1974). *Cultural democracy, bicognitive development and education.* Academic Press.

Ramirez, M., III., & Doell, S. R. (1982). *The Traditionalism–Modernist Inventory.* Unpublished manuscript, University of Texas at Austin.

Ramirez, M., III., Doell, S. R., Rodriguez, N. (n.d.). *Revised Traditionalism–Modernist Inventory.* Unpublished manuscript, University of Texas at Austin.

Ramirez, M., III, & Price–Williams, D. (1971). *The relationship of culture to educational attainment.* Center for Research in Social Change and Economic Development, Rice University.

Rappaport, J. (1977). *Community psychology: Values, research, and action.* Holt, Rinehart and Winston.

Readsura Decolonial Editorial Collective (in random order: Ratele, K., Reddy, G., Adams, G., & Suffla, S. (2022) Decoloniality as a social issue for psychological study. *Journal of Social Issues, 78*, 7–26.

Reed, E. S., & Gaines, S. O., Jr. (1997). Not everyone is "different–from–me": Toward an historico-cultural account of prejudice. *Journal of Black Psychology, 23*, 245–274.

Reich, S. M., Riemer, M., Prilleltensky, I., & Montero, M. (Eds.). (2007). *International community psychology: History and theories.* Springer Science + Business Media. https://doi.org/10.1007/978–0–387–49500–2

Reis, H. T. (2007). Steps toward the ripening of relationship science. *Personal Relationships, 14*(1), 1–23. https://doi.org/10.1111/j.1475-6811.2006.00139.x.

Reis, H. T., Capobianco, A., & Tsai, F.-F. (2002). Finding the person in personal relationships. *Journal of Personality, 70*(6), 813–850. 10.1111/1467-6494.05025.

Reis, H. T., Sheldon, K. M., Gable, S. L., Roscoe, J., & Ryan, R. M. (2000). Daily well–being: The role of autonomy, competence, and relatedness. *Personality and Social Psychology Bulletin, 26*(4), 419–435. https://doi.org/10.1177/0146167200266002

Reisenzein, R., Hildebrandt, A., & Weber, H. (2020). Personality and emotion. In P. J. Corr & G. Matthews (Eds.), *The Cambridge handbook of personality psychology* (2nd ed., pp. 81–99). Cambridge University Press.

Rendon, M. (2008). The vicissitudes of affect in Horney's theory. *International Review of Psychoanalysis*, *17*, 158–168.

Richeson, J. A., Rucker, J. M., & Brown, X. (2025) Race and racism. In D. T. Gilbert, S. T. Fiske, & W. B. Mendes (Eds.), *The handbook of social psychology* (6th ed.). Situational Press. https://doi.org/10.70400/AZGB1537

Ridgeway, D., & Hare, R. D. (1981). Sensation seeking and psychophysiological responses to auditory stimulation. *Psychophysiology*, *18*, 613–618.

Rilling, M. (2000). John Watson's paradoxical struggle to explain Freud. *American Psychologist*, *55*, 301–312.

Roberts, R., Phinney, J., Masse, L., Chen, Y., Roberts, C., & Romero, A. (1999). The structure of ethnic identity in young adolescents from diverse ethnocultural groups. *Journal of Early Adolescence*, *19*, 301–322.

Robins, R. W., & John, O. P. (1997). The quest for self-insight: Theory and research on accuracy and bias in self-perception. In R. Hogan, J. A. Johnson, & S. R. Briggs (Eds.), *Handbook of personality psychology* (pp. 649–679). Academic Press.

Robinson, M. D., & Sedikides, C. (2009). Traits and the self: Toward an integration. In P. J. Corr & G. Matthews (Eds.), *The Cambridge handbook of personality psychology* (pp. 457–472). Cambridge University Press.

Robinson, T. N., Jr., & Zahn, T. P. (1983). Sensation seeking, state anxiety and cardiac and EDR orienting reactions. *Psychophysiology*, *20*, 465.

Rogers, C. R. (1951). *Client-centered therapy: Its current practice, implications and theory.* Constable.

Rogers, C. R. (1959). A theory of therapy, personality, and interpersonal relationships as developed in the client-centered framework. In S. Koch (Ed.), *Psychology: A study of a science* (Vol. 3, pp. 184–256). McGraw-Hill.

Rogers, C. R. (1961). *On becoming a person: A therapist's view of psychotherapy.* Constable.

Rosenberg, M. (1965). *Society and the adolescent self-image.* Princeton University Press.

Rosenberg, M. (1989). *Society and the adolescent self-image* (rev. ed.). Princeton University Press.

Ross, L., Lepper, M., & Ward, A. (2010). History of social psychology: Insights, challenges, and contributions to theory and applications. In S. T. Fiske, D. T. Gilbert, & G. Lindzey (Eds.), *Handbook of social psychology* (5th ed., Vol. 1, pp. 3–50). John Wiley & Sons, Inc.

Rotter, J. B. (1954). *Social learning and clinical psychology.* Prentice-Hall.

Rotter, J. B. (1966). Generalized expectancies for internal versus external control of reinforcement. *Psychological Monographs, 80* (1, Whole No. 609).

Rotter, J. B. (1975). Some problems and misconceptions related to the construct of internal versus external control of reinforcement. *Journal of Consulting and Clinical Psychology*, *48*, 56–67.

Rowe, D. C. (1997). Genetics, temperament, and personality. In R. Hogan, J. Johnson, & S. Briggs (Eds.), *Handbook of personality psychology* (pp. 367–386). Academic Press.

Rusbridger, R. (2012). Affects in Melanie Klein. *International Journal of Psychoanalysis, 93*, 139–150.

Rusbult, C. E., & Van Lange, P. A. M. (2003). Interdependence, interaction and relationships. *Annual Review of Psychology, 54*, 351–375. https://doi.org/10.1146/annurev.psych.54.101601.145059

Rusbult, C., Verette, J., Whitney, G., Slovik, L., & Lipkus, I. (1991). Accommodation processes in close relationships: Theory and preliminary evidence. *Journal of Personality and Social Psychology, 60*, 53–78.

Rutter, M., & Silberg, J. (2002). Gene–environment interplay in relation to emotional and behavioral disturbance. *Annual Review of Psychology, 53*, 463–490.

Ryan, R. M., Bradshaw, E. L., & Deci, E. L. (2019). Motivation. In R. J. Sternberg & W. E. Pickren (Eds.), *The Cambridge handbook of the intellectual history of psychology* (pp. 391–411). Cambridge University Press.

Ryan, R. M., & Deci, E. L. (2000a). Self–determination theory and the facilitation of intrinsic motivation, social development, and well–being. *American Psychologist, 55*, 68–78.

Ryan, R. M., & Deci, E. L. (2000b). The darker and brighter sides of human existence: Basic psychological needs as a unifying concept. *Psychological Inquiry, 11*, 319–338.

Ryan, R. M., & Deci, E. L. (2001). On happiness and human potentials: A review of research on hedonic and eudaimonic well-being. *Annual Review of Psychology, 52*, 141–166.

Ryan, R. M., & Frederick, C. (1997). On energy, personality, and health: Subjective vitality as a dynamic reflection of well-being. *Journal of Personality, 65*, 529–565.

Ryff, C. D. (1989). Happiness is everything, or is it? Explorations on the meaning of psychological well-being. *Journal of Personality and Social Psychology, 57*, 1069–1081.

Ryff, C. D. (1995). Psychological well–being in adult life. *Current Directions in Psychological Science, 4*, 99–104.

Ryff, C. D., & Keyes, C. L. M. (1995). The structure of psychological well–being revisited. *Journal of Personality and Social Psychology, 69*, 719–727.

Ryff, C. D., & Singer, B. (1998a). Human health: New directions for the next millennium. *Psychological Inquiry, 9*, 69–85.

Ryff, C. D., & Singer, R. (1998b). The contours of positive mental health. *Psychological Inquiry, 9*, 1–28.

Ryff, C. D., & Singer, B. (2008). Know thyself and become what you are: A eudaimonic approach to psychological well-being. *Journal of Happiness Studies, 9*, 13–39.

Sabogal, F., Marín, G., Otero-Sabogal, R., VanOss Marín, B., & Pérez-Stable, E. J. (1987). Hispanic familism and acculturation: What changes and what doesn't? *Hispanic Journal of Behavioral Sciences*, *9*(4), 397–412.

Salzinger, K. (2008). Skinner's *Verbal Behavior. International Journal of Psychology and Psychological Therapy*, *8*, 287–294.

Sanches de Oliviera, G., & Baggs, E. (2023). *Psychology's WEIRD problems.* Cambridge University Press.

Sanchez, G. I. (1932). Group differences and Spanish-speaking children – a critical review. *Journal of Applied Psychology*, *16*(5), 549–558. https://doi.org/10.1037/h0072844

Sandoval-Norton, A. H., & Shkedy, G. (2019). How much compliance is too much compliance: Is long-term ABA therapy abuse? *Cogent Psychology*, *6*, e1641258.

Sappington, A. A. (1989). The Third Force and the psychology of effective functioning. *The Humanistic Psychologist*, *17*, 56–63.

Sartre, J.-P. (1956). *Being and nothingness: An essay on phenomenological ontology.* Routledge. (Original work published 1943)

Sartre, J.-P. (1996). *Existential psychoanalysis.* Gateway Editions. (Original work published 1953)

Saville, P., & Blinkhorn, S. (1981). Reliability, homogeneity and the construct validity of Cattell's 16 Personality Factor Questionnaire (16PF). *Personality and Individual Differences*, *2*, 325–333.

Schellenberg, J. A. (1978). *Masters of social psychology.* Oxford University Press.

Schneider, K. J. (2011a). Humanistic psychology's chief task: To reset psychology on its rightful existential–humanistic base. *Journal of Humanistic Psychology*, *51*, 436–438.

Schneider, K. J. (2011b). Toward a humanistic positive psychology: Why can't we just get along? *Existential Analysis*, *22*, 32–38.

Schneider, K. J. (2015). Rediscovering awe: A new front in humanistic psychology, psychotherapy, and society. In K. J. Schneider, J. F. Pierson, & J. F. T. Bugental (Eds.), *The handbook of humanistic psychology: Theory, research, and practice* (2nd ed., pp. 73–81). Sage.

Schuerger, J. M., Zarella, K. L., & Hotz, A. S. (1989). Factors that influence the temporal stability of personality by questionnaire. *Journal of Personality and Social Psychology*, *56*, 777–783.

Schunk, D. H. (1991). Self-efficacy and academic motivation. *Educational Psychologist*, *26*, 207–231.

Seligman, M., & Csikszentmihalyi, M. (2000). Positive psychology: An introduction. *American Psychologist*, *55*, 5–14.

Sellers, R. M., Rowley, S. A. J., Chavois, T. M., Shelton, J. N., & Smith, M. A. (1997). Multidimensional Inventory of Black Identity: A preliminary investigation of reliability and construct validity. *Journal of Personality and Social Psychology, 73*, 805–815.

Sellers, R. M., Smith, M. A., Shelton, J. N., Rowley, S. A. J., & Chavous, T. M. (1998). Multidimensional model of racial identity: A reconceptualization of African American racial identity. *Personality & Social Psychology Review, 2*, 18–39.

Shadel, W. G., Cervone, D., Niaura, R., & Abrams, D. B. (2004). Developing an integrative social–cognitive strategy for personality assessment at the level of the individual: An illustration with regular cigarette smokers. *Journal of Research in Personality, 38*, 394–419.

Sheehy, N. (2004). *Fifty key thinkers in psychology*. Routledge.

Sheffield, S. (1959). Edwin Ray Guthrie: 1886–1959. *American Journal of Psychology, 72*, 642.

Sheldon, K. M., & Schuler, J. (2015). Agency and its discontents: A two–process perspective on basic psychological needs and motives. In M. Mikulincer & P. R. Shaver (Eds.), *APA handbook of personality and social psychology* (Vol. 4: Personality processes and individual differences, pp. 167–187). American Psychological Association.

Shiner, R. L. (2015). The development of temperament and personality traits in childhood and adolescence. In M. Mikulincer & P. R. Shaver (Eds.), *APA handbook of personality and social psychology* (Vol. 4: Personality processes and individual differences, pp. 85–105). American Psychological Association.

Shiner, R. L., Buss, K. A., McClowry, S. G., Putnam, S. P., Saudino, K. J., & Zentner, M. (2012). What is temperament now? Assessing progress in temperament research on the twenty-fifth anniversary of Goldsmith et al. (1987). *Child Development Perspectives, 6*, 436–444.

Shostrom, E. (1964). An inventory for the measurement of self–actualization. *Educational and Psychological Measurement, 24*, 207–218.

Shostrom, E. L. (1974). *POI manual*. EdITS/Educational and Industrial Testing Service.

Shostrom, E. L. (1975). *Personal Orientation Dimensions*. EdITS/Educational and Industrial Testing Service.

Shweder, R. A., & Sullivan, M. A. (1993). Cultural psychology: Who needs it? *Annual Review of Psychology, 44*, 497–523. https://doi.org/10.1146/annurev.ps.44.020193.002433

Silvia, P. J., & Eddington, K. M. (2012). Self and emotion. In M. R. Leary & J. P. Tangney (Eds.), *Handbook of self and identity* (2nd ed., pp. 425–445). New York: Guilford Press.

Simpson, J. A., & Campbell, L. (2013a) The blossoming of relationship science. In J. A. Simpson and L. Campbell (Eds.), *The Oxford handbook of close relationships* (online ed.). Retrieved on March 3, 2026, from https://doi.org/10.1093/oxfordhb/9780195398694.013.0001

Simpson, J. A., & Campbell, L. (2013b). The waving of the relationship flag. In J. A. Simpson and L. Campbell (Eds.), *The Oxford handbook of close relationships* (online ed.). Retrieved on March 3, 2026, from https://doi.org/10.1093/oxfordhb/9780195398694.013.0001

Skinner, B. F. (1938). *The behaviour of organisms: An experimental analysis*. D. Appleton Century Company.

Skinner, B. F. (1950). Are theories of learning necessary? *Psychological Review*, *57*, 193–216.

Skinner, B. F. (1957). *Verbal behavior*. Appleton–Century–Crofts.

Skinner, B. F. (1974). *About behaviorism*. Knopf.

Skinner, B. F (1976). *Walden two*. Macmillan. (Original work published 1948)

Sleeth, D. B. (2006). The self and the integral interface: Toward a new understanding of the whole person. *The Humanistic Psychologist*, *34*, 243–261.

Slife, B. D., & Barnard, S. (1988). Existential and cognitive psychology: Contrasting views of consciousness. *Journal of Humanistic Psychology*, *28*, 119–136.

Smiler, A. P. (2011). Sexual strategies theory: Built for the short term or the long term? *Sex Roles*, *64*, 603–612.

Smith, G. M. (1967). Usefulness of peer ratings of personality in education research. *Educational and Psychological Measurement*, *27*, 967–984.

Smith, G. T., & Guller, L. (2015). Psychological underpinnings to impulsive behavior. In M. Mikulincer & P. R. Shaver (Eds.), *APA handbook of personality and social psychology* (Vol. 4: Personality processes and individual differences, pp. 329–350). American Psychological Association.

Smith, T. H., & Eikeseth, S. (2011). O. Ivar Lovaas: Pioneer of Applied Behavior Analysis and intervention for children with autism. *Journal of Autism and Developmental Disorders*, *41*, 375–378.

Snyder, M., & Cantor, M. (1998). Understanding personality and social behavior: A functionalist strategy. In D. T. Gilbert, S. T. Fiske., & G. Lindzey (Eds.), *The handbook of social psychology* (4th ed., Vol. 1, pp. 635–679). McGraw-Hill.

Snyder, M., & Ickes, W. (1985). Personality and social behavior. In G. Lindzey and E. Aronson (Eds.), *Handbook of social psychology* (3rd ed., Vol. 2, pp. 883–947). Random House.

Snyder, P. J., Kaufman, R., Harrison, J., & Maruff, P. (2010). Charles Darwin's emotional expression "experiment" and his contribution to modern neuropharmacology. *Journal of the History of the Neurosciences*, *19*, 158–170.

Soto, C. J., & John, O. P. (2017a). Short and extra–short forms of the Big Five Inventory–2: The BFI–2–S and BFI–2–XS. *Journal of Research in Personality*, *68*, 69–81. https://doi.org/10.1016/j.jrp.2017.02.004

Soto, C. J., & John, O. P. (2017b). The next Big Five Inventory (BFI–2): Developing and assessing a hierarchical model with 15 facets to enhance bandwidth, fidelity, and predictive power. *Journal of Personality and Social Psychology, 113*, 117–143.

Spence, J. T. (1985). Gender identity and its implications for the concepts of masculinity and femininity. In T. B. Sonderegger (Ed.), *Nebraska Symposium on Motivation 1984* (pp. 59–95). University of Nebraska Press.

Spence, J. T. (1993). Gender–related traits and gender ideology: Evidence for a multifactorial theory. *Journal of Personality and Social Psychology, 64*, 624–635.

Spence, J. T., Deaux, K., & Helmreich, R. L. (1985). Sex roles in contemporary society. In G. Lindzey & E. Aronson (Eds.), *Handbook of social psychology* (3rd ed., pp. 149–178). Random House.

Spence, J. T., & Helmreich, R. L. (1978). *Masculinity and femininity*: University of Texas Press.

Spence, J. T., Helmreich, R. L., & Holahan, C. K. (1979). Negative and positive components of psychological masculinity and femininity, and their relationship to self-reports of neuroticism and acting out behavior. *Journal of Personality and Social Psychology, 37*, 1673–1682.

Spence, J. T., Helmreich, R. L., & Sawin, L. L. (1980). The Male–Female Relations Questionnaire: A self-report inventory of sex role behaviors and preferences and its relationships to masculine and feminine personality traits, sex role attitudes, and other measures. *JSAS Catalog of Selected Documents in Psychology, 10*, 87.

Spence, J. T., Helmreich, R., & Stapp, J. (1973). A short version of the Attitudes toward Women Scale (AWS). *Bulletin of the Psychonomic Society, 2*, 219–220.

Spence, J. T., Helmreich, R., & Stapp, J. (1974). The Personal Attributes Questionnaire: A measure of sex role stereotypes and masculinity–femininity. *JSAS Catalog of Selected Documents in Psychology, 4*, 43–44.

Spence, K. W. (1956). *Behavior theory and conditioning*. Yale University Press.

Spranger, E. (1928). *Types of men. The psychology and ethics of personality.* Niemeyer.

Stagner, R. (1937). *Psychology of personality*. McGraw–Hill.

Stagner, R. (1948). *Psychology of personality* (2nd ed.). McGraw–Hill.

Stagner, R. (1961). *Psychology of personality* (3rd ed.). McGraw–Hill.

Stagner, R. (1974). *Psychology of personality* (4th ed.). McGraw–Hill.

Staudinger, U. M. (2020). The positive plasticity of adult development: Potential for the 21st century. *American Psychologist, 75*, 540–553.

Steele, H., & Steele, M. (1998). Attachment and psychoanalysis: Time for a reunion. *Social Development, 7*, 92–119.

Stevens, R. (2008). *Sigmund Freud: Examining the essence of his contribution.* Palgrave.

Still, A. (1986). E. C. Tolman: A centenary symposium. *British Journal of Psychology, 77*, 513–515.

Stone, B. L. (2000). *Robert Nisbet: Communitarian traditionalist.* ISI Books.

Strickland, B. R. (1989). Internal–external control expectancies: From contingency to creativity. *American Psychologist, 44,* 1–12.

Sullivan, H. S. (1953). *The interpersonal theory of psychiatry.* Norton.

Sullivan, H. S. (1954). *The psychiatric interview.* Norton.

Sullivan, H. S. (1966). *Conceptions of modern psychiatry.* Norton. (Original work published 1947)

Swann, W. B., Jr. (1983). Self–verification: Bringing social reality into harmony with the self. In J. Suls & A. G. Greenwald (Eds.), *Psychological perspectives on the self* (Vol. 2, pp. 33–66). Erlbaum.

Swann, W. B., Jr., & Bosson, J. K. (2010). Self and identity. In S. T. Fiske, D. T. Gilbert, & G. Lindzey (Eds.), *Handbook of social psychology* (5th ed., Vol. 1, pp. 589–628). John Wiley & Sons, Inc.

Szalma, J. L. (2020). Basic needs, goals and motivation. In P. J. Corr & G. Matthews (Eds.), *The Cambridge handbook of personality psychology* (pp. 330–338). Cambridge University Press.

Tabachnick, B. G., & Fidell, L. S. (2007). *Using multivariate statistics* (5th ed.). Allyn and Bacon.

Tajfel, H. (1981). *Human groups and social categories.* Cambridge University Press.

Tajfel, H., & Turner, J. C. (1979). An integrative theory of intergroup conflict. In W. G. Austin & S. Worchel (Eds.), *The social psychology of intergroup relations* (pp. 33–37). Brooks/Cole.

Tantam, D. (2015). The contribution of female existential philosophers to psychotherapy. *Existential Analysis, 26,* 36–48.

Taormina, R. J., & Gao, J. H. (2013). Maslow and the motivation hierarchy measuring satisfaction of the needs. *The American Journal of Psychology, 126,* 155–177.

Tate, C. C. (2013). Addressing conceptual confusions about evolutionary theorizing: How and why evolutionary psychology and feminism do not oppose each other. *Sex Roles, 69,* 491–502. https://doi.org/10.1007/s11199-012-0226-3

Tauvon, L. (2001). A comparison of psychoanalytic and psychodramatic theory from a psychodramatist's perspective. *Counselling Psychology Quarterly, 14,* 331–355.

Taylor, E. (1991). William James and the humanistic tradition. *Journal of Humanistic Psychology, 31,* 56–74.

Taylor, E. (1999). William James and Sigmund Freud: "The future of psychology belongs to your work." *Psychological Science, 10,* 465–469.

Taylor, E. (2000). "What is man, psychologist, that thou art so unmindful of him?" Henry A. Murray on the historical relation between classical personality theory and humanistic psychology. *Journal of Humanistic Psychology, 40,* 29–42.

Taylor, E. (2010). William James and the humanistic implications of the neuroscience revolution: An outrageous hypothesis. *Journal of Humanistic Psychology, 50*, 410–429.

Taylor, S., & Workman, L. (2021). *Cognitive psychology: The basics.* Routledge.

Tellegen, A. (1982). *Multidimensional Personality Questionnaire.* University of Minnesota Press.

Terman, L. M., & Miles, C. C. (1936). *Sex and personality: Studies in masculinity and femininity.* McGraw-Hill.

Thibaut, J. W., & Kelley, H. H. (1959). *The social psychology of groups.* John Wiley.

Thomson, J. A. K. (1955). *The ethics of Aristotle: The Nicomachean ethics.* Penguin.

Thompson, C. M. (1953). Towards a psychology of women. *Pastoral Psychology, 4*, 29–38.

Thorndike, E. L. (1905). *The elements of psychology.* A. G. Seiler.

Thorndike, E. L. (1911). *Animal intelligence: Experimental studies.* Macmillan.

Thorndike, E. L. (1917). *Thorndike arithmetics* (Books, 1, 2, & 3). Rand McNally.

Titchener, E. B. (1902). *Experimental psychology: A manual of laboratory practice.* MacMillan & Co.

Todes, D. P. (1997). Pavlov's physiological factory. *Isis, 88*, 205–246.

Tolman, E. C. (1924). The inheritance of maze-learning ability in rats. *Journal of Comparative Psychology, 4*, 1–18.

Tolman, E. C. (1932). *Purposive behavior in animals and men.* Century.

Tolman, E. C. (1938). The determinants of behavior at a choice point. *Psychological Review, 45*, 1–41.

Tolman, E. C. (1948). Cognitive maps in rats and men. *Psychological Review, 55*, 189–208.

Tosi, D. J., & Lindamood, C. A. (1975). The measurement of self-actualization: A critical review of the Personal Orientation Inventory. *Journal of Personality Assessment, 39*, 215–224.

Trivers, R. L. (1972). Parental investment and sexual selection. In B. Campbell (Ed.), *Sexual selection and the descent of man* 1871–1971 (pp.136–179). Aldine.

Tudor, K. (2010). Person-centered relational therapy: An organismic perspective. *Person-Centered & Experiential Psychotherapies, 9*, 52–68.

Tupes, E. C., & Christal, R. E. (1961). Recurrent personality factors based on trait ratings. *USAF ASD Technical Report*, 61–97.

Tyng, C. M., Amin, H. U., Saad, M. N. M., & Malik, A. S. (2017). The influences of emotion on learning and memory. *Frontiers in Psychology, 8*, Article 1454.

Umana-Taylor, A.J. (2012). Ethnic identity. In S. J. Schwartz, K. Luyckx, & V. L. Vignoles (Eds.), *Handbook of identity theory and research* (pp. 755–774). Springer-Verlag.

Umana-Taylor, A. J., Yazedijan, A., & Bamaca-Gomez, M. (2004). Developing the Ethnic Identity Scale: Using Eriksonian and social identity perspectives. *Identity, 4*, 9–38.

Unger, R. K. (1979). Toward a redefinition of sex and gender. *American Psychologist, 34*, 1085–1094.

US Department of Labor Office of Policy Planning and Research (1965). *The Negro family: The case for national action*. US Department of Labor.

Van Dijken, S., van der Veer, R., van Ijzendoorn, M., & Kuipers, H.-J. (1998). Bowlby before Bowlby: The sources of an intellectual departure in psychoanalysis and psychology. *Journal of the History of the Behavioral Sciences, 34*, 247–269.

Van Lange, P. A. M., & Balliet, D. (2015). Interdependence theory. In M. Mikulincer, P. R. Shaver, J. A. Simpson, & J. F. Dovidio (Eds.), *APA handbook of personality and social psychology: Vol. 3. Interpersonal relations* (pp. 65–92). American Psychological Association. https://doi.org/10.1037/14344-003.

Verkuyten, M. (2005). *The social psychology of ethnic identity*. Psychology Press.

Vernon, P. E., & Allport, G. W. (1931). A test for personal values. *Journal of Abnormal and Social Psychology, 26*, 231–248.

Villarreal, R., Blozis, S. A., & Widaman, K. F. (2005). Factorial invariance of a Pan–Hispanic familism scale. *Hispanic Journal of Behavioral Sciences, 27*(4), 409–425. https://doi.org/10.1177/0739986305281125

Voeks, V.W. (1950). Formalization and clarification of a theory of learning. *The Journal of Psychology, 30*, 341–362.

Von Hilsheimer, G., & Quirk, D. A. (2006). Origin of EEG biofeedback for remediating misbehavior. *The Behavior Analyst Today, 7*, 492–507.

Wade, N. J., Sakurai, K., & Gyoba, J. (2007). Wither Wundt? *Perception, 36*, 163–166.

Wahlsten, D. (1999). Single-gene influences on brain and behavior. *Annual Review of Psychology, 50*, 599–624.

Walker, E., Kestler, L., Bollini, A., & Hochman, K. M. (2004). Schizophrenia: Etiology and course. *Annual Review of Psychology, 55*, 401–430.

Walkey, F. H. (1979). Internal control, powerful others, and chance: A confirmation of Levenson's factor structure. *Journal of Personality Assessment, 43*, 532–535.

Walsh, R., Teo, T., & Baydala, A. (2014). *A critical history and philosophy of psychology: Diversity of context, thought, and practice*. Cambridge University Press.

Warner, M. S. (2009). Defense or actualization? Reconsidering the role of processing, self and agency within Rogers' theory of personality. *Person-Centered & Experiential Psychotherapies, 8*, 109–126.

Wasserman, E. A., & Miller, R. R. (1997). What's elementary about associative learning? *Annual Review of Psychology, 48*, 573–607.

Watson, D., Clark, L. A., & Tellegen, A. (1988). Development and validation of brief measures of positive and negative affect: The PANAS scales. *Journal of Personality and Social Psychology, 54*, 1063–1070.

Watson, J. B. (1913). Psychology as the behaviorist views it. *Psychological Review, 20*, 158–177.

Watson, J. B. (1916). The place of the conditioned reflex in psychology. *Psychological Review, 23*, 89–116.

Watson, J. B., & Raynor, R. (1920). Conditioned emotional reactions. *Journal of Experimental Psychology, 3*, 1–14.

Weeks, M. (2014). *Heads up: Psychology*. DK Publishing.

Wei, M., Russell, D. W., Mallinckrodt, B., & Vogel, D. L. (2007). The Experiences in Close Relationship Scale (ECR) – Short Form: Reliability, validity, and factor structure. *Journal of Personality Assessment, 88*, 187–204.

Weiner, B. (2010). The development of an attribution–based theory of motivation: A history of ideas. *Educational Psychologist, 45*, 28–36.

Weiss, A., & Deary, I. J. (2020). The trait approach. In P. J. Corr & G. Matthews (Eds.), *The Cambridge handbook of personality psychology* (pp. 31–43). Cambridge University Press.

Wertheimer, M. (1945). *Productive thinking*. Harper.

West, S. G., & Finch, J. F. (1997). Personality measurement: Reliability and validity issues. In R. Hogan, J. A. Johnson, & S. R. Briggs (Eds.), *Handbook of personality psychology* (pp. 143–164). Academic Press.

Westen, D. (1992). The cognitive self and the psychoanalytic self: Can we put our selves together? *Psychological Inquiry, 3*, 1–13.

Westen, D., & Chang, C. (2000). Personality pathology in adolescence: A review. *Adolescent Psychiatry, 25*, 61–100.

Wheeler, M., Kern, R. M., & Curlette, W. L. (1986). Factor analytic scales designed to measure Adlerian lifestyle themes. *Journal of Individual Psychology, 42*, 1–16.

Whitbourne, S. K., & Waterman, A. S. (1979). Psychosocial development in young adulthood: Age and cohort comparisons. *Developmental Psychology, 15*, 373–378.

White, S. C., Gaines, S. O., Jr., & Jha, S. (2012). Beyond subjective well–being. *Journal of International Development, 24*, 763–766.

White, W. F. (1993). From S-R to S-O-R: What every teacher should know. *Education, 113*, 620–629.

Wicker, A. W. (1969). Attitudes versus actions: The relationship of verbal and overt behavioral responses to attitude objects. *Journal of Social Issues, 25*, 41–78.

Widiger, T. A., ed. (2017). *The Oxford handbook of the Five Factor Model.* Oxford University Press.

Widiger, T. A., & McCabe, G. A. (2020). Personality in clinical psychology. In P. J. Corr & G. Matthews (Eds.), *The Cambridge handbook of personality psychology* (pp. 451–462). Cambridge University Press.

Wiggins, J. S. (1979). A psychological taxonomy of trait–descriptive terms: The interpersonal domain. *Journal of Personality and Social Psychology, 37,* 395–412.

Wiggins, J. S. (1991). Agency and communion as conceptual coordinates for the understanding and measurement of interpersonal behavior. In W. M. Grove & D. Ciccetti (Eds.), *Thinking clearly about psychology: Vol. 2. Personality and psychopathology* (pp. 89–113). University of Minnesota Press.

Wiggins, J. S. (1995). *Interpersonal Adjective Scales professional manual.* Psychological Assessment Resources, Inc.

Wiggins, J. S. (with Behrends, R. S., Ben-Porath, Y. S., Blatt, S. J., Costa, P. T., Jr., Gurtman, M. B., McAdams, D. P., Piedmont, R. L., Pincus, A. L., & Trobst, K. K.) (2005). *Paradigms of personality assessment.* Guilford Press. (Original work published 2003)

Wiggins, J. S., & Holzmuller, A. (1978). Psychological androgyny and interpersonal behavior. *Journal of Consulting and Clinical Psychology, 46,* 40–52

Wiggins, J. S., & Pincus, A. L. (1992). Personality: Structure and assessment. *Annual Review of Psychology, 43,* 473–504.

Wiggins, J. S., Steiger, J. H., & Gaelick, L. (1981). Evaluating circumplexity in personality data. *Multivariate Behavioral Research, 16,* 263–289.

Wiggins, J. S., & Trapnell, P. D. (1997). Personality structure: The return of the Big Five. In R. Hogan, J. Johnson, & S. Briggs (Eds.), *Handbook of personality psychology* (pp. 737–765). Academic Press.

Wiggins, J. S., Trapnell, P., & Phillips, N. (1988). Psychometric and geometric characteristics of the Revised Interpersonal Adjective Scales (IAS–R). *Multivariate Behavioral Research, 23,* 517–530.

Wilt, J., & Revelle, W. (2009). Extraversion. In M. R. Leary & R. H. Hoyle (Eds.), *Handbook of individual differences in social behavior* (pp. 27–45). Guilford.

Wilt, J., & Revelle, W. (2017). Extraversion. In T. A. Widiger (Ed.), *The Oxford handbook of the Five Factor Model* (pp. 57–81). Oxford University Press.

Windholz, G. (1992). Pavlov's conceptualization of learning. *The American Journal of Psychology, 105,* 459–469 .

Windholz, G., & Lamal, P. A. (1986). Priority in the classical conditioning of children. *Teaching of Psychology, 13,* 192–195.

Winnicott, D. (1931). *Clinical notes on disorders of childhood.* Heinemann.

Winter, D. G. (1997). Allport's life and Allport's psychology. *Journal of Personality, 65,* 723–731.

Wise, J. B. (2007). Testing a theory that explains how self-efficacy beliefs are formed: Predicting self-efficacy appraisals across recreation activities. *Journal of Social and Clinical Psychology, 26*, 841–848.

Wise, J. B. (2008). Using the Knowledge-and-Appraisal Personality Architecture to predict self-efficacy within individual persons. *Psychological Reports, 103*, 406–410.

Witkin, H. A., Dyk, R. B., Fattuson, H. F., Goodenough, D. R., & Karp, S. A. (1962). *Psychological differentiation: Studies of development.* Wiley.

Witkin, H. A., & Goodenough, D. R. (1981). Cognitive styles: Essence and origins. Field dependence and field independence. *Psychological Issues, 51*, 1–141.

Witkin, H. A., Lewis, H. B., Hertzman, M., Machover, K., Meissner, P. B., & Wapner, S. (1972). *Personality through perception: An experimental and clinical study.* Harper. (Original work published 1954)

Wong, P. T. P. (2005). Existential and humanistic theories. In J. C. Thomas, & D. L. Segal (Eds.), *Comprehensive handbook of personality and psychopathology* (pp.192–211). John Wiley & Sons, Inc.

Wood, W., & Eagly, A. H. (2010). Gender. In S. T. Fiske, D. T. Gilbert, & G. Lindzey (Eds.), *Handbook of social psychology* (Vol. 1, 5th ed., pp. 629–667). Wiley.

Wrightsman, L. S. (1981). Personal documents as data in conceptualizing adult personality development. *Personality and Social Psychology Bulletin, 7*, 367–385.

Wundt, W. (1910). *Principles of physiological psychology.* Swan Sonnenschein & Co. (Original work published 1874)

Wundt, W. (1973). *An introduction to psychology.* Arno Press. (Original work published 1911)

Yarkoni, T. (2015). Neurobiological substrates of personality: A critical overview. In M. Mikulincer & P. R. Shaver (Eds.), *APA handbook of personality and social psychology* (Vol. 4: Personality processes and individual differences, pp. 61–83). American Psychological Association.

Yee, A. H., Fairchild, H. H., Weizmann, F. & Wyatt, G. E. (1993). Addressing psychology's problem with race. *American Psychologist, 48*, 1132–1140.

York, G. K., III. (2009). Localization of language function in the twentieth century. *Journal of the History of the Neurosciences, 18*, 283–290.

Zeaman, D., & Radner, L. (1953). A test of the mechanisms of learning proposed by Hull and Guthrie. *Journal of Experimental Psychology, 45*, 239–244.

Zeiler, K. (2013). A phenomenology of excorporation, bodily alienation, and resistance: Rethinking sexed and racialized embodiment. *Hypatia, 28*, 69–84.

Zerbe, K. J. (1990). Through the storm: Psychoanalytic theory in the psychotherapy of anxiety disorders. *Bulletin of the Menninger Clinic, 54*, 171–183.

Zuckerman, M. (1969). Theoretical formulations. In J. P. Zubek (Ed.), *Sensory deprivation* (pp. 407–432). Appleton-Century-Crofts.
Zuckerman, M. (1971). Dimensions of sensation seeking. *Journal of Consulting and Clinical Psychology, 36*, 45–52.
Zuckerman, M. (1984). Sensation seeking: A comparative approach to a human trait. *Behaviour and Brain Sciences, 7*, 413–471.
Zuckerman, M. (1990). The psychophysiology of sensation seeking. *Journal of Personality, 58*, 313–339.
Zuckerman, M., & Cloninger, C. R. (1996). Relationships between Cloninger's, Zuckerman's and Eysenck's dimensions of personality. *Personality and Individual Differences, 21*, 283–285.
Zuckerman, M., Eysenck, S. B. G., & Eysenck, H. J. (1978). Sensation seeking in England and America: Cross–cultural, age, and sex comparisons. *Journal of Consulting and Clinical Psychology, 46*, 139–149.
Zuroff, D. C. (1986). Was Gordon Allport a trait theorist? *Journal of Personality and Social Psychology, 51*, 993–1000.

INDEX

For Product Safety Concerns and Information please contact our EU representative GPSR@taylorandfrancis.com
Taylor & Francis Verlag GmbH, Kaufingerstraße 24, 80331 München, Germany

www.ingramcontent.com/pod-product-compliance
Lightning Source LLC
LaVergne TN
LVHW050428301026
851387LV00044B/1305

9781032989808